Christian Monastic Life in Early Islam

Edinburgh Studies in Classical Islamic History and Culture

Series Editor: Carole Hillenbrand

A particular feature of medieval Islamic civilisation was its wide horizons. The Muslims fell heir not only to the Graeco-Roman world of the Mediterranean, but also to that of the ancient Near East, to the empires of Assyria, Babylon and the Persians; and beyond that, they were in frequent contact with India and China to the east and with black Africa to the south. This intellectual openness can be sensed in many inter-related fields of Muslim thought, and it impacted powerfully on trade and on the networks that made it possible. Books in this series reflect this openness and cover a wide range of topics, periods and geographical areas.

Titles in the series include:

The Body in Arabic Love Poetry
Jokha Alharthi

Arabian Drugs in Early Medieval Mediterranean Medicine
Zohar Amar and Efraim Lev

Towards a History of Libraries in Yemen
Hassan Ansari and Sabine Schmidtke

The Abbasid Caliphate of Cairo, 1261–1517
Mustafa Banister

The Medieval Western Maghrib
Amira K. Bennison

Christian Monastic Life in Early Islam
Bradley Bowman

Keeping the Peace in Premodern Islam
Malika Dekkiche

Queens, Concubines and Eunuchs in Medieval Islam
Taef El-Azhari

Islamic Political Thought in the Mamluk Period
Mohamad El-Merheb

The Kharijites in Early Islamic Historical Tradition
Hannah-Lena Hagemann

Medieval Damascus
Konrad Hirschler

A Monument to Medieval Syrian Book Culture
Konrad Hirschler

The Popularisation of Sufism in Ayyubid and Mamluk Egypt
Nathan Hofer

Defining Anthropomorphism
Livnat Holtzman

Making Mongol History
Stefan Kamola

Lyrics of Life
Fatemeh Keshavarz

Art, Allegory and the Rise of Shiism in Iran, 1487–1565
Chad Kia

The Administration of Justice in Medieval Egypt
Yaacov Lev

The Queen of Sheba's Gift
Marcus Milwright

Ruling from a Red Canopy
Colin P. Mitchell

Islam, Christianity and the Realms of the Miraculous
Ian Richard Netton

The Poetics of Spiritual Instruction
Austin O'Malley

Sacred Place and Sacred Time in the Medieval Islamic Middle East
Daniella Talmon-Heller

Conquered Populations in Early Islam
Elizabeth Urban

edinburghuniversitypress.com/series/escihc

Christian Monastic Life in Early Islam

Bradley Bowman

EDINBURGH
University Press

Edinburgh University Press is one of the leading university presses in the UK. We publish academic books and journals in our selected subject areas across the humanities and social sciences, combining cutting-edge scholarship with high editorial and production values to produce academic works of lasting importance. For more information visit our website: edinburghuniversitypress.com

Edinburgh University Press Ltd
The Tun – Holyrood Road
12 (2f) Jackson's Entry
Edinburgh EH8 8PJ

First published in hardback by Edinburgh University Press 2021

Typeset in 11/15 Adobe Garamond by
Servis Filmsetting Ltd, Stockport, Cheshire and
printed and bound by CPI Group (UK) Ltd,
Croydon, CR0 4YY

A CIP record for this book is available from the British Library

ISBN 978 1 4744 7968 4 (hardback)
ISBN 978 1 4744 7969 1 (hardback)
ISBN 978 1 4744 7970 7 (webready PDF)
ISBN 978 1 4744 7971 4 (epub)

Contents

Figures

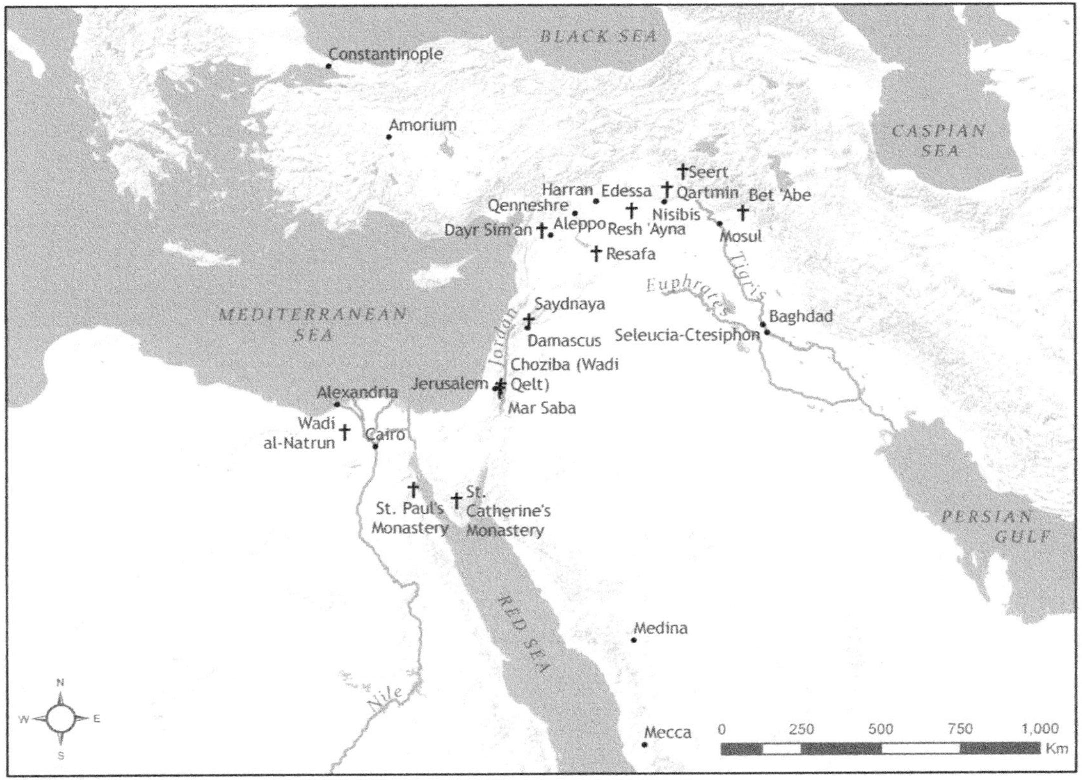

Map of monastic centres and regions of monastic importance across the Near East.
Credit: Donald Biddle, GISP, University of Louisville Center for Geographic Information Sciences.

Introduction

The title for the opening chapter of this book was inspired by a phrase within the *Kitāb al-ruhbān* (*The Book of Monks*), authored by the ninth-century Muslim moralist Ibn Abī al-Dunyā (d. 894 CE). Ibn Abī al-Dunyā, a well-regarded scholar of early Islamic mysticism and an ascetic himself, here provides considerable insight into Muslim views of Christian monasticism by detailing encounters between Muslim ascetics, or *zuhhād*, and their monastic counterparts. The text itself is essentially a collection of edifying sayings, short stories, and dialogues that demonstrate monastic wisdom, ever situating a Muslim sage as the recipient of that knowledge. The particular passage, from which the first chapter owes its title, depicts a monk insisting to his novice that only in a withdrawal into nature, turning away from humanity, can the ascetic truly reach spiritual serenity. The sage admonishes:

> Until the disciple of God seeks refuge in the bosoms of the mountains and the wombs of the wadīs and caverns, taking shelter with the wild beasts, settling at their watering holes and eating from the gardens of trees in its shade, he will not see that a blessing, complete as this one, is laid before him.
>
> . . . ḥattā yāwā murīd allāh ilā aknāf al-jibāl wa-buṭūn al-awdiya w-l-ghīrān yaẓallu maʿa al-waḥsh yaridu muwāridahā, yaʾkulu min ajinnat al-shajar fī aẓillihā, lā yarā fī dhālika anna al-niʿma atamma ʿalā aḥadin minhā ʿalayhi.[1]

While being credited with well over a hundred treatises, primarily concerned with themes such as the virtue of humility, fasting, fear of the divine, and the admonition of the physical world, it is instructive that a religious scholar such as Ibn Abī al-Dunyā would exhibit this degree of concern about a text emphasising the merits of Christian monastic devotion. We therefore see within the *Kitāb al-ruhbān* a model for a piety-driven existence that offers little in the way of discernible confessional barriers, rather suggesting a kind of nebulous religious context in which many groups could exchange concepts of righteousness and spirituality. The monks featured by Ibn Abī al-Dunyā are not expressly characterised as 'denominational' Christians, meaning that there is no discussion of Christology or particular theological principles to be found throughout the entirety of the work. The Christian ascetics and hermits recounted in *The Book of Monks* simply offer advice on achieving a pious lifestyle, a regiment that like-minded Muslims could have perhaps most empathised with and embraced.

My research seeks to participate in this ongoing discussion of confessional fluidity, as well as overlapping religious contours, during the early centuries of Islam in the Near East. The investigation here is carried out with specific attention to Christian monastic life within a Muslim political milieu. Even following the turbulent transition from Byzantine hegemony to Islamic authority across the Levant in the middle of the seventh century, Christian monasteries of the region displayed continued vitality and sustainability for centuries under Islamic rule. While it has been widely acknowledged that Christian monasticism continued to flourish across Iraq, Syria-Palestine and North Africa well into the Islamic period, the question remains as to the precise nature of the relationship between monastic communities and Muslim society. These disparate populations appear to have not only established a relatively harmonious coexistence, but also facilitated a collective exchange of ideas, interests and concerns across would-be confessional divides. A considerable range of medieval texts from the Byzantine Greek, Syriac and Arabic traditions (including hagiographies, historical chronicles, geographical treatises and works of poetry) indeed demonstrate a palpable Muslim fascination with Christian asceticism and monasticism.

I would argue that this fascination with Christian monastic life was articulated through a fluid, piety-centred movement at the rise of Islam that did not rigidly distinguish between sectarian groups. Ultimately this would suggest an overlapping of confessional affiliation within nascent Islam, revealing a relatively amorphous religious context that closely reflected the flexible identifications within late antique Christianity. Such ambiguity would echo throughout the following centuries of the Islamic period, manifesting itself in Muslim appreciation, interest, and at times, participation in Christian monastic life. The overarching proposal of the research is thus less a matter of religious tolerance, than a suggestion for confessional synthesis between like-minded religious groups throughout the period. This potential ecumenism, as it is explored in the monograph, would have been based upon the sharing of core tenets concerning piety and righteous behaviour. Such fundamental attributes of the Christian eremitic existence, long associated with monasticism in the East, would have perhaps served as a mutually inclusive common ground for Muslim and Christian communities of the period.

The theoretical underpinning of this research was largely inspired by the work of Fred Donner and his proposal for a 'Believers' movement at the dawning of the Islamic period. As Donner has suggested most recently in *Muhammad and the Believers: At the Origins of Islam*, the earliest expression of such a 'Believers' drive, which would eventually come to be known as *Islam*, would have potentially included both Jews and Christians. The absolute mandate for personal piety would have been a primary directive of the incipient community, a society which Donner has defined as 'a separate group of righteous, God-fearing monotheists, separate in their strict observance of righteousness from those around them', yet decidedly non-sectarian in nature.[2]

Utilising this basic premise, the research here attempts to refine the principle by addressing a particular group of Christians within this more complex, multi-confessional framework, that is, the monastic communities of the Near East. While Donner's argument may well have applied across broader religious boundaries, it seems that the emphasis on piety might have had an even greater bearing on the possible spiritual kinship between Christian monks and their Muslim, and/or 'Believer', counterparts. Just as the monk had been understood as a standard of righteousness par excellence in the late antique Christian environment, so the image remained virtually unchanged into the Islamic period, an appreciation for the wisdom and piety of the monk being transferred into a new religious matrix. The captivation of such figures, carrying even more weight within a community characterised by its absolute fervour for righteousness, would have naturally extended to their houses of worship as well as dwelling places.

The 'Believers' proposition, it should also be noted, deals with a rather narrow window of ecumenism in a historical sense, exclusively relating to the origins period and early state formation within Islam. This confessional fluidity that characterised the intital impulse of the movement, according to Donner's template, then subsided in the late seventh century under the caliph ʿAbd al-Malik ibn Marwān (r. 685–705). Under pressure to reassert Umayyad control and reaffirm their legitimacy in the wake of two devastating civil wars, the ruling elite began to lay the foundations of Islam as we recognise it today.[3] Ambitious projects such as the commissioning of the Dome of the Rock[4] and epigraphic changes in coinage[5] were clearly implemented with a public religious ideology in mind, perhaps simultaneously signalling the official pronouncement of Islam as the basis of the state as well as creating a partition between, at least what might have been seen as, rival confessional groups.[6] By the time of the Second Fitna, we could include among these competing constituencies more than just Christian groups within Umayyad lands, but also ʿAlid or Shīʿī factions, as well as Kharijites – each of the latter groups laden with their own claims to authority. To these internal political struggles should be added a renewed hostility with Byzantium, under Justinian II (c. 692–3). All of these aforementioned trials, witnessed by the Marwānid regime, are reflected in the innovations carried out by ʿAbd al-Malik and undoubtedly shaped by the growing necessity to establish a distinct self-identity that could reinforce the dynasty on religious grounds.[7]

The crystallisation of an unambiguous confessional identity, as far as could be accomplished by ʿAbd al-Malik and his successors, however, speaks to a strictly institutional model. As Donner acknowledges, the programme of delineating religious boundaries would have been gradual outside of the administrative structure.[8] A communal acceptance, or even recognition, of barriers like these would have necessarily taken decades or longer to mature on the local level. I would suggest that the continued Muslim fascination with Christian monastic life is a corollary to precisely such an ongoing process. Though measures adopted by the Islamic state may have indeed sought to demarcate confessional lines, the intimate collaboration between monastic communities and piety-minded Muslims remained strong for many years. Ibn

Abī al-Dunyā's *Kitāb al-ruhbān* should be appreciated as a testament to a kind of 'residual, ecumenical *īmān*'[9] that endured well beyond the seventh century.

This study intends to present a survey of Christian monastic life in the Near East, focusing on the early centuries of the Islamic era. This opening chapter frames the discussion to follow by acquainting readers with the scholarship concerning Christian communities, and more specifically monastic life, under Muslim rule in the early Islamic centuries. In introducing the methodology behind my research, I also draw on examinations into broader fields of Late Antiquity and early Islamic history relating to 'identity' or 'self-identity' of various religious groups. The recent discourse in scholarship to recognise over-lapping confessional boundaries and shifting religious identities, from the Christianisation process in North Africa and Egypt to the blending of Christian, Zoroastrian and Muslim communities in early Islamic Persia, is utilised to support my claims that monastic life may indeed serve as a window into Islamic theology and inter-confessional relations in the formative centuries.

On the practical level this will involve an elucidation of official Muslim administrative policy toward such institutions, including the parameters for taxation, maintenance, construction and security measures. The next two sections of this research attempt to draw parallels and distinctions to previous Byzantine attitudes toward monasteries in the Near East. The second chapter particularly directs attention to the condition of monastic communities in their late antique context through the early to middle seventh-century period of the Islamic conquests. The main idea here is to present a contrast between the fortunes of monastic communities on the eve of the conquest era and directly following the initial Muslim occupation of the region. The following chapter will concentrate on the legal and administrative strategies exhibited toward monasteries in the early caliphal and Umayyad periods. Given the variety of Christian confessional positions in the region at this time, falling under the broad rubric of Chalcedonian and Miaphysite communities, the necessary question arises concerning the extent of uniformity for Muslim policy over divergent Christian groups. In other words, one of the issues is concerned with whether or not the official position of the Muslim court was in any way different with respect to the dogmatic principles of a specific confessional community.

In connection to this line of inquiry it has been suggested that the Chalcedonian Christians of the region, who maintained a theological allegiance to the church in Byzantium, were more burdened by the transition to Muslim authority than were their Miaphysite neighbours.[10] Does this however imply a deliberate policy toward this community or was it merely the result of an increasingly difficult means of communication and support across imperial borders? In addition, to be taken into consideration is the discrepancy between official policies of the state regarding non-Muslim communities and the practical administrative procedures carried out on the local level toward such confessional groups, which appears to have had some measure of variation depending on location and time.[11]

As will be demonstrated in the third chapter, the variations mentioned above included, at times, rather oppressive measures against monasteries – though even in these instances, the oppression appears to be principally economic in nature. The information for this section primarily comes from Christian ecclesiastical sources, which would have of course been invested in documenting the hardships of local institutions. Even in such events, however, the overall picture that emerges indicates a considerable leniency and respect in dealing with monasteries. As stated by Alphonse Mingana with respect to issues of religious tolerance under the early caliphates:

> The need has always been felt for an authoritative statement throwing light on the relations between official Islam and official Christianity at the time when Islam had power of life and death over millions of Christian subjects. Individual Christians may have suffered persecution at the hands of individual Muslims; isolated cases of Christian communities suffering hardships through the fanaticism of a provincial governor, or jurist, or the hallucinations of a half-demented sheikh or mullah are also recorded in history . . . but such incidents, however numerous, are to be considered infractions of the law, and the men who brought them about were breakers of the law . . . however imperfect official Islam may have been in some social aspects, statutory intolerance was not among its defects.[12]

While Mingana's statement could be said to apply quite generally to the treatment of non-Muslim populations under the early caliphates, the episodic persecution of monasteries was indeed largely subject to the wills of particularly harsh local officials, rather than any institutionalised policies for monastic governance. Indeed, it would appear that the fate of monastic communities was intimately bound to the stability of the Muslim state, in terms of security and protective measures granted from time to time by the central administration.

Chapter 4 examines the diverse nature of Muslim interest in Christian monasteries during the medieval Islamic period. According to a variety of contemporary accounts, Muslim visitation to monasteries often involved wine consumption and licentious behaviour on the part of the elites. While not dismissing this possibility, this research suggests that there was often a greater religious dimension to Muslim fascination with monastic sites. Sacred shrines throughout the late antique Levant had, after all, been held in esteem for their hospitality and miraculous powers long before the arrival of Islam. This examination contends that Muslim interest in such Christian shrines and monasteries represents a dynamic, flexible confessional environment at the dawning of Islam. The pious spirit of pilgrimage and *ziyāra*/visitation was simply transferred into a new religious context, one that was defined by its fluid character and amorphous sectarian lines. It was this form of popular Muslim fascination which prompted the composition of numerous texts dealing with monks and their monasteries in the Islamic period. While much of this Muslim literary corpus on monasteries is no longer extant, it is in itself instructive that this type of writing constituted such a presence in the literature of that time. The tenth-century compendium of Ibn al-Nadīm, the *Fihrist*, for example, lists five books by Muslim authors dedicated to Christian monasteries – although these works unfortunately do not survive intact.[13]

Some of the most important remaining material on monasteries is found in the *Kitāb al-diyārāt* (*Book of Monasteries*) of al-Shābushtī (d. 1008), which has preserved earlier accounts relating, in part, to Muslim-Christian interaction at monasteries.[14] In addition to this, there are numerous references to monasteries in other forms of prose literature, historical narratives and geographical works in the Islamic tradition. All of this clearly suggests a certain interest in monastic communities; the particular implications and interpretations of such an interest will form the basis of the fourth and fifth sections of the research.

Certain examples of these later texts from the Islamic literary tradition generally propose that attraction and visitation to monasteries corresponded to Muslim participation in illicit activities, such as the consumption of wine and fornication. Some of this material devoted to monastery excursions has been categorised as a sub-genre of ʿAbbāsid wine poetry/*khamriyya*.[15] While Christian monasteries were indeed recognised for their vineyards and production of wine in the Levant of Late Antiquity,[16] there could perhaps have been an additional, more spiritual purpose for Muslim visitation to such environs and interest in monasticism. Inasmuch as Christian monasteries were known for their storehouses of wine, they were also repositories of learning, often containing libraries of ecclesiastical texts and theological scholarship.[17] The intellectual activity of monks throughout this period has been widely recognised, in terms of the preservation of classical works, the copying of manuscripts, and compositions of historical and hagiographical material.[18]

It seems that a curiosity in such matters, as well as an increasing interest in ascetic practices and liturgical celebrations, would have likewise served as a factor in the allure of monasticism on behalf of the popular culture in the early Islamic period. There are, after all, various accounts in the aforementioned literature that depict Muslims in attendance for Christian ceremonies at monasteries and churches, albeit the explanations for such outings are generally not overtly justified in religious terms.[19] Even the deeply religious ʿUmar ibn ʿAbd al-Azīz (r. 717–20), typically considered the most pious of the Umayyad caliphs, is said not only to have led Muslim prayers in a Christian church,[20] but visited and was buried at Dayr Simʿān (Monastery of St Simeon) in northern Syria.[21] Accounts like this seem to suggest that there was more going on at the monasteries than just revelry and merrymaking. In reality it would appear that visitation and pilgrimage to Christian shrines, undertaken by the Muslim devout throughout the Middle Ages, possessed a decidedly greater pietistic dimension. In an article concerning medieval Arabic literature relating to monasteries, Gérard Troupeau arrived at a similar conclusion, stating:

> À lire les ouvrages relatifs aux couvents, on a l'impression que ceux-ci étaient surtout fréquentés par des oisifs, des buveurs et des débauchés qui appartenaient aux classes les plus hautes et les plus riches de la société:

> califes, grands personnages de la cour, hauts fonctionnaires de l'empire, accompagnés de leurs commensaux, de leurs poètes, de leurs musiciens et de leurs chanteuses. En fait, ce n'est pas tout à fait exact, et il semble bien que la clientèle musulmane des couvents chrétiens comprenaient des gens de tous les milieux, et même des milieux simples, qui s'y rendaient en toute honnêteté . . . À mon avis, ces raisons sont de deux sortes: des raisons profanes et des raisons religieuses.[22]

While previous sections of this book have been devoted to demonstrating the flexible parameters for monastic existence as well as substantiating an elevated religious and social prominence for monastic communities throughout the early Islamic period, the question remains, however, as to precisely why these institutions and their guardians would have been accorded such a privileged position within Islam during its formative era. In other words, what was the origin of this reverence for Christian ascetic communities that appears to have been transferred into a Muslim context? In turn, what can this tell us about the nature of Islam and confessional distinctions in the early period? In an attempt to answer such a query, the final chapter of this book will posit that the ultimate source of early Muslim interest in monasteries is articulated through an inclusive, piety-centred religious orientation that extends from the late antique period.

This project overall involves a critical examination of primary texts, spanning a variety of genres, confessional backgrounds and linguistic compositions – utilising Greek, Arabic and Syriac sources from the late antique and early medieval periods. From the Christian tradition there exists a substantial corpus of historical chronicles, statutes for monastic life, *typica* documents (foundational charters for monasteries), ecclesiastical literature, theological treatises and hagiographical material which provide valuable information concerning the state of Christian communities in the Near East. In addition to the classical histories, local chronicles and *futūḥ* literature within the Muslim historiographical tradition, which provide some details on Christians during the conquest and consolidation of Muslim rule, other materials which specifically relate to inter-confessional relations with Christians, legislation on non-Muslim populations, the depiction of monasticism and/or asceticism in Islam, geographical works containing information on monasteries, and specific elements within the *adab* genre of Arabic literature will be addressed in this analysis.[23]

Admittedly, the intrinsic shortcoming in such an endeavour is the relative paucity of documentary historiographical evidence, of an exclusively archival nature from the Muslim side,[24] regarding inter-confessional relations from the earliest period of Islam. Insofar as this reflects well-known issues from within the Islamic tradition itself, it should be conceded that many of the classical Arabic texts examined here are not contemporary with the events they describe. In many cases they are, in fact, several centuries removed from the foundational era of Islam. The question as to the historical validity of such source material lingers,[25] particularly regarding the potentially anachronistic tendencies that may or may not suggest concerns of later times.[26] Despite the debate over the merits and accuracy of the Islamic historiographical traditions, it seems prudent to attempt to glean from them what one can, especially as they relate to inter-confessional contacts in the early period. However, even then, the relations between religious groups are not generally of primary concern to classical Muslim authors. This is precisely where evidence from the Christian tradition must be employed, where possible, to provide a fuller depiction of social, political and religious interactions between communities.[27] Important information can likewise be gathered from the considerable corpus of late antique and early Islamic papyri, the vast majority of which was produced in Egypt. While the papyri records are often concerned with fiscal receipts, land leases and the like, these kinds of documents do serve as supplements to a much wider social history that includes confessional relations.[28]

A considerable body of modern research has been dedicated to the study of Christian communities under Muslim authority during the early Islamic period. Strictly speaking, however, the particular status of monasticism and monasteries within this context has received only limited attention. This study will therefore necessarily require a synthesis of information contained within a broad scope of disparate materials, in an attempt to present a historical reconstruction of monastic communities for the transitional period in question. The range of such materials that are pertinent to this research can be categorised into the following broad genres of study: social and ecclesiastical/sectarian histories and studies of *dhimmī* populations,[29] theological and doctrinal aspects of Christian life under Muslim rule,[30] Christian ascetic and monastic practices,[31] studies on the Islamic conquest period and the final stages of Byzantine rule in the Levant,[32] Byzantine policies and Muslim legislation on monasteries,[33] and archaeological research relating to monastic complexes and churches from this period.[34]

In terms of studies that have focused the discussion on Christian monks and/or monasteries within an Islamic historical context, of which there are relatively few, the first that should be mentioned here is the article by Troupeau, entitled 'Les Couvents Chrétiens dans la Littérature Arabe'.[35] Troupeau, primarily using the *Kitāb al-diyārāt* of al-Shābushtī as a guide, presents a concise evaluation of the relationship between the Muslim populace and monasteries in the early Islamic period. The term 'populace', in terms of the examples from al-Shābushtī, incorporates characters across wide social strata, including caliphs, court officials, imperial functionaries, poets, musicians and singers. Throughout this process he cites numerous accounts within *Kitāb al-diyārāt* of Muslim visitation to monasteries, to which he suggests a few sociological conclusions for such ventures.

The first is that the monasteries of the Near East would have served as perfect locales for relaxation, away from the hustle and bustle of the towns and cities.[36] To this point, al-Shābushtī typically begins his chapters on monasteries with descriptions of the topographical beauty of the gardens, vineyards and orchards, and serene atmosphere of monasteries. The second reason, according to Troupeau, is for the purposes of intoxication, which is forbidden in Islam, for which monasteries were also the ideal places, generally secluded and quite apart from the more austere elements within the Muslim community.[37] The final explanation relates to the hospitality of monastic institutions, in which even Muslim travellers could expect accommodation.[38] This description of the monastery-hostel is perhaps also plausible, in that providing a secure and comfortable environment for way-side pilgrims and travellers appears to be a typical characteristic of monastic custom.[39] Muslims often journeyed to monasteries, Troupeau further explains, specifically to take part in Christian feasts and celebrations. This was not only due to the paucity of such holy days in the Islamic calendar, but also with respect to the richness of liturgical services in that domain.[40]

A second article which should be taken into account is 'Monasteries

Through Muslim Eyes: The Diyārāt Books',[41] by Hilary Kilpatrick. This work, which uses Troupeau's article as its point of departure, is primarily interested in the depiction of monasteries as a literary motif in classical Arabic wine-poetry. The main sources for such an examination are, again, the *Kitāb al-diyārāt* as well as the *Kitāb al-aghānī* (*Book of Songs*) of al-Iṣfahānī (d. 972). Aside from the recounting of various other examples of Muslims attending monasteries and involvement in Christian ceremonies, Kilpatrick does not seem to be interested in the possible religious implications of such activities. Interestingly, her argument against Troupeau's theory for legitimate Muslim interest in monastic rituals on an inter-confessional level is based on the suggestion that many of the Muslims who were allegedly taking part in Christian traditions, were indeed likely to have been descended from Christian families. She dismisses this as a mere illustration of popular forms of religion, actually remnants of previous religious affiliation, and is for her thus a 'moot point'.[42] This, however, is precisely the interest of the research here in attempting to determine the relationship between these complex and fluid systems of confessional identities.

A third sample of scholarship on this subject is found in 'Monks, Monasteries and Early Islam',[43] by Elizabeth and Garth Fowden. This article is essentially a survey tracing the importance of monasticism in the Near East from the eve of Islam into the Umayyad period. The main point of the article is that Christian monasticism continued to flourish within an Islamic political milieu, essentially due to the nature of reverence accorded to such ascetics and holy men in the historical context of Late Antiquity. While certain episodic disturbances to monasteries did occur in this period, examples being occasional looting and pillaging of a site, the article maintains that there is even archaeological evidence for restoration and establishments of new monasteries under Muslim rule.[44] The complicated interpretation of monasticism on the part of Muslim theologians is also addressed, often involving conflicting images of the monk in *hadīth* literature, ranging from appreciation of ascetic values exhibited by monks to strict condemnation of their celibacy. This article likewise provides several examples of Muslim visitation to monasteries, although interestingly enough, al-Shābushtī is not mentioned as a source. With these topics having been explored, the general solution to the relationship between monasteries and the Muslim community, as this article suggests, rests in the authority of the exemplars of piety and their reputation being transmitted from the late antique period into a Muslim context.

Related pieces of contemporary scholarship have focused more on the interpretation of monasticism within the Qur'ān itself. Works by Jane McAuliffe,[45] Daniel J. Sahas,[46] Louis Massignon[47] and Edmund Beck[48] represent the most relevant of these studies. Though these examinations form different conclusions as to the image of the monk in Muslim scripture and exegesis,[49] they all focus the discussion on the pietistic inclination of Near Eastern monastic communities and its possible effects on the development of early Islamic religious practices.

The 2009 book entitled *Violence and Belief in Late Antiquity: Militant Devotion in Christianity and Islam*[50] by Thomas Sizgorich also addresses the theme of monasticism and its interpretations in the early Islamic period, albeit from a very different perspective than the aforementioned studies. His thesis relates to Christian monks as figures of warrior-ascetics in the late antique period: on the fringes of society waging not only a spiritual battle against the forces of evil, but also at times an armed struggle against politico-religious opponents. This transmission of the holy warrior ideal and models of militant piety, according to Sizgorich, appear in the evolution of *jihād* as a tenet of Islam and a subdivision of the practice of *zuhd*, Muslim asceticism.[51] While the argument has merit, particularly as it relates to a slightly later period in Islamic history,[52] it is a decidedly separate approach from the one here. The concern of this research will focus more on aspects of an inward struggle for personal righteousness – a spiritual striving, or *jihād*,[53] toward a piety-centred existence. This type of struggle, rather than one predicated on militancy, appears to have been where the example of Christian monks would have exerted the most influence in the formative period of Islam. As further examples will contend, Muslim interest in monasteries was intimately connected to a reverence for the righteous monastic lifestyle. It is in this pietistic sense that the tenth-century religious scholar al-Malaṭī makes an appraisement of monks as 'believers who have made a fervent effort to practice their religion' (*al-mujtahidīn fī dīnihim*).[54]

The plan of analysis here will attempt to construct a framework for the relationship between Christian monasteries and Muslim authority/popular interest. While the initial sections of the material will involve practical administrative measures for the governance of monastic communities, the latter portions will attempt to provide interpretations for Muslim interest in monasteries on a more popular and possibly religious level – invoking questions with regard to the degree of rigidity for confessional distinctions in the early Islamic period. At this point, it appears plausible that there is more to this relationship than monasteries merely serving as hostelries and wayside *ḥawānīt* (taverns)[55] for amusement-seeking Muslims.

In closing, it is perhaps fitting to refer to a similar reasoning by Jane McAuliffe, who has offered a familiar plan for the lingering, developmental process of self-definition in the early Islamic period on the basis of textual criticism of the Qurʾān and *tafsīr*, stating:

> From its inception Islam has lived with other religions. Its emergent self-definition evolved through a process of differentiation from other contemporary belief systems. As textual attestation to this process, Islam's foundational Scripture offers abundant evidence of varied interreligious concerns and connections. For example, a primary theological assessment created the fundamental categorization of believer/unbeliever, while further particularization recognized such groupings as Christians, Jews, Majūs, Sābiʾūn, idolators, and so on. Those generations of scholars who then explicated the Qurʾan sought and stabilized the referents for these terms as they elaborated the theological judgments to which they found textual allusion. From this interplay of the Qurʾan and its exegesis arose a fluctuating ethos of interreligious perspectives, prescriptions, and proscriptions.[56]

Notes

1. MS Rampur 565 *al-Muntaqā min kitāb al-ruhbān*, fol. 190b, section 4, lines 24–6. I would like to acknowledge Abusad Islahi, the archivist at the Raza Library of Rampur, India, for making digital scans of the manuscript available to me. I am profoundly appreciative of his efforts. This manuscript was also partially edited by Ṣalāḥuddīn al-Munajjed under the title 'Morceaux choisis du Livre des Moines', *Mélanges* 3 (MIDEO: Institut Dominicain D'Études Orientales du Caire, 1956), 349–58.
2. Fred Donner, *Muhammad and the Believers: At the Origins of Islam* (Cambridge, MA: Belknap Press of Harvard University Press, 2010), 69.
3. Ibid. 220–1. Jeremy Johns has similarly argued for a truly centralised adminis-

trative apparatus beginning only at the time of ʿAbd al-Malik, hence the absence of any definitive, imperial ideological statements prior to the late seventh century. Before the reign of ʿAbd al-Malik, in the author's own words, 'The polity that found itself ruling the conquests was a loose confederation of Arab tribes, not a hegemonic state.' See Johns, 'Archaeology and the History of Early Islam: The First Seventy Years', *Journal of the Economic and Social History of the Orient* 2003, 411–36 at 418. For an alternate view of state formation in the early Islamic period, one that posits an earlier phase of bureaucratic and administrative policies, see Clive Foss, 'A Syrian Coinage of Muʿāwiya?', *Revue Numismatique* 158 (2002), 353–65. Robert Hoyland has addressed both of these contrasting positions in 'New Documentary Texts and the Early Islamic State', *Bulletin of the School of Oriental and African Studies* 69:3 (2006), 395–416.

4. For interpretations regarding the construction of the Dome of the Rock, see Nasser Rabbat, 'The Meaning of the Umayyad Dome of the Rock', *Muqarnas* 6 (1989), 12–21; Oleg Grabar, *The Shape of the Holy: Early Islamic Jerusalem* (Princeton, NJ: Princeton University Press, 1996); Marcus Milwright, *The Dome of the Rock and its Umayyad Mosaic Inscriptions* (Edinburgh: Edinburgh University Press, 2016); and Amikam Elad, 'Why did ʿAbd al-Malik Build the Dome of the Rock? A Re-examination of the Muslim Sources', *Bayt al-Maqdis* (1993), 33–58.
5. Jere L. Bacharach, 'Signs of Sovereignty: The 'Shahāda', Qurʾanic Verses, and the Coinage of ʿAbd al-Malik', *Muqarnas* 27 (2010), 1–30.
6. One might also be tempted to see some of the early martyrological accounts of Muslim converts to Christianity, or apostates, against such a contextual backdrop. See Christian Sahner, *Christian Martyrs Under Islam: Religious Violence and the Making of the Muslim World* (Princteon, NJ: Princeton University Press, 2018), 90. Here, Sahner discusses the execution of Peter of Capitolias on the orders of al-Walīd ibn ʿAbd al-Malik.
7. Bacharach, 'Signs of Sovereignty', 24–5.
8. Donner, *Muhammad and the Believers*, 221–2.
9. I am indebted to an anonymous reviewer for suggesting this phrasing.
10. Hugh Kennedy, 'Islam', in *Interpreting Late Antiquity: Essays on the Post-Classical World*, eds G. W. Bowersock, Peter Brown and Oleg Grabar (Cambridge, MA: Belknap Press of Harvard University, 2001), 219–37. This suggestion stems from the possibility that these particular Christian communities may have perhaps been seen as a 'fifth column' or Byzantine agents of a sort by Muslim authorities due to their connection to Constantinople.

11. See Michael Morony, 'Religious Communities in Late Sassanian and Early Muslim Iraq', *Journal of the Economic and Social History of the Orient* 17 (1974), 113–35.
12. See 'Introductory Note' in 'A Charter of Protection Granted to the Nestorian Church in A.D. 1138, by Muktafi II, the Caliph of Baghdad', ed. A. Mingana, *Bulletin of the John Rylands Library*, 10 (1926), 127–33.
13. Ibn al-Nadīm, *Kitāb al-fihrist*, ed. M. Ridā Tajaddud, 3rd edn (Beirut: Dār al-Masīrah, 1988).
14. Al-Shābushtī, *Kitāb al-diyārāt*, ed. Kūrkīs ʿAwwād, 3rd edn (Beirut: Dār al-Rāʾid al-ʿArabī, 1986). The editor's introduction also provides a long list of medieval authors writing on monasteries, some of which formed the source material for al-Shābushtī.
15. Robert Irwin, *Night and Horses and the Desert: An Anthology of Classical Arabic Literature* (New York: Anchor Books, 2001), 123.
16. Philip Mayerson, The Wine and Vineyards of Gaza in the Byzantine Period', *Bulletin for the American Schools of Oriental Research* 257 (Winter 1985), 75–80.
17. Ruth Mackenson, 'Background of the History of Moslem Libraries', *The American Journal of Semitic Languages and Literatures* 52:2 (January 1936), 194. The author also claims that the use of churches and monasteries as schools in the East had a direct influence on the development of mosque schools in Islam.
18. Hippolyte Delehaye, 'Byzantine Monasticism', in *Byzantium: An Introduction to East Roman Civilization*, eds N. H. Baynes and H. St L. B. Moss (Oxford: Clarendon Press, 1961), 136–65.
19. The *Diyārāt* of al-Shābushtī contains several instances of such occurrences at monasteries; for one example, see the celebration of the *First Sunday of the Great Fast*/Lent at Dayr al-Khawāt on page 93. Further demonstrations of this type of religious interaction are given by Adam Mez in *The Renaissance of Islam* (London: Luzac and Co., 1937). It is perhaps of some relevance as well that even as late as the thirteenth/fourteenth century Ibn Taymīyya chastised his contemporary Muslim community for involvement in Christian festivals and feasts. In his *Iqtiḍāʾ al-ṣirāt al-mustaqīm: mukhālafat aṣḥāb al-jaḥīm*, Ibn Taymīyya explains that his criticism is on the basis that they were non-*Sunna* sanctioned activities and scandalous forms of 'popular religion'. See Jacques Waardenburg, 'Official and Popular Religion in Islam', *Social Compass* 25 (1978), 315–41; Charles D. Matthew, 'A Muslim Iconoclast (Ibn Taymīyyeh) on the "Merits" of Jerusalem and Palestine, *Journal of the American Oriental Society* 56:1 (March, 1936), 1–21; *A Muslim Theologian's Response to Christianity: Ibn Taymiyya's al-*

Jawab al-Sahih, ed. and trans. Thomas F. Michel (Delmar, NY: Caravan Books, 1984), for further explanation.

20. Ibn Saʿd, *Ṭabaqāt al-kabīr* (11 vols) (Cairo: Maktabat al-Khanjī, 2001), vol. 7, 374; see also Suliman Bashear, 'Qibla Musharriqa and Early Muslim Prayer in Churches', *The Muslim World* 81:3–4 (1991), 268–82.
21. The account of ʿUmar's death at Dayr Simʾān is recorded in Tabarī's *Taʾrīkh al-rusūl waʾl mulūk*, Leiden edition 1362–1363 (Leiden: Brill, 1879–1901). The burial account is also preserved in other places, yet there is some confusion over the precise name and location of the monastery.
22. G. Troupeau, 'Les Couvents Chrétiens dans la Littérature Arabe', in *Études sur le christianisme arabe au Moyen Âge*, Variorum Collected Series 515 (London: Variorum, 1995), 265–79 at 270–1.
23. Certain caveats remain, however, concerning the utilisation of the aforementioned material, as there are often issues relating to the nature of their subject matter (i.e. the use of hagiographies, martyriologies, polemic/apologetic treatises or prose literature for historical insight) as well as questions of reliability based on historical and geographical provenance.
24. Chase Robinson discusses the issue of archival preservation in the opening chapter of *Islamic Historiography* (Cambridge: Cambridge University Press, 2003).
25. Donner has aptly noted that scholarly debates over these historiographical issues 'have hung like an ominous cloud over the field almost from the moment scholars began scientifically to work it'. See introduction by Fred Donner, vii–xvii, in ʿAbd al-ʿAzīz al-Dūrī, *The Rise of Historical Writing Among the Arabs* (Princeton, NJ: Princeton University Press, 1983).
26. As Stephen Humphreys has concisely put it, 'If our goal is to comprehend the way in which Muslims of the late 2nd/8th and 3rd/9th centuries understood the origins of their society, then we are well off indeed. But if our aim is to find out "what really happened" – i.e., to develop reliably documented answers to modern questions about the earliest decades of Islamic society – then we are in trouble.' See Humphreys, *Islamic History: A Framework for Inquiry* (Princeton, NJ: Princeton University Press, 1991), 69.
27. Such was the impetus behind Robert Hoyland's *Seeing Islam as Others Saw It: A Survey and Evaluation of Christian, Jewish, and Zoroastrian Writings on Early Islam* (Princeton, NJ: The Darwin Press, 1997).
28. Hugh Kennedy, 'Introduction', in *Documents and the History of the Early Islamic World*, eds Alexander T. Schubert and Petra M. Sijpesteijn (Leiden and Boston: Brill, 2015), 1–7.

29. Hugh Kennedy, 'The Melkite Church from the Islamic Conquest to the Crusades: Continuity and Adaptation in the Byzantine Legacy', in *The 17th International Byzantine Congress, Major Papers* (New Rochelle, NY: A. D. Caratzas, 1986), 325–43; G. J. Reinink, *Syriac Christianity under Late Sassanian and Early Islamic Rule* (London: Ashgate Variorum, 2005); François Nau, *Documents pour servir à l'histoire de l'Église nestorienne, Patrologia Orientalis* tome 13, fasc. 2 (Paris: Firmin-Didot, 1919); J. M. Fiey, *Chrétiens Syriaques sous les Abbassides surtout à Baghdad, 749–1258*, Corpus Scriptorum Christianorum Orientalium t. 59 (Louvain: Secrétariat du Corpus SCO, 1980); Robert Schick, *The Christian Communities of Palestine from Byzantine to Islamic Rule* (Princeton, NJ: Darwin Press, 1995); Milka Levy-Rubin, 'The Reorganization of the Patriarchate of Jerusalem in the Early Muslim Period', *ARAM* 15 (2003), 197–226; Arthur Vööbus, 'The Origin of the Monophysite Church in Syria and Mesopotamia', *Church History* 42:1 (March 1973), 17–26; Andrew Palmer, *Monk and Mason on the Tigris Frontier: the Early History of Tur 'Abdin* (Cambridge: Cambridge University Press, 1990).
30. Sidney Griffith, *Arabic Christianity in the Monasteries of Ninth-Century Palestine* (Aldershot: Ashgate Variorum, 1992), *The Beginnings of Christian Theology in Arabic: Muslim-Christian Encounters in the Early Islamic Period* (Aldershot: Ashgate Variorum, 2002), 'Michael, the Martyr and Monk of Mar Sabas Monastery, at the Court of the Caliph 'Abd al-Malik; Christian Apologetics and Martyrology in the Early Islamic Period', *ARAM* 6:1 (1994); Andrew Louth, 'Palestine under the Arabs 650–750: The Crucible of Byzantine Orthodoxy', in *Holy Land, Holy Lands and Christian History*, ed. R. N. Swanson (Rochester, NY: Ecclesiastical History Society, 1998); A. A. Vasiliev, 'The Iconoclast Edict of the Caliph Yazid II, A.D. 721', *Dumbarton Oaks Papers* 9 (1956), 23–47; Daniel J. Sahas, 'Cultural Interaction during the Umayyad Period. The "Circle" of John of Damascus', *ARAM* 6:1 (1994), 35–66.
31. The most relevant works here are Arthur Vööbus, *History of Asceticism in the Syrian Orient: A Contribution to the History of Culture in the Near East*, vol. III, CSCO t. 81 (1988); Derwis J. Chitty, *The Desert a City: An Introduction to the Study of Egyptian and Palestinian Monasticism under the Christian Empire* (Crestwood, NY: St Vladimir's Seminary Press, 1995); Sebastian Brock, in addition to several works relating to the Syrian Church, the article 'Early Syrian Asceticism', *Numen* 20 (April 1973), 1–19, is of primary interest to this theme; Robert Kirschner, 'The Vocation of Holiness in Late Antiquity', *Vigiliae Christianae* 38 (1984), 105–24; Peter Brown, *Society and the Holy in*

Late Antiquity (Berkeley and Los Angeles, CA: University of California Press, 1982).

32. Fred Donner, *The Early Islamic Conquests* (Princeton, NJ: Princeton University Press, 1981); Walter Kaegi, *Byzantium and the Early Islamic Conquests* (Cambridge: Cambridge University Press, 1992); Hugh Kennedy, 'The Last Century of Byzantine Syria: a Reinterpretation', *Byzantinische Forshungen* 10 (1985), 141–83; Irfan Shahid, *Byzantium and the Arabs in the Sixth Century* (Washington, DC: Dumbarton Oaks Research Library and Collection, 1995); Robert Schick, 'Jordan on the Eve of the Muslim Conquest A.D. 602–634', in *La Syrie de Byzance à L'Islam VII–VIII Siècles*, eds P. Cavinet and J.-P. Rey-Coquais (Damascus: Institute Français de Damas, 1992), 107–19; Elizabeth Fowden, *The Barbarian Plain: Saint Sergius between Rome and Iran* (Berkeley, CA: University of California Press, 1999).
33. Peter Charanis, 'Monastic Properties and the State in the Byzantine Empire', *Dumbarton Oaks Papers* 4 (1948), 53–118; Charles A. Frazee, 'Late Roman and Byzantine Legislation on the Monastic Life from the Fourth to the Eighth Centuries', *Church History* 51:3 (September 1982), 263–79; John Philip Thomas, *Private Religious Foundations in the Byzantine Empire* (Washington, DC: Dumbarton Oaks, 1987); Daniel C. Dennett, *Conversion and the Poll Tax in Early Islam* (Cambridge, MA: Harvard University Press, 1950); Antoine Fattal, *Le Statut Légal des Non-Musulmans en Pays D'Islam* (Beirut: L'Institut de Lettres Orientales de Beyrouth, 1958); A. J. Tritton, *The Caliphs and Their Non-Muslim Subjects* (London: Frank Cass & Co., 1970).
34. Yizhar Hirschfeld, *The Judean Desert Monasteries in the Byzantine Period* (New Haven, CT: Yale University Press, 1992); Yoram Tsafrir, 'Monks and Monasteries in Southern Sinai', in *Ancient Churches Revealed*, ed. Y. Tsafrir (Jerusalem: Israel Exploration Society, 1993), 315–33; Geoffrey King, 'Two Byzantine Churches in Northern Jordan and their Re-use in the Islamic Period', *Damaszener Mitteilungen* 1 (1983), 111–36; Michele Piccirillo, 'The Umayyad Churches of Jordan', *Annual of the Department of Antiquities in Jordan* 28 (1984), 333–41.
35. Troupeau, 'Les Couvents', 271.
36. Ibid. 271.
37. Ibid. 271.
38. Ibid. 273.
39. John Binns, *Ascetics and Ambassadors of Christ: The Monasteries of Palestine 314–631* (Oxford: Clarendon Press, 1994), 54–5.

40. Ibid. 54–5.
41. Hilary Kilpatrick, 'Monasteries Through Muslim Eyes: The Diyārāt Books', in *Christians at the Heart of Islamic Rule: Church Life and Scholarship in 'Abbasid Iraq*, ed. David Thomas (Leiden: Brill, 2003), 19–37.
42. Kilpatrick, 'Monasteries', 25.
43. Elizabeth and Garth Fowden, 'Monks, Monasteries and Early Islam', in *Studies on Hellenism, Christianity and the Umayyads*, eds G. Fowden and E. K. Fowden, *Melethmata* 37 (Athens: Diffusion de Boccard, 2004), 149–74.
44. Ibid. 149–74.
45. Jane McAuliffe, *Qur'anic Christians: An Analysis of Classical and Modern Exegesis* (Cambridge: Cambridge University Press, 1991). Chapter 9, entitled 'Compassion, Mercy, and Monasticism', 260–84, deals extensively with this theme.
46. Daniel J. Sahas, 'Monastic Ethos and Spirituality and the Origins of Islam', in *Acts of the XVIIIth International Congress of Byzantine Studies*, eds I. Ševčenko and G. Litavrin (Shepherdstown, WV: Byzantine Studies Press, 1996), issue 2, 27–39.
47. Louis Massignon, 'The Vocation of Monasticism', in *Essays on the Origins of the Technical Language of Islamic Mysticism*, trans. Benjamin Clark (Notre Dame, IN: University of Notre Dame Press, 1997).
48. Edmund Beck, 'Das Christliche Mönchtum Im Koran', *Studia Orientalia* 13:3 (1946), 3–29.
49. Massignon, for instance, is more interested in the development of Islamic mysticism and its connection to the legacy of monasticism in the Near East.
50. Thomas Sizgorich, *Violence and Belief in Late Antiquity: Militant Devotion in Christianity and Islam* (Philadelphia, PA: University of Pennsylvania Press, 2009), as a reformulation of his doctoral dissertation 'Monks, Martyrs and Mujāhidūn: Militant Piety in Late Antiquity and Early Islam' (unpublished dissertation from the University of California Santa Barbara, 2005).
51. Ibid. 168–70.
52. The largely 'Abbāsid period of frontier warfare, which Michael Bonner has covered in *Aristocratic Violence and Holy War: Studies in the Jihad and the Arab-Byzantine Frontier* (New Haven, CT: American Oriental Society, 1996).
53. See Reuven Firestone, 'Jihād', in *The Blackwell Companion to the Qur'ān*, ed. A. Rippin (Oxford: Blackwell Publishing, 2006), 308–20 at 311. The term *jihād* is discussed in a range of meanings: from the more explicit example of a defen-

sive war to protect the community, to a more nuanced interpretation relating to a personal effort towards righteousness.

54. Muḥammad ibn Aḥmad al-Malaṭī, *Die Widerlegung der Irrgläubigen und Neuerer, von Abū l-Husain Muhammad ibn Aḥmad al-Malatī*, ed. Sven Dedering, Biblioteca Islamica vol. 9 (Leipzig and Istanbul: Brockhaus, 1936), 122. The root *j-h-d* is used in this context specifically to denote the effort in pietistic observance.
55. The description of monasteries as places of wine-drinking and amusement is also mentioned by Muhammad Manazir Ahsan, *Social Life Under the Abbasids 786–902* AD (London: Longman Press, 1979), 271, on the basis of accounts in *Kitāb al-aghānī* and *Kitāb al-diyārāt*.
56. Jane Dammen McAuliffe, 'Christians in the Qur'an and Tafsīr', in *Muslim Perspectives of Other Religions: A Historical Survey*, ed. Jacques Waardenburg (Oxford: Oxford University Press, 1999), 105–21 at 105.

1

The Wombs of the Wadīs: An Inquiry into Christian Monastic Life of the Medieval Islamic Era

Defining Confessional Boundaries

A June 2009 *National Geographic* article entitled 'Arab Christians: The Forgotten Faithful' provides a vivid description of contemporary Muslim visitation to the Christian shrine of Ṣaydnāyā near Damascus. Cross-confessional interest in the Greek Orthodox Convent of Our Lady, constructed in the fifth century above the town of Ṣaydnāyā, has persisted since the Middle Ages.[1] The location's renown is owed to the presence of a purportedly miraculous icon of the Virgin Mary, known locally as the *shaghūra* or 'famed one' in Syriac. The image of the Holy Mother, attributed to Saint Luke, has long been believed to possess curative powers.[2] Even during the tumultuous period between the twelfth to thirteenth centuries, the Crusader chronicler Jacques of Vitry writes not only of Christians, but throngs of 'Saracens' that appeared as devotees to the shrine.[3] This place has maintained its spiritual allure for those in need amongst both the Christian and Muslim communities of the region until the present day. As witnessed by the *National Geographic* reporter, the scene that unfolds before the icon is one of deep and emotional veneration. In the words of a Muslim woman who had come to the shrine from Damascus with her ailing child, 'I am a Muslim, but a long time ago my family was Christian. I believe in the prophets – Muslim, Jewish and Christian – and I believe in Mary. I have come here so that my boy will be healed.'[4]

This type of interreligious contact has been exhibited since the earliest days of Islam in a variety of manners and locales. While there are pockets in which customs such as this continue, they appear to have been considerably more widespread in the medieval world. The research here will focus on Christian monasteries of the Near East as prominent centres for contact and communication between religious traditions in the formative period of the Muslim community. Just as the modern-day scene recounted above at Ṣaydnāyā presents a challenge to traditionally interpreted, strictly defined denominational barriers, the early Muslim concern for monastic sites and sanctuaries would appear to suggest a certain religious ecumenism within the late antique Mediterranean tradition. Instead of interpreting early Muslim fascination with monastic life as a facet of tolerance toward Christians in the broader sense, which has been well documented in contemporary scholarship, the phenomenon should then be viewed as a genuine synthesis of confessional factions based upon certain shared, core spiritual values.[5]

Given the recent trend in scholarship concerning the question of 'identity'[6] in the late antique and early Islamic Near East, the issue of confessional boundaries becomes all the more salient. This period, after all, has been increasingly characterised as an era of ebbing barriers, applying to both the general dissolution of imperial borders[7] as well as the mutability of social frontiers between the fifth and seventh centuries. The academic discourse has thus shifted from the older, more stringent view that this period represents a conclusive 'decline',[8] with its outlook firmly fixed upon the late Roman administrative centre, to a more transitional interpretation based largely on cultural and religious contours.[9] The cross-cultural pollination of religious ideas, extending across political divides, has become a consistent feature of contemporary research within the field of late antique studies.[10] This nuanced understanding of pliable frontiers has yielded additional inquiries into the manner in which various groups would have self-identified, with regard to political, linguistic, geographic and religious factors. An examination of identity, or self-identity, in the late antique Near East often hinges upon the obscured confluence of a Byzantine/Hellenistic past, a Greek/Coptic/Syriac Christian or Jewish cultural heritage, and the emergence of a new Islamic regional polity.[11]

Richard Miles has observed that identities in this context are not necessarily static, fastened to a 'fixed' reality, but are rather quite dynamic and subject to change depending on a group's recognition of itself as a collective in a particular situation. As he suggests, 'It is possible to have an overarching single identity, but it will always be made up of several, if not myriad, separate identities, some of which may be contradictory.'[12] The argument clearly acknowledges the fluid nature of identities throughout the late antique period, allowing for an overlapping of the self-identity construct. Most crucial, however, is the insistence that the concept could be applied to religious orientations that may appear to be, on the surface, paradoxical.

In his work on late antique Christianity in North Africa, Éric Rebillard has advocated for precisely this type of tiered or multilayered understanding of confessional distinction. In the specific context of Carthage, inasmuch as many Christians of Tertullian's era would have identified themselves as belonging to a voluntary community, one that had abandoned the world of the Roman Empire in preference for the church,[13] it seems that neither Christians nor pagans considered religious allegiance any more important a social indicator than other factors. In terms of dress, language, gesture, occupation, education and involvement in cultural activities, there does not seem to be much evidence for concrete barriers to demarcate a completely separate 'Christian world', in which more ancient, indigenous beliefs and newly shaped Christian elements would have been mutually exclusive. The identification between such groups would have commonly been shared, superseding the construct of confessional divisions.[14] Rebillard concludes this discussion by offering:

> Christianness was only one of the many affiliations that mattered in everyday life, and we should not assume that the degree of groupness associated with the Christian category was as high, stable, and consistent as Tertullian claims it should be. We need therefore to take into consideration that Christians, as the other inhabitants of the Roman Empire, did not belong to only one collectivity that determined their identity.[15]

If we can accept the idea that religious boundaries would have been sensitively negotiated in a late antique Christian context, can the same inference not be drawn for the emergence of Islam in the middle of the seventh century? The processes of this suggested *blurred* ecclesiastical margin would have remained much the same as had existed in the earlier periods.[16] As a consequence of flexible confessional barriers between Christians and their Muslim counterparts at the beginnings of social interaction, we see a discernible trepidation over exclusively demarcating religious divisions in the legal and literary texts of the following centuries. The hardening of confessional distinctions was, after all, a progression that has been traced from approximately the same period within the Muslim caliphates and the world of Syriac-speaking Christianity, in terms of polemical literature and legal statutes. Such a concern on the part of both Muslim and Christian theologians, originating in the ninth century and continuing beyond, would therefore suggest that rigid confessional barriers had yet to be fully recognised in the initial periods of contact.[17]

Michael Penn has specifically pointed to legal tracts from the Syriac tradition that bear witness to this attempt at defining borders between Muslim and Christian, demonstrating a shift in attitudes from the seventh century onwards in addressing issues like inter-marriage, interaction with officials, participation in religious rites, and visitation to holy places.[18] This would indicate a later, systematic reaction to the situation that had prevailed on the local level from the dawn of interchange between communities, revealing that 'Syriac authors were much more interested in patrolling the boundaries between Christianity and Islam than were most of their audience'.[19] Here we must include the crucial observation offered by Jack Tannous that such confessional fluidity was facilitated by the rather 'simple and compatibilist' view of religious doctrine held by the eastern Christian masses throughout the late antique and early Islamic period. These common people, or the 'audience' that Penn refers to, were not, after all, professional theologians and exercised only a limited understanding of scripture, sanctioned rituals or dogma.[20] Consequently, the intersecting and overlapping of sacramental rites between religious communities should come as no surprise for the period in question.

Cannot the same be said for the first generations of Muslims as well? We should concede that the fledgling *umma* would not have overwhelmingly been comprised of religious scholars, and those who did seek to earnestly follow the Prophet's convictions undoubtedly came into contact with other religious communities that espoused comparable tenets. This connection to varieties of Christian communities, Jews and Zoroastrians invariably had an impact on the development of Islamic theology and doctrine. In the words of Tannous:

> The earliest Christian-Muslim interactions took place in a Near East characterized by widespread ignorance of and selective regard – if not outright disregard – for the Qur'ān and for the Prophet's teaching and behavior, even as the understanding of these things and their import among the religiously engaged members of his community were undergoing development and change. It was in such a setting that the notional followers of the Prophet had to answer questions from members of other religious groups and Muslim leaders had to make cultic and doctrinal decisions about the practical implications of Muḥammad's preaching.[21]

In line with this statement from Tannous, Christian Sahner's work on 'conversion' in this period makes it clear that 'the line between religious conversion and cultural assimilation was often very blurry'.[22] We should not forget either that a significant majority of those whom embraced the message of Muḥammad en masse, only did so after the *Hijra* and ensuing military triumphs of the Medina period.[23] It seems reasonable to suggest that these 'converts' too would have necessarily held a cursory awareness of what that 'conversion' actually meant in theological terms. While a sincere adoption of Muḥammad's teachings cannot, of course, be dismissed, other factors also played a role – particularly, reasons of political expediency amongst the Meccan aristocracy. An argument for the latter could surely be made regarding a number of prominent figures in the early Islamic tradition, including Khālid ibn al-Walīd, 'Amr ibn al-'Āṣ, and Abū Sufyān – all of whom, for some time, had vehemently opposed the message before ultimately being reconciled by virtue of their 'conversion'. The question could then be raised whether or not such a superficial understanding of religious doctrines contributed to the *Ridda* Wars (the Wars of Apostasy), which broke out across the Arabian penninsula following the death of the Prophet. These wars, which pitted the nascent Muslim community against a host of 'would-be rival prophets',[24] demonstrate the fragile balance between political allegiance to Medina and a genuine adherence to the spiritual principles laid forth by Muḥammad.[25]

In terms of Christians living under Muslim rule, Tannous rightly points out that this was a period of Near Eastern history in which the 'mosque was in the shadow of the Church, or better yet, Churches'.[26] As time moved forward and groups became increasingly intertwined, it would have been perceived as all the more obligatory, on the part of each culture's intellectual and spiritual elite, to erect doctrinal walls to differentiate religious communities. Partially this would have perhaps been in an effort to ingratiate one's own sectarian group to regional authorities, at the expense of one's larger co-religionist population. In an evolving struggle to define one's own cultic community in explicit terms, it was perhaps most expedient to envision certain other theologies and rituals in stark contrast or opposition. The same can be said of the historical process for self-identification among Christian sectarian groups throughout the fifth to eighth centuries in the Near East.[27] There is little indication that groups commonly referred to in the texts of this period as 'Nestorian', 'Chalcedonian' or 'Jacobite' presented a movement of theological solidarity in the face of Muslim rule, often in its place resorting to polemical confrontations with each other in an effort to limit the porous boundaries of inter-sectarian contact.[28]

The fact that there were internal ecclesiastical attempts to regulate sectarian contact unmistakably reinforces that boundaries were being ignored and that such indiscretions were a concern for clergy. The eighth-century Syriac *Chronicle of Marūthā*, for example, illustrates the sharing of the Eucharist and other ceremonies between Nestorian and Miaphysite communities in Mesopotamia between the mid-sixth to mid-seventh century, as well as recording visits by members of the Sassanian court to monasteries. Even as the text further explains that the monk Marūthā (d. 649), the metropolitan of Takrīt, put an end to the inter-confessional ritual involvement among rival Christian groups,[29] the demonstration remains that sectarian lines could be blurred on the local level. The fact that higher ecclesiastical authorities would have been the champions of delineating such boundaries should come as no surprise.

In examining a similar phenomenon of 'imagined boundaries', David Frankfurter has focused his work on the development of Christianity in late Roman Egypt. In this case, the syncretism of local traditional Egyptian cults with a rising tide of Christian practice hindered any absolute delineation between communities.[30] By questioning the familiar and tidy terms like 'conversion' in a late antique Egyptian context, Frankfurter's work has demonstrated that 'popular' or 'lived' spiritual praxes would necessarily undermine the more official directives of an organised church.[31] On the local level, therefore, communal ritual and religious observance would have often possessed their own agency, expressed through a variety of syncretic customs, quite aloof from any unyielding, institutional oversight.[32]

It is worth noting that Frankfurter begins his book, *Christianizing Egypt*, with a compelling textual example of this overlapping between what might be termed 'pagan' mythological remnants and Christian motif. Here a translation is provided of a seventh-century papyrus document containing healing invocations, perhaps unexpectedly recording the name of 'Jesus Horus, the son of Isis', as the central figure within the incantation. The example of the papyrus passage is then followed by questions of its interpretation: What would an enchantment like this mean for the overtly Christian society that produced it? Does the phrasing within the document simply hint at the survival of negligible archaic elements from a pagan past, or does it represent a more organic fusion of local abandoned rites with emerging Christian traditions? With these issues in mind, the remainder of his study examines the artificial, or imposed, distinction between 'popular religion' and 'proper religion' in this particular historical situation. In doing so, as he claims,

> we begin to find religion as it was lived, Christianity in its local constructions . . . Christianity in Egypt of the fifth, sixth, and seventh centuries amounted to a framework within which mothers and scribes, artisans and holy men, priests and herdsmen experimented with diverse kinds of religious material and traditions.[33]

In his work on conversion to Islam during the early period, Richard Bulliet has sketched comparable issues in attempting to evaluate the process of religious change over time. It would undoubtedly have been a rather slow process and would have varied considerably from region to region.[34] In this case attempting to measure the adoption of Islam within a given community setting, within the first two centuries of Muslim rule, is rendered all the more complicated because it was 'more a matter of social behavior than religious belief'.[35] By looking at early testimonials and personal conversion accounts from the Islamic tradition, Bulliet concludes that there would have been no documentary proof, sacramental performance or catechetical preparation to indicate the character of conversion in this context; rather, it would likely have been based on social behaviour as the qualifier. However, a change in the nature of conversion would eventually take place which emphasised belief, or theology, above practice, but not until some time around the fourth Islamic century. Particularly in the earlier period, there is no textual evidence to suggest that learning the Qurʾān or being knowledgeable of its subject matter plays any role in conversion.[36] We cannot therefore presuppose that an early initiate could necessarily have held any significant comprehension of doctrinal barriers or dogma that partitioned one's old religion from a new one. As Bulliet succinctly puts it, 'In a sense, a convert first became a member of the Muslim community and later discovered, or tried to discover, what it meant to be a Muslim.'[37] The early Muslim creed on balance, in its most fundamental form, was to affirm the existence of the one God[38] and reinforce the duty of mankind to be pious in this endeavour.[39]

This would seem especially applicable to the initial phases of contact with Christian and Jewish populations, whose basic theologies would have been in relative conjunction. This argument clearly allows for considerable fluctuations in confessional self-identity during the period in question, to the extent that one might then contend that the very notion of definable religious barriers, as a method of verifying conversion or designating the other in early Islam, would become somewhat dubious. We must take into account the potential knowledge of doctrinally specific beliefs on the local level, the difference in vernacular languages of various religious groups in the initial contact period, and the continued intimate social interaction between religious communities. Again, this fluid process concerns *lived religion*, as it would have been understood and practised by common people on the ground, not withstanding the differing judgements of erudite theologians.

Both Frankfurter and Michael Morony, albeit from the differing vantage points of Egypt and Iraq respectively, appropriately link the commemoration of saints and holy figures, along with visitation to their shrines and monasteries, as essential to the conception of Christian identity in this period.[40] While reverence for particular heroes of the faith could sustain a group's collective memory, we cannot insist that shrines within this religious landscape would have been in any way confessionally exclusive. They were often, as Frankfurter suggests, social sites where diverse communities would come into contact with each other for celebrations and feast days.[41] The mystique of the holy man was situated at the core of this religious landscape, attracting the common masses, both those initiated into explicit confessional backgrounds as well as the uninitiated, for pilgrimage to his tomb, shrine or monastery. These figures that Peter Brown refers to as representatives for 'the locus of the supernatural'[42] supplied more rural communities with *fixed points*, in the form of monasteries, shrines and martyria around which communication networks revolved.[43]

The basic components that constituted ritual activity in such holy places, such as the lighting of candles, making supplicatory offerings, and prostrations were altogether part of the public fabric of traditions in the wider Near East and Mediterranean world. Josef Meri has described these rites as

> common to all and were arguably intrinsic to 'religion' itself in this part of the world. The universality of a 'prophet' as a figure of holiness is suggested, indeed, by those occasions on which Muslims, Jews, and Christians venerated together at common shrines.[44]

This kind of interreligious contact within the *sacred topography* appears to have been remarkably widespread throughout the medieval world, with Ṣaydnāyā serving as an excellent example of its continuation into modern times.[45] For Christians in the late Roman period it seems as though visitation to sacred places and to holy individuals were linked in a sense of coterminous piety.[46] The early pilgrim's desire to not only see biblical sites but to actually interact with living holy figures, was envisioned as the most vivid way of truly experiencing sacred text. Travel to hallowed destinations often then began at monasteries, with monks being relied upon as guides within the sacred topography and transmitters of spiritual wisdom along the way.[47] The *Itinerarium Egeriae*, a late fourth-century pilgrimage account from the Latin West, depicts precisely this kind of circuit that begins at Nitria, continues through the Thebaid, across Sinai, and ultimately arrives in Palestine via monastic assistance.[48]

The profound influence of eastern Christian asceticism on regional cultural and religious life within the period of Late Antiquity has long been recognised. To this end, the era has been characterised as 'the age of the holy man and ascetic'[49] of the Near East, where a multitude of Christian monasteries and hermitages dotted the landscape of the Levant and North Africa. To these ascetic figures was attributed the capacity to navigate both the mundane, human existence as well as the immaterial world of the spiritual.[50] In the early Christian imagination, holy men served as reminders of the divine presence in the world, providing testimony of God's proximity to mankind through the charisma of the ascetic himself, the potency of his intercessory prayers, and/or the miracles conducted through his agency.[51] Referring to them as 'arbiters of the holy', Peter Brown has suggested that,

> throughout the Christian world of the fifth and sixth century, the average Christian believer was encouraged to draw comfort from the expectation that, somewhere, in his own times, even, maybe, in his own region, a chosen few of his fellows had achieved, usually through prolonged ascetic labour, an exceptional degree of closeness to God.[52]

The impact of the mystic and holy man continued into the early Islamic period, exerting a broad-ranging influence across a variety of religious communities. Garth Fowden makes the intransience of the holy man's mystique within this transitional era clear in the statement, 'the monk came to stand emblematically for the Christian faith as a whole – such was the powerful role played by asceticism during Muhammad's lifetime'.[53]

Monasteries were in turn the institutional expression of the ascetic ideal, forming the 'spiritual and intellectual axis'[54] of their local communities. In many examples from early eastern monastic literature it appears that the space chosen for ascetic practice was often charged with as much meaning as the actual ritual exercises that took place there.[55] The planning and construction of monastic space was therefore seen as a metaphor for the instructions of ascetic life, including individual and communal aspects of this praxis.[56] In terms of the perception by the local populations and their religious experience, the monastery as an entity would have commonly been considered a wellspring of sanctity, the site and its surroundings being imbued with holiness by virtue of the ascetics within its walls.[57]

As the Syriac text of the *Book of Life* recounts concerning the ascetic fame of the fifth-century monks of the monastery at Qartmin,[58]

> Men thronged to this place in multitudes and in their regiments to become proven monks and saintly men, able to work powers and marvels with great

> signs and amazing feats, true disciples of holy masters . . . who is there indeed that is equal to the task of relating their protracted fasting, their ceaseless prayers, their abstinence and asceticism.[59]

Contemporary hagiographers and hymnists within the Syriac tradition commonly equate the hardships endured by monks with a life of combat in the arena, styling the monk himself as an 'athlete' in the spiritual sense.[60] The esteem for certain elements of the monastic life, particularly with respect to eastern monasticism and the severity of its ascetic tenets,[61] permeated across confessional boundaries in the late antique world.

While the fifth to seventh centuries represent the climax of monastic activity in the region, it is well documented that many of these monasteries continued to flourish throughout these regions after the Islamic conquests of the seventh century. Even amidst the turbulent regime change, shifting from Byzantine Christian to Muslim rule, there is virtually no evidence for widespread destruction of Christian religious institutions or places of worship in this transitional era.[62] Though it appears that the construction of new monasteries stagnated during this period, in contrast to the previously intense phases of Christian building activity under the Byzantines, archaeological data suggests that many of the pre-existing monasteries continued to function and prosper under Muslim authority.[63]

This research will contend that the interaction between the monasteries of the region and the early Muslim community suggests a vague confessional milieu in which certain collective beliefs, such as an emphasis on rigorous piety, would have been the key determinant in the shaping of Muslim interest in the preservation and appreciation for the monastic lifestyle. There has been a considerable volume of scholarly literature dedicated to the pivotal role of monks and ascetics within the pietistic domain of Late Antiquity,[64] demonstrating their standing as representatives of popular forms of Christian devotion in the East and symbols of an alternative to the more structured practices of the imperial Church.[65] The spiritual function of monastic communities was, however, merely one component to their significance and influence upon the state and its citizenry. Such figures had physically withdrawn from society, yet the monasteries and hermitages they inhabited were often the settings of political and theological debates that had wide-ranging consequences across the Byzantine world.[66]

As an outsider to the traditional public life, having earned reputations for unyielding honesty, wisdom and impartiality, the holy man also served as an ideal mediator of local quarrels. Mundane disputes involving lawsuits over taxation and debts, aside from more spiritual matters, periodically included a monastic presence.[67] This melange of asceticism with political activism was personified in the figure of Simeon Stylites, the fifth-century pillar saint of northern Syria. According to the *Historia religiosa*, Simeon was celebrated not only for his working of miracles and feats of self-mortification, but also for his mediation efforts between temporal authorities and the troubled populace.[68] There were others as well that became renown for defending the peasantry against ruthless tax-collectors and landowners.[69] As Alice-Mary Talbot has commented, 'It is one of the great paradoxes of Byzantine civilization that the monasteries that were established to enable Christian ascetics to renounce the material values and kinship bonds of the secular world soon became a microcosm of Byzantine social structure.'[70]

Just as the boundary between the coenobitic monk behind monastery walls and the Christian ascetic hermit are somewhat opaque in this period,[71] the discussion necessarily involves the interface between Christian and Muslim manifestations of asceticism and the Islamic doctrinal position on monasticism. The prestige of ascetic figures, in a multitude of guises throughout this period, would itself seem to have traversed certain doctrinal barriers. If we acknowledge this potential flexibility and fluidity of exchange across confessional divides at the genesis of Islam, it seems reasonable that Jewish, Christian and other vague monotheistic traditions, anchored in comparable tenets, could have been incorporated into such a movement. The argument, in other words, suggests a somewhat amorphous, pietistic milieu in which core theological and moralistic concepts would have necessarily superseded precise confessional allegiances.[72] Rather than examining this phenomenon as an initiative based entirely on newly formed religious principles, the rise of Islam can perhaps best be viewed as a constituent to the larger context of the period or 'as a continuation of the pietistic tendency found in Near Eastern religions in the late antique period'.[73] The demand for personal righteousness and pious action, visible throughout the Qur'ān by virtue of a multitude of mandates,[74] perhaps most accords with the traditional tenets of eastern monastic life in Late Antiquity. One might argue that the early Muslim view of Christian monastic communities should be less characterised as religious toleration, but more in the vein of confessional overlapping and ambiguity. The absolute imperative for piety amongst the early Muslim *umma*, as well as the appreciation of this principle in outlying groups, can be seen as the tie that further bound these traditions together.

The issue of what precisely this *piety* meant for the early Islamic community might likewise be explained by virtue of its Qur'ānic context. The overriding concern in Muslim holy scripture is that mankind has a duty to be pious 'as a religious obedience – which, in the Qur'anic terms, means submission (*islām*) to God's revealed law for men: belief in one God and the Last Judgment, performance of basic ritual duties – prayer, fasting, righteous and modest manner'.[75] The theme of piety and morality is such a constant, in terms of its unqualified injunction within the Qur'ān, it may be concluded that this was indeed 'the essence of Muḥammad's message'.[76] As the main tenets above imply, this strict code of ethical conduct rooted in monotheism would have unavoidably held a more ecumenical basis, rather than possessing any conspicuous confessional distinction at that moment in time.

Monasteries within Caliphal Lands

As an extension of this convergence between the solitary and lay masses, missionary endeavours would likewise become an essential feature of the ascetic existence in the East. Levantine and Mesopotamian monasticism in particular played a fundamental role in the 'life of ideas',[77] involving the active participation of monks in the Christianisation of Arab nomadic tribes and the dissemination of Christian intellectual culture to the so-called 'barbarian' peoples along the fringes of society.[78] This also produced the quite tangible effects of establishing settlements within the wild places of the imperial borderlands, facilitating a greater interaction between desert nomads and villages.[79] From the period of the early fourth to late sixth century, the institution of monasticism experienced a remarkable expansion across the Roman and Byzantine world. From its origins in Egypt under St Antony in the late third century, it further spread throughout adjacent Syria-Palestine under Hilarion and Epiphanius in the mid-fourth century, widening its diffusion in the West by the early fifth century.[80] It is clear that these ascetic movements achieved a remarkable following during the late antique period, attracting many thousands to the hermitic and/or monastic lifestyle; J. M. Fiey estimated that monks constituted a full third of the Syriac-speaking Christian population of Iraq in this period.[81]

Yet, determining an approximate number for institutions in a certain locale within a given time frame is difficult,[82] as is estimating the numbers of monks in residence.[83] Particularly regarding its eastern contexts, the classifications of monastic existence varied considerably, ranging from great *coenobia* with hundreds of residents to hermitages consisting of merely a few communal ascetics. The prospect of verifying the number of monasteries is made all the more obscure due to what Fiey refers to as 'displaced monasteries',[84] whereby monks would have at times been forced to move their entire communities for security reasons. In turn, these relocated monasteries often appear in the texts with the same name as the original establishments, adding to some confusion over the number of monasteries in a given region. Bearing these uncertainties, an illustration for the scale of monastery construction at its summit has been provided by the archaeological investigations of Hirschfeld, who suggested that there could have been as many as 3,000 monks inhabiting some sixty monasteries within a ten-square-mile area of the Judean desert.[85] A seventh-century Armenian source counts nearly seventy monastic sites in and around Jerusalem.[86]

In terms of the monasteries located throughout Palestine in general, Vailhé lists more than 100 known *laurae* and other forms of monasteries in existence prior to the Persian invasion in the early seventh century.[87] Based on more recent excavations, Doron Bar was able to identify the remains of more than 170 monasteries across the Palestinian countryside in the Byzantine period.[88] Fiey, in turn, was able to confirm the existence of approximately 150 East Syriac monasteries in Iraq and the surrounding regions into the beginnings of the Islamic period.[89] Using a sixth-century Syriac document containing the signatures of Miaphysite abbots together with the names of their monasteries, Shahîd was able to verify the existence of 137 monasteries in Provincia Arabia.[90] The geographical lexicon of Yāqūt (d. 1229), the *Muʿjam al-buldān*, provides separate entries for nearly 200 monasteries within Islamic domains.[91] Additionally, the Muslim author al-Shābushtī

(d. 1008) provides information concerning fifty-three monasteries, still in operation during Islamic times, scattered throughout the Levant, Iraq and Egypt in his *Kitāb al-diyārāt* (*Book of Monasteries*).[92] The historian al-Maqrīzī (d. 1442) suggested that there were 100 monasteries in the Wadī al-Natrūn of Lower Egypt alone on the eve of the conquest period.[93]

These monasteries in question, while technically under the legal supervision of local Muslim officials, appear to have continued to operate according to their own established rules of conduct and independent hierarchical structures. That the internal administration of monasteries continued to be quite self-regulating is not to suggest that they were irrelevant to the political mechanisms of the state, as they did continue to occupy an important position within the social structure of the empire. Their enduring significance was partially due to the fact that the bulk of their subject population remained Christian well into the Islamic period. However, their impact was not confined to the Christian strata alone within the Muslim state, as it seems that monasteries maintained significant import to the caliphal administration and its intellectual infrastructure as well, perhaps being appropriately described as 'intermediaries' within that society.[94]

The Nestorian complex of Dayr Qunnā for example, located south of Baghdad on the banks of the Tigris, was renown for its monastic school and is reported to have trained generations of secretaries and functionaries for the ʿAbbāsid court.[95] The intellectual activity of monks throughout this period has been widely recognised in terms of the preservation of classical works, the copying of manuscripts, and compositions of historical and hagiographical material;[96] this use of monasteries as schools and repositories of learning in turn had a direct influence on the development of the Muslim library and madrasa.[97] As a component of these philosophical endeavours, it has been suggested that contacts between Muslim ascetics and the Christian monastic communities, scattered throughout Syria, Arabia and Iraq, helped to shape the principles of early Islamic mysticism.[98]

The function of monasteries as places of healing, along with the perception that monks possessed certain pharmaceutical knowledge or medical training, had been a common feature of the late antique world.[99] It seems that the scholarly pursuit of physically curative properties was therefore often blended with the search for spiritually curative practices.[100] This fusion of bodily healing with religion is demonstrated in the case of the famous School of Edessa in this period, where the leading field of study and faculty belonged to theology, while the second most important field was reserved for medicine.[101] This recognition likewise continued within an Islamic context.[102] The traditionally isolated and rural settings for monasteries, particularly as in the case of many of the Levantine monastic communities, served to promote their association with hospices for the sick and places of asylum in times of disease. An account preserved in the *Ansāb al-ashrāf* of al-Balādhurī (d. 892 CE) records that even the caliph Hishām (r. 723–43) sought refuge from a plague at a rural monastery in Syria, apparently remote enough to be safe from the spreading disease.[103]

Muslim interest in monastic life was not restricted to purely theological or academic pursuits. Popular fascination with monasteries engendered an entire sub-field in medieval Arabic literature, primarily envisioning Christian monasteries as places of retreat and merrymaking for Muslim elites. While much of this Muslim literary corpus on monasteries is no longer extant, it is in itself instructive that this type of writing constituted such a presence in the literature of that time.[104] Art and architectural projects of the early Islamic period can also provide evidence for the continued socio-economic gravity of monastic settlements within that society. Several of the Umayyad royal *quṣūr* (palaces), particularly those located in the desert areas of the Levant, were constructed adjacent to monasteries or above ruined monastic sites. The Monastery of Saint Theodore for example, located in the hills above Damascus, was confiscated by the Umayyads and turned into a residential palace.[105] The Umayyad caliph al-Walīd I (d. 715) is reported to have retired to Dayr Murrān, another expropriated monastery near the capital, seeking relief from his maladies.[106] The caliph Hishām established a residence at Ruṣāfa that was near the monastery of the basilica dedicated to Saint Sergius, one of the most important holy men for the Levantine Arabs of Late Antiquity.[107] These desert *quṣūr*, like the monasteries founded before them, were strategically located according to the topography; while physically removed from the greater part of society, they were still close to water supplies and in proximity to the major trade routes, allowing the Umayyads to keep close watch on the Bedouin tribes of the region.[108]

In discussing the foundation of Sāmarrāʾ under the Caliph al-Muʿtaṣim,

Figure 1.1 Ruṣāfa (Sergiopolis) – Church of St Sergius. Credit: Judith McKenzie/ Manar al-Athar photo-archive, Oxford 2013.

the tenth-century historian al-Masʿudī demonstrates that the practice of imperial construction near monastic settlements extended into the ʿAbbāsid period as well. According to al-Masʿūdī's *Murūj al-dhahab*, the search for pristine land upon which to construct his new imperial capital led the caliph to the site of an ancient Christian monastery along the eastern banks of the Tigris. As he was so taken with the fertility of the soil and the tranquility of the locale, al-Muʿtaṣim arranged to purchase the land from the monks in residence for the sum of 4,000 dinars.[109] It also seems that this was not just a rural phenomenon, as even the towers of the complex that would eventually be incorporated into the Great Mosque in Damascus had once been a place of retreat for Christian monks.[110]

The natural beauty of these monastic estates, particularly in their pastoral settings, was clearly one facet to the allure of such venues expressed by classical Muslim authors. The accounts of the various monasteries contained in the *Muʿjam al-buldān* of Yāqūt (d. 1229) as well as the entries in al-Shābushtī's (d. 1009) *Diyārāt* provide ample evidence for adoration on this basis. These sources frequently combine detailed descriptions of the magnificence of structures within the compounds with poetic odes dedicated to the marvellous topography of the environs, including orchards and vineyards.[111] In addition to the aesthetic charm, the Muslim commentators also observed the economic benefits to monasteries possessing these estates. For the listing of the Monastery of Mar Mārī, for example, al-Shābushtī reports that

> the monastery is located sixteen parasangs (*farsakhan*) from Baghdad . . . it is a beautiful place with splendid cultivated lands, containing a hundred cells (*qillāya* from the Greek κελλὶον) for monks and ascetics, each one having his own cell . . . and around these cells there is a garden, which produces a great yield in fruit, dates and olives, generating a revenue of around two hundred and fifty dinars.[112]

When the caliph Hishām travelled to a Syrian monastery to escape the plague, as mentioned previously, he was so taken by the richness of the fruits from its orchards that he attempted to purchase the garden from a monk there.[113] Yāqūt, citing an extraordinary example of monastic wealth in the Islamic period, informs that the complex of Dayr Simʿān in northern Syria was so large that it measured roughly half the size of the royal palace in Baghdad (*dār al-khilāfa*) and maintained a revenue of 400,000 dinars yearly.[114] Though not determined in the text, this remarkable economic capacity was presumably the result of a mixture of trade, pilgrimage and agricultural projects. The Monastery of Bar Ṣawmā, located near Malatya along the Byzantine frontier, likewise maintained a profitable economic enterprise based on pilgrimage that extended into the Islamic period; it was said to have held 'many monks, who delivered ten thousand dinars each year to the Byzantine emperor from the revenues of pilgrims'.[115] In an interesting addition, Yāqūt claims that among these visitors that supplied the monastery with funds were Muslims who had come to Dayr Bar Ṣawmā to make their vows.[116]

The hagiographical text of the *Life of Saint Sheʿmūn* (Simeon) *of the Olives*, Syrian Orthodox Bishop of Harran in the early eighth century, also demonstrates the continued economic vitality of monasteries and their landed endowments in the early Islamic period. According to his biography, Simeon had been the superior of a monastery in the region of Tur Abdin prior to his confirmation as bishop in the year 700 CE. During his time as superior he was said to have purchased 'hamlets, villages, courtyards, shops, mill-stones, gardens and orchards' and dedicated them to the monastery of Qartmin.[117] He then planted 12,000 olives, a feat which earned him the sobriquet 'of the olives', and hired agricultural workers to look after the fields. From the abundance produced in these fields he was able to supply the nearby monasteries and churches with oil.[118] Accounts like these certainly suggest that the economic activity of monastic communities, in part based on their management of agricultural estates, was still an important feature of the local economy into the Islamic period. As late as the eleventh century, the writings of the travelling Nestorian physician Ibn Buṭlān illustrate the persistence of the fertile topography of northern Syria in conjunction with its continued monastic presence, describing the landscape as full of monasteries, hermits' cells, flourishing villages, cultivated fields, streams and gardens.[119]

The Curious Conversion of Salmān al-Fārisī as a Lens into Monasticism

The impact of Christian monasticism and asceticism in the late antique Near East was not limited by sectarian constraints. To the contrary, this particular facet of Christian devotion, long honoured within the Roman/Byzantine sphere for piety and austerity, seems to have held significant interest for Muslim chroniclers, hagiographers, Qur'ānic exegetes, and theologians as well. In attempting to explain this cross-confessional interest, we should now turn to the narrative of Salmān al-Fārisī/'the Persian' and his conversion to Islam, as recounted in the eighth-century *Sīra* of Ibn Isḥāq (the earliest extant biography of the Prophet Muḥammad), as a lens into this kind of laudatory interpretation of Christian monasticism by early Muslims. It is my proposition here that Salmān's conversion story holds a crucial key for determining the view of Christian monasticism held by Muslim theologians and exegetes in the early centuries of Islam. In this account, Salmān performs the role of a seeker of religious knowledge, studying under various Christian teachers and monks while making a great arc across the Near East, ultimately acknowledging the perfection of Islam. This quest, in many ways, mirrors the spiritual sojourns of eastern monasticism in Late Antiquity.[120] The central question that emerges is how this regard for monasticism, transcending doctrinal barriers, relates to the formation of the early Muslim community and the prospect of inter-confessional flexibility within its earliest stages.

The figure of Salmān the Persian is most generally recognised, in terms of his contribution to Islamic history, as one of the earliest non-Arab converts to Islam, being an important source of *ḥadīth* transmission as a member of the *ṣaḥāba* or Companions of the Prophet, and for his strategic planning amidst the Battle of Trench (*al-khandaq*) in the year 627 CE.[121] Over time, his legacy came to enjoy great prominence amongst Shīʿī traditionalists as well as the mystical orders. The Iṣfahānī background of Salmān, in particular, became ever more emphasised as the Muslim population of Persia began to flourish in the subsequent centuries, with his tomb in Ctesiphon maintaining important status as a place of visitation until the modern period.[122]

The examination here will be concerned with Salmān's initial embrace of Islam and the monks that bear considerable responsibility as his devotional guides along the path. This conversion narrative within the *Sīra* of Ibn Isḥāq casts Christian holy men as intercessors between confessional distinctions, which not only seems to express an appreciation for Christian asceticism but can perhaps as well be interpreted within a larger framework of a piety-driven, nebulous spirituality that characterises the early Islamic movement. Although the decisive point of accepting Islam comes in Medina, at the feet of the Prophet himself, Christian ascetics provide the critical direction within the narrative. The crux of the account may therefore lend itself to the proposition for a synthesis between certain facets of late antique Christianity and emergent Islam, in which monasticism appears as an 'intermediary stage'.[123] The over-lapping of religious identities in such a case hinges upon shared tenets of righteousness, but without a rigidly defined dogmatic structure.

This analysis contends that the ultimate source of early Muslim interest in Christian monastic life was articulated through an inclusive, piety-centred religious orientation that extends from the late antique period. It is from within this zeitgeist of Late Antiquity,[124] laden with themes of veneration for 'holy men' and ascetic figures,[125] that flexible parameters for confessional identity would come to be a defining characteristic of devotion. This inclination, at least in its nascency, may perhaps be considered a component of an early 'Believers' movement.[126] In turn, membership within such a group of *muʾminūn*, or 'believers', would have been based upon a shared core of spiritual principles but without regard to exclusive sectarian identities. The most essential concepts therein would include a rigid monotheism, faith in a Final Judgement, and the acceptance of messengers from God.[127] The movement likewise seems to have emphasised the inherent immorality of their current age, thus the great focus on a certain and looming apocalyptic reckoning.[128]

Simply acknowledging the concepts was, however, not enough for inclusion into the category of *muʾminūn*. As stated by Fred Donner,

> The Qurʾan makes it clear that to be a true Believer mere intellectual acceptance of these ideas was not sufficient; one also had to live piously. According to the Qurʾan, our status as creatures of God demands pious obedience to His word; we should constantly remember God and humble ourselves before Him in prayer.[129]

Seeing themselves as existing in a world where iniquity was endemic, they strove to differentiate their group by expression of a loftier moral standard based not only on belief, but on righteous conduct as well.[130] Just as submission and humbleness before God was interpreted as a key element within this morality, the proposed piety-centred community would therefore have maintained a profound sense of humility as a fundamental criterion for genuine belonging. In terms of practice and ritual of such a precept, which accords with 'living piously', the traditional tenets of late antique monasticism would seemingly translate with relative ease into this kind of religious matrix. One of the crucial implications here is the prospect for pliability and fluidity of exchange across confessional divides, in part relating to Christian and Muslim theological interaction in a somewhat vague, pietistic climate.[131]

There have been several contemporary studies on the references to Christian monks and the interpretation of Christian monasticism in early Islamic literature.[132] The terms *ruhbān*, or 'monks', and *rahbāniyya*, 'monasticism', appear throughout various Muslim literary genres of this period, including geographical texts, historical chronicles, poetry, theological treatises, hagiographies, discourses on Muslim asceticism, and *ḥadīth* scholarship. While one cannot argue that the medieval Muslim commentators held one, definitive position on the merits of this Christian institution, it should be stated that the practice of monasticism clearly held genuine fascination for Muslims throughout this period. Moreover, it appears to have been generally regarded in a positive light, particularly in discussions concerning the wisdom, rigour and virtue associated with *rahbāniyya*.[133]

When the term *ruhbān* appears in verse 82 of *Sūrat al-māʾida*, for example, the Qurʾānic exegete al-Ṭabarī (d. 923) insists that the implicit approbation of monastic life is owed to the fact that their core beliefs are so comparable to those of the Muslim faithful (*fa-hum lā yab'dūna min al-mū'minīn*).[134] Because these men practice such grace in their religion, the Christians as a whole will be more likely to be counted in fellowship with Muslims (*bi-qurb mawaddatihim li-ahl al-īmān bi-llāhi wa-rasūlihi*).[135] Though these figures may not speak for the entirety of practitioners, their personal sense of devotion provides some sense of kinship. The passage from the Qur'ān states:

> You will find the people most intensely hostile to the believers are the Jews and pagans, and that the nearest in affection to them are those that say: 'we are Christians' (*alladhīna qālū innā Naṣāra*). That is because there are priests (*qissīsīn*) and monks (*ruhbān*) among them who are free from arrogance (*lā yastakbirūna*). (*Sūrat al-mā'ida* 5:82)

The ninth-century Muslim essayist al-Jāḥiẓ, when writing of this passage from *Sūrat al-mā'ida*, establishes an even more specific point of reference to these monks that resonates between their Qur'ānic interpretation and certain vignettes within the *Sīrat Rasūl Allāh* of Ibn Isḥāq (d. 767).[136] The monks who guide Salmān al-Fārisī to Islam in the *Sīra*, mentioned by al-Jāḥiẓ below, will be of primary interest to this proposal for flexible confessional identities in the early Islamic period.

> In this verse itself there is the best proof that God did not mean these particular Christians and their like, those being the Melkites and Jacobites. Rather, He meant only the kind like Baḥīrā and the likes of those monks whom Salmān served (*wa-innamā 'ana ḍarb Baḥīrā wa-ḍarb al-ruhbān alladhīna kāna yakhdimuhum Salmān*).[137]

These figures associated with Salmān, according to al-Jāḥiẓ, are therefore distinct from the more reprehensible Christians identifying themselves as either Chalcedonians/Melkites (*al-milkāniyya*) or Jacobites (*al-ya'qūbiyya*).[138] It would then appear that individual monks, perhaps those adhering to a particularly strict asceticism and disavowing a distinct confessional allegiance, formed a kind of 'middle ground' in the early and classical Muslim understanding. In this way their version of religious devotion seems to be interpreted as a more faithful rendering of the original *dīn 'Isā* (the religion of Jesus) and its precursor, the *dīn Ibrāhīm* (the religion of Abraham), as opposed to the more popular forms of Christianity. The intrinsic purity offered by the monastic life had also previously been judged, by Christian figures such as St Ephrem, as the only measure of sincere Christianity.[139] For certain Muslim commentators as well, these monks would represent the last vestiges of a 'true Christianity', which was not only untainted by the corrupted teachings of the Church but also receptive to the prophethood of Muḥammad.[140]

The justification offered by al-Ṭabarī for this spiritual connection is the 'presence of those among them that are steadfast in their duties to God; those that have entered monastic life in monasteries and hermitages, and are wise in their knowledge of scripture and practice the recitation of their texts'.[141] The exegesis here is quite lucid, placing the monastic tenets of solemnity and learning in a close parallel to those of the Muslim community. It is furthermore the consummate humility of the institution, thus avoiding haughtiness, which serves as a key determinant for religious virtue. Such themes are revisited in the account of Salmān's journey to Islam. Inasmuch as the guides of Salmān are openly demonstrated to be Christians, their degree of wisdom and piety sets them apart from the larger Christian community, transferring them into a more fluid confessional environment.

The report of Salmān is included among other conversion stories and/or testimonials that might best be termed 'annunciation narratives'.[142] Mecca, the contextual backdrop, is depicted here in the *Sīra* as a place with some degree of religious discontent on the eve of Islam, drawing attention to certain religiously conscious individuals and their quest for a higher truth than that offered by the traditional Arabian paganism.[143] Though several of these seekers embrace Christianity, this section does also recognise the existence of the *ḥanīfiyya*[144] as a primordial, abstract monotheism that is distinct from either Judaism or Christianity.[145] Julius Wellhausen interpreted this pre-Islamic *ḥanīfiyya* as a 'religion of seekers' that emerged from 'a mood which was widespread throughout Arabia in the period before Muḥammad and dominated many of the most noble spirits . . . the ground was then prepared for the emergence of Islam'.[146] By way of example, the story of Zayd ibn ʿAmr's pursuit of the *ḥanīfiyya*, the religion of Abraham, takes him from pagan Mecca and across the whole of Iraq before meeting with a Christian monk at Balqāʾ, in Syria. The monk then reveals to Zayd that a prophet is now arising in Arabia, his own ancestral homeland, that will deliver the *dīn Ibrāhīm*.[147]

As demonstrated with the example of Zayd ibn ʿAmr, these vignettes are highlighted by acknowledgements of the predestined arrival of Muḥammad from pagan, Jewish and Christian observers. Uri Rubin has suggested a highly biblical framework that consciously situates Muḥammad in an ancient pattern of prophetic annunciation.[148] Among the various groups that recognise the advent of this new Arabian prophet, Christians appear to be the most receptive to the message. The episodes are not solely cast in the *Sīra* as a foretelling of Muḥammad's future emergence, but rather at times apply to a recognition of the Prophet in his own lifetime. Both the well-known story of Bāḥīrā[149] and the account of Salmān's conversion fall into this latter category. It is of some note that both the *Ṭabaqāt al-kabīr* of Ibn Saʿd (d. 845) and the *Ḥilyat al-awliyāʾ* of Abū Nuʿaym al-Iṣfahānī (d. 1038) provide similar versions of this story in biographical entries for Salmān al-Fārisī.[150]

The exposition begins with Salmān recounting, in first-person narrative style, his youth in the village of Jayy, near Iṣfahān. His early years unfold under the watchful eye of his father, a local *dihqān* and ardent practitioner of Zoroastrianism (*al-majūsīya*). Over time, Salmān began to be drawn toward the Christian faith that he witnessed being practised in the neighbouring communities, a move that he himself claims was initially brought about because of the beauty of their liturgical chanting (*fa-samiʿatu aṣwātahum fīhā wa-hum yuṣallūna*).[151] When Salmān asks the Christians about the foundations of their tradition, they reply that its origins lay 'in Syria' (*thuma qultu lahum: ayna aṣl hādhā al-dīn? Qālū: bi-Shām*). Learning that his son had spent time in a church, Salmān's father became outraged. After being scolded by his father for this perceived betrayal of his Magian birthright and being forbidden to leave the house lest these unwelcome influences continue their advance, Salmān conspires with a group of travelling Christian merchants to escape into the wider world and flees into Syria. Upon his arrival at the Bilād al-Shām, he began inquiring about men of knowledge[152] and suitable places to learn more about the faith. He was thus directed to a local bishop (*usquf*), a man recognised for his erudition in the faith, and became an attendant in the bishop's church.

In due course, however, Salmān discovered that the bishop was 'an evil man' (*wa-kāna rajul sūʾ*), using alms money (*ṣadaqa*) granted to the church for his own personal treasury and withholding funds for the poor. Even as

Salmān's hatred for such an affront was swelling, the corrupt bishop died and was subsequently replaced by a virtuous appointee. This new master continued the religious education of the young Persian. So profound was the affection between the disciple and teacher that Salmān declares

> I have never seen a man, who was not praying the five prayers that was more righteous (*afḍal*), more ascetic (*azhad*) in religion, more committed to the Hereafter (*arghib fi-l-ākhira*), or more constant through night and day, than this man. I loved him more than I had ever before loved another.[153]

The above passages in the *Sīra* reflect the limitations of a uniform interpretation of monasticism that we find in the Qur'ān. Accordingly, in this stage of the narrative, Salmān witnesses both the righteous and iniquitous types of monks. The charge lain upon this first figure of refusing to grant alms money to the local Christians, which prompts Salmān's castigation of him as an 'evil man', resonates with a negative assessment of monasticism in the Qur'ān. A similar condemnation on the basis of greed is delivered in *Sūrat al-tawba*, stating:

> O Believers, many are the rabbis and monks who devour the wealth of the people in falsehood and hinder them from the path of God. To those that gather up gold and silver and do not spend it in the cause of God, announce for them a woeful punishment. (*Sūrat al-tawba* 9:34)

The concurrence here between the *Sīra* and the Qur'ān is an excellent example of the dual function of the Ibn Isḥāq text, which is simultaneously an attempt to demonstrate a linear chronology of the Prophet's life in biographical fashion as well as, to some extent, to provide exegesis on the holy scripture of the Qur'ān.[154] Wansbrough has commented on this exegetical technique, stating: 'the extracts (serial and isolated) from scripture provided the framework for extended *narratio*; and parabolic, in which the *narratio* was itself the framework for frequent if not continuous allusion to scripture'.[155] These juxtapositions of monastic virtues and vices in the *Sīra* represent a microcosm for the view of monasticism in the Qur'ān, providing commentary on the more general verses on the basis of specific episodes from the life of the Prophet. In effect then, the narrative serves as an explanation for both assessments of monasticism in the sacred text. Still, it should be stressed that the honourable qualities of the monks within the account outweigh the negative sentiments. The disparity here is shown directly through individual qualities of several righteous monks contrasted with a single immoral example.

Upon the deathbed of his beloved teacher, Salmān is directed to seek out his next virtuous master. At this point in the narrative the dying man explains that most others have abandoned or distorted the true religion (*baddalū wa-tarakū akthar mā kānū ʿalayhi*), so it is therefore necessary to embark on another journey to find the remaining, genuinely righteous men of the faith.[156] This instruction sets Salmān upon a great circuit of travel, studying with various holy men throughout the region: first to al-Mawṣil, then to Naṣībīn, then on to ʿAmmurīya in Byzantine territory. The cycle of an aged master pointing the way to distant, further guides is replicated in this portion of the narrative. At the death of his teacher in ʿAmmurīya, Salmān is confronted with the possibility that there are none left who still abided by this spiritual manner of life. Just before he expires, however, the master refers him to an unnamed prophet who will arise among the Arabs and whose advent is at hand. It is therefore in this land, the land of the Arabs, that the Persian will finally be able to end his long search for spiritual enlightenment. This prophet, according to the venerable old man, will be dispatched carrying the religion of Abraham (*wa-huwa mabʿūth bi-dīn Ibrāhīm*)[157] and will migrate between two lava fields set amongst palm groves.[158]

This account detailing the conversion of Salmān al-Fārisī to Islam may, of course, be interpreted in a variety of ways. The proposition that the narrative represents a polemical attitude,[159] in which Islam is demonstrated as being superior to Christianity – in other words, the final phase in the journey toward true religious fulfilment – is reasonable at first glance. Such would be a powerful admonition of Christianity indeed, coming from the mouths of learned Christian monks themselves. Bearing the details of the text in mind however, it would appear that simply viewing the story as a polemic leaves much to be answered. The merits of Christianity, after all, are not dealt with explicitly and there is a notable absence of any kind of theological or Christological debate within the narrative.[160] There is likewise no judgement on the institution of monasticism here, the only criticism being that one of these teachers is not conducting his office in a righteous manner. By contrast, the other masters that educate Salmān are overwhelmingly seen in a favourable light. One might expect a straightforward polemic to take a stance on these concerns.

In a more nuanced interpretation, Jaakko Hämeen-Anttila has suggested the story to be a device detailing the gradual corruption of Christianity in its historical context. While perhaps the great majority of Christians had fallen away from the original teachings of Christ, there did endure a select few that adhered to the authentic message. The Christians that guide Salmān were therefore to be seen as the last remaining 'real followers of Christ – growing old and dying out',[161] just in time for the next and final revelation to appear. In this respect, the proposal by Hämeen-Anttila could be integrated into a model for an early *muʾminūn* movement, one in which certain groups would be included among the 'believers' not necessarily on the basis of their theology, but by austerity, righteousness and pious standard of living. Where the argument for a polemical reading of the story moreover insists upon a tangible delineation between the two faiths, with one necessarily superseding the other, the contention here leans more toward a synthesis of traditions that places its focal point on the ascetics themselves and their manner of living. The fact that Ibn Isḥāq casts Christian monks as the virtual signposts on the road to Islam contributes significantly to our understanding of how piety-minded Muslims perceived monasticism in an ecumenical sense – in my mind, revealing the 'residual, ecumenical *īmān*' that was previously mentioned. If these learned and devout Christian figures, according to the narrative, steer their acolyte toward the feet of Muḥammad – which not only results in Salmān's conversion but his consecration amongst the ranks of the *ṣaḥāba* – what does this suggest concerning strictly defined confessional barriers in this period? The Christian monks in this account are not only righteous, but they are virtually proto-Muslims or fellow 'Believers' as well. We will return to this narrative in the final chapter of the book with a more complete interpretation of its importance to understanding medieval Muslim views of monasticism.

Notes

1. Ḥabīb Zayyāt, *Khabāyā al-zawāyā min taʾrīkh Ṣaydnāyā/ Histoire de Saidanaya* (Ḥarīṣā: Imprimerie de Saint Paul, 1932), Documents inédits pour server à l'histoire du patriarcat Melkite d'Antioche 3, 12–14. The building had apparently served both monks and nuns in residence until the eighteenth century.

2. There is believed to be a blessed oil secreted from the icon which possesses healing properties. Zayyāt, *Khabāyā al-zawāyā*, 14–15.
3. Jacques de Vitry, *Histoire de l'Orient et des croisades pour Jérusalem*, ed. F. P. G. Guizot (Clermont-Ferrand: Paleo, 2005), 318. This chronicler would have surely been well acquainted with Marian devotion in its European context, such was the enormous popularity of shrines, relics, representations and church dedications associated with her by the end of the twelfth century. In many examples there were miracles associated with these items and locations, just as there were in the East. See Rachel Fulton, *From Judgment to Passion: Devotion to Christ & the Virgin Mary, 800–1200* (New York, NY: Columbia University Press, 2002), 201, 219–20, 224–5. While pre-Islamic references in Christian texts may generally refer to any Arab nomads with the catchall term *Σαρακηνοί*, the context of this account makes it quite clear that Jacques of Vitry is referring to Muslims. For more information on the term itself, see Philip Mayerson, 'The Word Saracen (Σαρακηνός) in the Papyri', *Zeitschrift für Papyrologie und Epigraphik* 79 (1989), 283–7.
4. Don Belt, 'Arab Christians: The Forgotten Faithful', *National Geographic* (June 2009), 92.
5. For what Fred Donner has characterised as a 'Believers movement', see 'From Believers to Muslims: Confessional Self-Identity in the Early Islamic Community', *al-Abhath* 50–1 (2002–3), 9–53 at 15–21. Donner has since expanded this thesis into a full monograph entitled *Muhammad and the Believers: At the Origins of Islam* (Cambridge, MA: Belknap Press of Harvard University Press, 2010).
6. For an overview on the questions of 'identity', see 'Introduction' by Richard Miles in *Constructing Identities in Late Antiquity*, ed. Richard Miles (London and New York: Routledge Press, 1999), 1–15. Also relevant is *Tradition and Innovation in Late Antiquity*, eds F. M. Clover and R. S. Humphreys (Madison, WI: University of Wisconsin Press, 1989); *History and Identity in the Late Antique Near East*, ed. Philip Wood (Oxford: Oxford University Press, 2013); *Being Christian in Late Antiquity: A Fetschrift for Gillian Clark*, eds Carol Harrison, Caroline Humfress and Isabella Sandwell (Oxford: Oxford University Press, 2014); *Redefining Christian Identity: Cultural Interaction in the Middle East Since the Rise of Islam*, eds J. J. Van Ginkel, H. L. Murre-Van Den Berg and T. M. Van Lint, Orientalia Lovaniensia Analecta 134 (Leuven and Paris: Uitgeverij Peeters en Departement Oosterse Studies, 2005); and *Shifting Frontiers in Late Antiquity*, eds

Ralph W. Mathisen and Hagith S. Sivan (Aldershot: Ashgate Variorum, 1996).

7. David Olster has commented on this point that 'for most of the seventh century the Roman Empire could be said to have had no borders; Arabs and Slavs wintered or even worse, settled, in Roman territory; almost no territory in the Balkans or Asia Minor could be said to be behind a secure border'. See his article, 'From Periphery to Center: The Transformation of Late Roman Self-Definition in the Seventh Century', in *Shifting Frontiers in Late Antiquity*, ed. Ralph W. Mathisen and Hagith S. Sivan (Aldershot: Ashgate Variorum, 1996), 93–101 at 98.
8. The work of Peter Brown appeared at the genesis of this movement with *The World of Late Antiquity, AD 150–750* (New York, NY: Harcourt Brace Jovanovich, 1971). The origin of the project, as Brown admits, was a reaction to previous histories of the late Roman world. As he later stated, 'In the late 1960's, it seemed as if the past decades of scholarship on the social and cultural history of the later Roman empire had taken us not only a long way from the melancholy history of decline and fall, and of decay, that was associated with the names of Gibbon and Rostovtzeff. It had done more than that. It had taken us to the edge of a major discovery. It seemed as if it was possible to find, in the peculiar balance of fluidity and stability that characterized the social 'style' of the late empire, a clue to the unabated religious and cultural ferment which was so marked a feature of other aspects of the period.' See Peter Brown, 'So Debate: The World of Late Antiquity Revisited', *Symbolae Osloenses* 72:1 (1997), 5–30 at 15.
9. For a discussion of this shift in scholarship, see Robert Markus, 'Between Marrou and Brown: Transformations of Late Antique Christianity', in *Transformations of Late Antiquity: Essays for Peter Brown*, eds Philip Rousseau and Manolis Papoutsakis (London and New York: Routledge, 2016), 1–14. Garth Fowden also outlines this intellectual swing in academia, particularly in relation to how the rise of Islam fits into late antique studies; see *Before and After Muḥammad: The First Millennium Refocused* (Princeton, NJ: Princeton University Press, 2014), especially chapter 2 entitled 'Time: Beyond Late Antiquity', 18–49.
10. For works that specifically deal with this issue in its Near Eastern 'frontier' context, between the Roman/Byzantine Empire and Persia, see Elizabeth Fowden, *The Barbarian Plain: Saint Sergius between Rome and Iran* (Berkeley, CA: University of California Press, 1999); Richard Payne, *A State of Mixture:*

Christians, Zoroastrians, and Iranian Political Culture in Late Antiquity (Berkeley, CA: University of California Press, 2015); Matthew Canepa, *The Two Eyes of the Earth: Art and Ritual of Kingship between Rome and Sasanian Iran* (Berkeley, CA: University of California Press, 2017).

11. Ahmad Shboul and Alan Walmsley, 'Identity and Self-Image in Syria-Palestine in the Transition from Byzantine to Early Islamic Rule: Arab Christians and Muslims', *Mediterranean Archaeology* 11, Identities in the Eastern Mediterranean in Antiquity (1998), 255–87.
12. Miles, 'Introduction: Constructing Identities in Late Antiquity', 5.
13. The concept that 'Christians are made, not born' comes from a reading of Tertullian's *Apology* 18.4. See Andrew Louth, 'Fiunt, non nascuntur Christiani: Conversion, Community, and Christian Identity in Late Antiquity', in *Being Christian in Late Antiquity: A Fetschrift for Gillian Clark*, eds Carol Harrison, Caroline Humfress, and Isabella Sandwell (Oxford: Oxford University Press, 2014), 109–19.
14. Éric Rebillard, *Christians and Their Many Identities in Late Antiquity, North Africa 200–450* CE (Ithaca, NY: Cornell University Press, 2012), particularly chapter 1 entitled 'Setting the Stage: Carthage at the End of the Second Century', 9–33.
15. Ibid. 33.
16. Philip Michael Penn has devoted much attention to this cross-religious connection between early Islam and late antique Christianity in *Envisioning Islam: Syriac Christians and the Early Muslim World* (Philadelphia, PA: University of Pennsylvania Press, 2015), particularly the final chapter entitled 'Blurring Boundaries: The Continuum Between Early Christianity and Islam', 142–82.
17. Penn, *Envisioning Islam*, 152–4.
18. Ibid. 144–55.
19. Ibid. 155.
20. Jack Tannous, *The Making of the Medieval Middle East: Religion, Society, and Simple Believers* (Princeton, NJ: Princeton University Press, 2018), 225–60.
21. Ibid. 308–9.
22. Christian Sahner, 'Swimming Against the Current: Muslim Conversion to Christianity in the Early Islamic Period', *Journal of the American Oriental Society* 136:2 (2016), 265–84 at 266.
23. Tannous, *The Making of the Medieval Middle East*, 266. Here Tannous brings up an important point concerning the authenticity of spiritual conviction behind some of these early conversions to Islam.

24. For an overview on the *Ridda* campaign against rebel prophets in Arabia, see Fred Donner, *The Early Islamic Conquests* (Princeton, NJ: Princeton University Press, 1981), 82–90. For the operations against Musaylima, the 'false prophet' about whom the classical Muslim sources reveal the most information, see both Dale F. Eickelman, 'Musaylima: An Approach to the Social Anthroplogy of Seventh Century Arabia', *Journal of the Economic and Social History of the Orient* 10:1 (July 1967), 17–52 and M. J. Kister, 'The Struggle Against Musaylima and the Conquest of Yamāma', *Jerusalem Studies in Arabic and Islam* 27 (2002), 1–56.
25. Tannous, *The Making of the Medieval Middle East*, 266.
26. Ibid. 400–1. This statement acts as a counterpoint to Sidney Griffith's *The Church in the Shadow of the Mosque: Christians and Muslims in the World of Islam* (Princeton, NJ: Princeton University Press, 2008).
27. Michael Morony, 'History and Identity in the Syrian Churches', in *Redefining Christian Identity: Cultural Interaction in the Middle East Since the Rise of Islam*, eds J. J. Van Ginkel, H. L. Murre-Van Den Berg and T. M. Van Lint, Orientalia Lovaniensia Analecta 134 (Leuven: Uitgeverij Peeters en Departement Oosterse Studies, 2005), 1–34.
28. Ibid. 3.
29. Denha, *Histoire des Divines Actions de Saint Mar Marouta L'Ancien*, Syriac ed. F. Nau, *Patrologia Orientalis*, vol. 3, fasc. 1 (Paris, 1905), 75–6.
30. David Frankfurter, *Christianizing Egypt: Syncretism and Local Worlds in Late Antiquity* (Princeton, NJ: Princeton University Press, 2018), particularly chapters 2 and 3 focusing on ritual and the perception of holy figures and sacred shrines.
31. Frankfurter, *Christianizing Egypt*, chapter 1, 4–7.
32. Ibid. 5.
33. Ibid. 3.
34. See Richard Bulliet, *Conversion to Islam in the Medieval Period: An Essay in Quantitative History* (Cambridge, MA: Harvard University Press, 1979), 80–90. Bulliet here provides some rough percentage rates of conversion: for example, between 791 and 975, the conversion to Islam would have constituted approximately 68 per cent of the population of Iraq, while the process seems to have been accelerated in Iran. Also, see Wadi Z. Haddad, 'Continuity and Change in Religious Adherence: Ninth-Century Baghdad', in *Conversion and Continuity: Indigenous Christian Communities in Islamic Lands, Eighth to Eighteenth Centuries*, eds Michael Gervers and Ramzi

Jibran Bikhazi (Toronto: Pontifical Institute of Medieval Studies, 1990), 33–54.

35. Richard Bulliet, 'Conversion Stories in Early Islam', in *Conversion and Continuity: Indigenous Christian Communities in Islamic Lands, Eighth to Eighteenth Centuries*, eds Michael Gervers and Ramzi Jibran Bikhazi (Toronto: Pontifical Institute of Medieval Studies, 1990), 123–45 at 131.
36. Richard Bulliet, *Islam: The View from the Edge* (New York: Columbia University Press, 1994), 28–9.
37. Bulliet, 'Conversion Stories in Early Islam', 131.
38. Ibid. 128–31.
39. Fred Donner, *Narratives of Islamic Origins: The Beginnings of Islamic Historical Writing*, Studies in Late Antiquity and Early Islam 14 (Princeton, NJ: Darwin Press, 1998), 67.
40. Frankfurter, *Christianizing Egypt*, particularly chapter 4 'A Site of Blessings, Dreams, and Wonders: Traditions of the Saint's Shrine', 104–44, and Morony, 'History and Identity in the Syrian Churches', 29–33.
41. Frankfurter, *Christianizing Egypt*, 109.
42. Brown, *The World of Late Antiquity*, 100.
43. Greg Fisher and Philip Wood, 'Arabs and Christianity', with contributions from George Bevan, Geoffrey Greatrex, Basema Hamarneh, Peter Schadler and Walter Ward, in *Arabs and Empires before Islam*, ed. Greg Fisher (Oxford: Oxford University Press, 2015), 276–372 at 286.
44. Josef W. Meri, 'The Etiquette of Devotion in the Islamic Cult of Saints', *The Cult of Saints in Late Antiquity and the Middle Ages*, eds James Howard-Johnston and Paul Antony Hayward (Oxford University Press, 1999), 264–86 at 265.
45. It was not, however, limited to a Near Eastern context, as we also see the vestiges of overlapping religious divides in the numerous examples of Jewish visitation to Christian shrines in late medieval Europe. See Ephraim Shoham-Steiner, 'Jews and Healing at Medieval Saints' Shrines: Participation, Polemics, and Shared Cultures', *The Harvard Theological Review* 103:1 (January 2010), 111–29.
46. Georgia Frank, *The Memory of the Eyes: Pilgrims to Living Saints in Christian Late Antiquity* (Berkeley, CA: University of California Press, 2000), 7–10.
47. Ibid. 11–13.
48. *Itinerarium Egeriae*, eds P. Geyer and O. Cuntz, Corpus Scriptorum Series Latina 175–6 (Turnhout: Brepols Publishing, 1965) ending at Jerusalem

around 9.7 in the text. See also English translation by John Wilkinson, *Egeria's Travels to the Holy Land* (Warminster: Aris & Phillips, 1981).

49. Averil Cameron, *The Mediterranean World in Late Antiquity* AD *395–700* (London and New York: Routledge, 2012), 76.
50. For the parallels and contrasts to the conception of the holy man between the Hellenistic pagan and early Christian traditions, see Robert Kirschner, 'The Vocation of Holiness in Late Antiquity', *Vigiliae Christianae* 38:2 (June 1984), 105–24, and Garth Fowden, 'The Pagan Holy Man in Late Antique Society', *The Journal of Hellenic Studies* 102 (1982), 33–59.
51. Claudia Rapp has written on the power of the holy man as intercessor between human society and the sacred, which, according to her model, should be less focused on the 'spectacular miracles' than on the 'perceived efficacy of his prayer'. See '"For Next to God, you are my Salvation": Reflections on the Rise of the Holy Man in Late Antiquity', in *The Cult of Saints in Late Antiquity and the Middle Ages: Essays on the Contribution of Peter Brown*, eds James Howard-Johnston and Paul Antony Hayward (Oxford: Oxford University Press, 1999), 63–83 at 66.
52. Peter Brown, 'Holy Men', in *The Cambridge Ancient History*, vol. 14, eds A. Cameron, B. Ward-Perkins and M. Whitby (Cambridge: Cambridge University Press, 2001), 781–810 at 781. For a nuanced view of the holy man in this period, one that challenges Brown on his characterisation, see Philip Rosseau, 'Ascetics as Mediators and Teachers', in *The Cult of Saints in Late Antiquity and the Middle Ages: Essays on the Contribution of Peter Brown*, eds James Howard-Johnston and Paul Antony Hayward (Oxford: Oxford University Press, 1999), 45–62.
53. Elizabeth and Garth Fowden, 'Monks, Monasteries and Early Islam', in *Studies on Hellenism, Christianity and the Umayyads*, eds G. Fowden and E. K. Fowden, *Melethmata* 37 (Athens: Diffusion de Boccard, 2004), 153.
54. Gedaliahu Stroumsa, 'Religious Contacts in Byzantine Palestine', *Numen* 36:1 (June 1989), 16–42 at 32.
55. Caroline Schroeder, 'A Suitable Abode for Christ', *Church History* 73:3 (2004), 472–521. Moreover, the institution of monastic life was often viewed as a theological parallel to the community of Heavenly Jerusalem, the monastery being a symbol of the perfect religious life. See Kristi Copeland, 'The Earthly Monastery and the Transformation of the Heavenly City in Late Antique Egypt', in *Heavenly Realms and Earthly Realities in Late Antique Religions*, eds R. S. Boustan and A. Y. Reed (Cambridge: Cambridge University Press, 2004), 142–58.

56. Schroeder, 'A Suitable Abode for Christ', 477.
57. Mark S. Burrows, 'On the Visibility of God in the Holy Man: A Reconsideration of the Role of the Apa in the Pachomian Vitae', *Vigiliae Christianae* 41 (1987), 11–33. In the case of Pachomius and his monastic settlement, this particular saint becomes the 'fixed point' around which the new, ascetic society would develop. It is the saint's extraordinary *stabilitas*, or presence of the divine, that gathers the like-minded to his monastery. In other words, the 'new community exists because of the peculiar "locus" of the holy which is to be found in the person of the founder' (at 13).
58. Qartmin monastery is located in present-day southeastern Turkey, founded in the fifth century by Mar Samuel and his disciple Mar Simeon. See Andrew Palmer, *Monk and Mason on the Tigris Frontier: The Early History of Tur 'Abdin* (Cambridge: Cambridge University Press, 1990), 12.
59. *The Book of Life*, XXI, taken from the microfiche supplement to Palmer, *Monk and Mason*.
60. Arthur Vööbus, *A History of Asceticism in the Syrian Orient: A Contribution to the History of Culture in the Near East, Corpus Scriptorum Christianorum Orientalium*, vol. II (Louvain: Peeters, 1960), 256.
61. See Kirschner, 'The Vocation of Holiness in Late Antiquity', 109–14. This type of rigorous piety was pronounced in Christian asceticism by the absolute renunciation of the material world and even, at times, mortification of the flesh and abstinence from food or drink.
62. Robert Schick, *The Christian Communities of Palestine from Byzantine to Islamic Rule* (Princeton, NJ: Darwin Press, 1995), 96–7.
63. Yizhar Hirschfeld, *The Early Byzantine Monastery at Khirbet Ed-Deir in the Judean Desert: The Excavations in 1981–1987*, QEDEM 38 (Jerusalem: The Hebrew University of Jerusalem, 1999), 155.
64. Significant contributions to this field include Peter Brown, 'The Rise and Function of the Holy Man in Late Antiquity', *The Journal of Roman Studies* 61 (1971), 80–101; Derwis Chitty, *The Desert a City: An Introduction to the Study of Egyptian and Palestinian Monasticism under the Christian Empire* (Crestwood, NY: St Vladimir's Seminary Press, 1995); S. P. Brock, 'Early Syrian Asceticism', *Numen* 20:1 (April 1973), 1–19; Kirschner, 'The Vocation of Holiness in Late Antiquity', 105–24; Arthur Vööbus, *A History of Asceticism in the Syrian Orient: A Contribution to the History of Culture in the Near East* (2 vols) (Louvain: Corpus Scriptorum Christianorum Orientalium Secrétariat du Corpus, 1958–60).

65. W. H. C. Frend, 'The Monks and the Survival of the East Roman Empire in the Fifth Century', *Past and Present* 54 (1972), 3–24 at 6.
66. Stroumsa, 'Religious Contacts in Byzantine Palestine', 32.
67. Kirschner, 'The Vocation of Holiness in Late Antiquity', 110.
68. Theodoret of Cyrrhus, *Historia religiosa XXVI, Patrologia cursus completus*, Series Graeca, ed. Jacques-Paul Migne (Paris, 1857–89), col. 1484. See trans. Theodoret of Cyrrhus, *A History of the Monks of Syria* (Kalamazoo, MI: Cistercian Publications, 1985).
69. W. H. C. Frend, *The Rise of the Monophysite Movement: Chapters in the History of the Church in the Fifth and Sixth Centuries* (Cambridge: Cambridge University Press, 1972), 90.
70. Alice-Mary Talbot, 'A Monastic World', in *A Social History of Byzantium*, ed. John Haldon (Chichester: Wiley-Blackwell, 2009), 257–78 at 258.
71. See Brown, 'The Rise and Function of the Holy Man in Late Antiquity', 80–101.
72. Donner, 'From Believers to Muslims', 11. The central argument in the 'believers' thesis suggests that fluidity in interreligious discourse from this era corresponds to, or perhaps yields, the systematic development over time of a more clearly defined perception of confessional distinction within the early Islamic community. This formula is in relative accord with the conventional assessment for the hardening of sectarian lines which, though undergoing a process of formulation and delineation in the Umayyad period, appears to have been fundamentally realised in the transition from Umayyad to ʿAbbāsid authority in the middle of the eighth century. The 'believers' proposition can therefore ultimately be viewed as an important contribution to the study of Islamic origins within a religiously dynamic late antique context. This is in reference to assessments by historians such as Averil Cameron and Peter Brown, which have tended to interpret and historically situate the rise of Islam in its perceived indigenous context within Late Antiquity – that of an intellectually vibrant, religiously diverse and complex, ascetic and eschatologically minded culture of the Near East.
73. Donner, *Muhammad and the Believers*, 67.
74. Donner, *Narratives of Islamic Origins*, 67.
75. Ibid. 67.
76. Ibid. 75.
77. Stroumsa, 'Religious Contacts', 32.
78. François Nau, *Les Arabes Chrêtiens de Mésopotamie et de Syrie du VIIe au VIIIe Siècle* (Paris: Cahiers de la Société Asiatique, 1933), 17.

79. Greg Fisher and Philip Wood, 'Arabs and Christianity', 284–6.
80. Hippolyte Delehaye, 'Byzantine Monasticism', in *Byzantium: An Introduction to East Roman Civilization*, eds N. H. Baynes and H. St L. B. Moss (Oxford: Clarendon Press, 1961), 136–65 at 141.
81. J. M. Fiey, *Assyrie Chrétienne: Contribution à l'étude de l'histoire et de la géographie ecclésiastiques et monastiques du Nord de l'Iraq*, vol. I (Beirut: Imprimerie Catholique, 1965–8), 14–15.
82. A. H. M. Jones, *The Later Roman Empire 284–602: A Social, Economic and Administrative Survey*, vol. II (Norman, OK: University of Oklahoma Press, 1964), 930. This problem of enumeration is particularly evident in respect to the monasteries lying outside the Byzantine realm, at least after the seventh century. Those situated inside Byzantine territory, in operation at various times throughout the duration of the empire, have been estimated at more than 240 monasteries by Charanis, who in turn based his suggestion on the research of H.-G. Beck and R. P. B. Menthon. See Charanis, 'The Monk as an Element of Byzantine Society', *Dumbarton Oaks Papers* 25 (1971), 63–4.
83. Part of the problem with estimates is that the contemporary sources also appear to exaggerate the number of monks in residence at monasteries. For example, Cyril records as many as 10,000 monks gathering together in a church in Jerusalem: *Cyril of Scythopolis: The Lives of the Monks of Palestine* (Kalamazoo, MI: Cistercian Publications, 1991). Additionally, Theodoret of Cyrrhus suggests that 'in Egypt, some retreats have five thousand men each', which is possibly an allusion to Pachomius's monastery at Tabennisi that was said to have housed more than 5,000 monks under a single abbot. See Theodoret of Cyrrhus, *A History of the Monks of Syria* (Kalamazoo, MI: Cistercian Publications, 1985), 188.
84. Fiey, *Assyrie Chrétienne* 1, 19–20.
85. Yitzhar Hirschfeld, *The Judean Desert Monasteries in the Byzantine Period* (New Haven, CT: Yale University Press, 1992), 80–90.
86. A. K. Sanjian, 'Anastas Vardapet's List of Armenian Monasteries in Seventh-Century Jerusalem: A Critical Examination', *Le Muséon* 82:3–4 (1969), 265–92.
87. S. Vailhé, 'Répertoire Alphabétique des Monastères de Palestine', *Revue de l'Orient Chrétien* 4 (1899), 272–92.
88. Doron Bar, 'Rural Monasticism as a Key Element in the Christianization of Byzantine Palestine', *Harvard Theological Review* 98:1 (2005), 49–65 at 51.
89. Fiey, *Assyrie Chrétienne* 1, 13–15.

90. Irfan Shahîd, *Byzantium and the Arabs in the Sixth Century* (Washington, DC: Dumbarton Oaks Research Library and Collection, 1995–), vol. 2, 182–3.
91. Yāqūt, *Muʿjam al-buldān*, 5 vols (Beirut: Dār al-Sādir, 1955–57), see entry for *dayr* in vol. 2.
92. See al-Shābushtī, *Kitāb al-diyārāt*, ed. Kūrkīs ʿAwwād, 3rd edn (Beirut: Dār al-Rāʾid al-ʿArabī, 1986). Regionally, these consist of some forty monasteries in Mesopotamia and Iraq, three in Syria, and nine in Egypt.
93. Al-Maqrīzī, *Kitāb al-khiṭāṭ* (2 vols) (Bulāq al-Qāhira: Dār al-Ṭibāʿah al-Miṣriyya, 1853) vol. 1, 186.
94. Benedict Landron, 'Les Relations Originelles de l'est (Nestoriens) et Musulmans', *Parole de l'Orient* 10 (1981–2), 191–222 at 201.
95. Ibid. 202–3.
96. Delehaye, 'Byzantine Monasticism', 165.
97. Ruth Mackenson, 'Background of the History of Moslem Libraries', *The American Journal of Semitic Languages and Literatures* 52:2 (January 1936), 104–10.
98. Ofer Livne-Kafri, 'Early Muslim Asceticism and the World of Christian Monasticism', *Jerusalem Studies in Arabic and Islam* 20 (1996), 105–29.
99. Andrew Crislip, *From Monastery to Hospital: Christian Monasticism and the Transformation of Health Care in Late Antiquity* (Ann Arbor, MI: University of Michigan, 2005), 14. The author cites the monastery at Nitria as an example, stating that out of this large monastic settlement of some 5,000 monks, a number of them were practising physicians.
100. Hospitals and other healing institutions were commonly associated with churches and monasteries throughout the Byzantine period. See Dimitri Brady, 'Eastern Christian Hagiographical Traditions', in *The Blackwell Companion to Eastern Christianity*, ed. Ken Parry (Oxford: Wiley Blackwell Publishing, 2007), 420–1.
101. Cyril Elgood, *A Medical History of Persia and the Eastern Caliphate: From the Earliest Times until the Year* A.D. *1932* (Cambridge: Cambridge University Press, 1951), 44–5.
102. A. Tritton, *The Caliphs and the Their Non-Muslim Subjects: A Critical Study of the Covenant of ʿUmar* (London: Frank Cass & Co., 1970), 150–1.
103. See Lawrence Conrad, 'Historical Evidence and the Archaeology of Early Islam', in *Quest for Understanding: Arabic and Islamic Studies in Memory of Malcolm H. Kerr*, eds S. Seikaly, R. Baalbaki and P. Dodd (Beirut: American University of Beirut, 1991), 271. This is apparently from an unpublished section of the *Ansāb*.

104. The tenth-century compendium of Ibn al-Nadīm, the *Fihrist*, for example, lists five books dedicated to Christian monasteries, although these works unfortunately do not survive intact. See Ibn al-Nadīm, *Kitāb al-fihrist*, ed. M. Riḍā Tajaddud, 3rd edn (Beirut: Dār al-Masīrah, 1988). Some of the most important remaining material on monasteries is found in the *Kitāb al-diyārāt* (*Book of Monasteries*) of al-Shābushtī (d. 1008), which has preserved earlier accounts relating, in part, to Muslim-Christian interaction at monasteries. However, this material is more appropriate for the later chapters of this research.
105. I. Dick, 'La Passion Arabe de S. Antoine Ruwaḥ', *Le Muséon: revue d'études orientales* 74 (1961), 112.
106. Paulus Peeters, 'La Passion de St. Pierre de Capitolias', *Analecta Bollandiana* 57 (1939), 309–12. Though the medical treatment of al-Walīd at the monastery is not mentioned by al-Ṭabarī, it is recorded that the death of the caliph occurred at Dayr al-Murrān in the middle of Jumada II in the year 96 AH. See the *Taʾrīkh al-rusul waʾl-muluk* (5 vols) (Beirut: Dar al-Kutub al-ʿIlmiyya, 1987), vol. 3.
107. Fowden, *The Barbarian Plain*, 174–83.
108. See Elizabeth Fowden, 'Christian Monasteries and Umayyad Residences in Late Antique Syria', *Studies on Hellenism, Christianity, and the Umayyads*, ed. Garth and Elizabeth Fowden, *Meletemata* 37 (Athens, 2004), 175–92.
109. Al-Masʿūdī, *Murūj al-dhahab* (Beirut: Dār al-Maʿrifa, 2005), vol. 4, 49.
110. Nancy Khalek, *Damascus after the Muslim Conquest: Text and Image in Early Islam* (Oxford: Oxford University Press, 2011), 49.
111. This information generally comes at the beginning of the entries in both works, which start with the geographical location of the monastery and then proceed with descriptions of the environment.
112. Al-Shābushtī, *Kitāb al-diyārāt*, 265.
113. Conrad, 'Historical Evidence and the Archaeology of Early Islam', 271.
114. See the *Muʿjam al-buldān* 2, 517.
115. Ibid. 500.
116. Ibid. 500.
117. Sebastian P. Brock, 'The Fenqitho of the Monastery of Mar Gabriel in Tur ʿAbdin', *Ostkirchliche Studien* 28 (1979), 168–82 at 174–5. As well, Jack Tannous has devoted considerable attention to the ecclesiastical career of Simeon of the Olives. See Tannous, *The Making of the Medieval Middle East*, 181–5.
118. Ibid. 175–6.

119. Lawrence Conrad, 'Ibn Buṭlān in Bilād al-Shām: The Career of a Travelling Christian Physician', in *Syrian Christians Under Islam, the First Thousand Years*, ed. David Thomas (Leiden: Brill, 2001), 131–57 at 150. It should be noted that at the time of Ibn Buṭlān, a native of Baghdad, the regions that he is describing in this example, namely Antioch and its environs, were under Byzantine control. It is included here only to demonstrate the continued prosperity of the region, even in the wake of the transition from Muslim to Byzantine rule.
120. In part, these types of travels between late antique monastic communities were undertaken with the intention of collecting the wisdom of various sages and composing biographies of regional religious authorities. Such was the case with the fifth century *Lausiac History* of Palladius and the *Historia Religiosa* of Theodoret, among others. See discussion of 'Desert Ascetics and Distant Marvels' in Georgia Frank, *The Memory of the Eyes. Pilgrims to Living Saints in Christian Late Antiquity* (Berkeley and Los Angeles: University of California Press, 2000), 35–78. For Christian ascetics of the period this 'wandering' was perhaps also a method of *imitatio Christi*, taking scenes of travel in the life of Christ and the apostles as the highest form of religious devotion. See Daniel Caner, *Wandering, Begging Monks: Spiritual Authority and the Promotion of Monasticism in Late Antiquity* (Berkeley, CA: University of California Press, 2002), 14. For the connection between knowledge and travel in the pre-Christian era, see Ian W. Scott, 'The Divine Wanderer: Travel and Divination in Late Antiquity', in *Travel and Religion in Late Antiquity*, ed. Philip Harland (Waterloo, Ontario: Wilford Laurier University Press, 2011), 101–22.
121. See Josef Horovitz, 'Salmān al-Fārisī', *Der Islam* 12:3–4 (1922), 178–83, and Louis Massignon, *Salmân Pâk et les prémices spirituelles de l'Islam iranien* (Tours: Arrault, 1934).
122. Sarah B. Savant, *The New Muslims of Post-Conquest Iran: Tradition, Memory, and Conversion*, Cambridge Studies in Islamic Civilization (Cambridge: Cambridge University Press, 2013), 61–2. Also, Jaakko Hämeen-Anttila, 'The Corruption of Christianity: Salām al-Fārisī's Quest as Paradigmatic Model', *Studia Orientalia* 85 (1999), 115–26.
123. See Jane McAuliffe, *Qur'anic Christians: An Analysis of Classical and Modern Exegesis* (Cambridge: Cambridge University Press, 1991), specifically 240–59.
124. See Garth Fowden, *Empire to Commonwealth: Consequences of Monotheism in Late Antiquity* (Princeton, NJ: Princeton University Press, 1993), particularly the final chapter dealing with inherited traditions between early Islam and the Byzantine/Eastern Christian world.

125. A significant amount of scholarship has been composed on this subject. See Peter Brown, 'The Rise and Function of the Holy Man in Late Antiquity' [a reproduction of the 1971 *Journal of Roman Studies* article], in Brown, *Society and the Holy in Late Antiquity* (Berkeley, CA: University of California Press, 1982), 103–52; Kirschner, 'The Vocation of Holiness in Late Antiquity', 105–24; Vööbus, *A History of Asceticism in the Syrian Orient*; Sebastian Brock, in addition to several works relating to the Syrian Church, the article 'Early Syrian Asceticism', 1–19.
126. See Donner, 'From Believers to Muslims', 19–21. The core beliefs are mentioned as well in Donner's *Muhammad and the Believers*. It should, however, be admitted here that the 'Believers' model is not without its critics. See Robert Hoyland, 'Reflections on the Identity of the Arabian Conquerors of the Seventh-Century Middle East', *Al-ʿUṣūr al-Wusṭā* 25 (2017), 113–40, in which the author challenges the notion of a non-confessional, monotheistic society within the foundational period of Islam.
127. Donner, *Muhammad and the Believers*, 60–1.
128. Ibid. 66–7.
129. Ibid. 61.
130. Ibid. 66.
131. See note 72 above.
132. G. Troupeau, 'Les Couvents Chrétiens dans la Littérature Arabe', in *Études sur le christianisme arabe au Moyen Âge*, Variorum Collected Series 515 (London: Variorum, 1995), 265–79; Hilary Kilpatrick, 'Monasteries Through Muslim Eyes: The Diyārāt Books', in *Christians at the Heart of Islamic Rule: Church Life and Scholarship in ʿAbbasid Iraq*, ed. David Thomas (Leiden: Brill, 2003), 19–37; Elizabeth and Garth Fowden, 'Monks, Monasteries and Early Islam', 149–74; Suleiman Mourad, 'Christian Monks in Islamic Literature: A Preliminary Report on Some Arabic Apophthegmata Pratum', *Bulletin for the Royal Institute on Inter-Faith Studies* 6 (2004), 81–98; Elizabeth Fowden, 'The Lamp and the Olive Flask: Early Muslim Interest in Christian Monks', in *Islamic Cross Pollinations: Interactions in the Medieval Middle East*, eds Anna Akasoy, James Montgomery and Peter Pormann (Exeter: Gibb Memorial Trust, 2007), 1–28; Ofer Livne-Kafri, 'Early Muslim Asceticism and the World of Christian Monasticism', *Jerusalem Studies in Arabic and Islam* 20 (1996), 105–29; Christian Sahner, 'Islamic Legends about the Birth of Monasticism: A Case Study on the Late Antique Milieu of the Qurʾān and Tafsīr', in *The Late Antique World of Early Islam: Muslims Among Christians*

and Jews in the Eastern Mediterranean, ed. R. Hoyland (Princeton, NJ: Darwin Press, 2015), 393–435; Sidney Griffith, *Arabic Christianity in the Monasteries of Ninth-Century Palestine* (Aldershot: Ashgate Variorum, 1992), *The Beginnings of Christian Theology in Arabic: Muslim-Christian Encounters in the Early Islamic Period* (Aldershot: Ashgate Variorum, 2002), and 'Michael, the Martyr and Monk of Mar Sabas Monastery, at the Court of the Caliph ʿAbd al-Malik; Christian Apologetics and Martyrology in the Early Islamic Period', *ARAM* 6:1 (1994), 15–48.

133. Livne-Kafri, 'Early Muslim Asceticism and the World of Christian Monasticism', 105–7.
134. Al-Ṭabarī, *Jāmiʿ al-bayān ʿan taʾwīl āy al-Qurʾān* (15 vols) (Egypt: Dār al-Maʿārif), vol. 10, 505.
135. Ibid. 505.
136. There are several relevant studies on the development of the *Sīra*. See Uri Rubin, *The Eye of the Beholder: The Life of Muḥammad as Viewed By the Early Muslims* (Princeton, NJ: Darwin Press, 1995) and as editor, *The Life of Muḥammad, The Formation of the Classical Islamic World*, vol. 4 (Aldershot: Ashgate Variorum, 1998); John C. Rankin, *The Real Muḥammad: In the Eyes of Ibn Isḥāq* (TEI Publishing, 2013); Gregor Schoeler, *The Biography of Muḥammad: Nature and Authenticity* (London: Routledge Press, 2011); Muhammad Hamidullah, *Muhammad Ibn Ishaq: The Biographer of the Holy Prophet* (Karachi: Pakistan Historical Society, 1967); Gordon D. Newby, *The Making of the Last Prophet: A Reconstruction of the Earliest Biography of Muhammad* (Columbia: University of South Carolina Press, 1989).
137. Al-Jāḥiẓ, *Thalāth risāʾil*, ed. Joshua Finkel (Cairo: al-Matbaʿat al-Salafiyya, 1926), 14. Baḥīrā, the monk from Boṣtra, was commonly recognised as the first person to acknowledge the future prophetic significance of the young Muḥammad. See Rudolph Sellheim, 'Prophet, Chalif, und Geschichte: Die Muhammed-Biographie des Ibn Isḥāq', *Oriens* 18 (1965–6), 33–91; F. Nau, 'L'expansion nestorienne en Asie', *Annales du Musée Guimet*, tome 40 (Paris, 1913), 193–383; T. Nöldeke, 'Hatte Muḥammad christliche Lehrer?', *Zeitschrift der Deutschen Morgenländischen Gesellschaft* (1858), 699–708 at 704; Stephen Gero, 'The Legend of the Monk Baḥīrā, the Cult of the Cross, and Iconoclasm', in *La Syrie de Byzance à l'Islam, VIIe–VIIIe siècles* (Damascus: Institut Français de Damas, 1992), 47–58; Barbara Roggema has also greatly contributed to the interpretation of the Baḥīrā narrative as it appears in both Muslim and Christian sources, in *The Legend of Sergius/Baḥīrā: Eastern*

Christian Apologetics and Apocalyptic in Response to Islam (Leiden and Boston: Brill, 2009).

138. The Melkites and Jacobites are also specifically targeted by the ninth-century theologian Abū ʿĪsā al-Warrāq. See *Early Muslim Polemic against Christianity: Abū ʿĪsā al-Warrāq's 'Against the Incarnation'*, ed. David Thomas (Cambridge: Cambridge University Press, 2002).
139. John Meyendorff, *Imperial Unity and Christian Divisions: The Church 450–680 A.D.* (Crestwood, New York: St Vladimir's Seminary Press, 1989), 83.
140. Roggema, *The Legend of Sergius/Baḥīrā*, 37.
141. Al-Ṭabarī, *Jāmiʿ al-bayān*, 505.
142. Rubin, *The Eye of the Beholder*, 21–2, 44–53. Cf. Hämeen-Anttila, 'The Corruption of Christianity', 116–17.
143. Walid A. Saleh, 'The Arabian Context of Muḥammad's Life', *The Cambridge Companion to Muḥammad*, ed. Jonathan E. Brockopp (Cambridge: Cambridge University Press, 2010), 21–38 at 31.
144. G. R. Hawting has taken this problematic term as an identification of pure monotheism, a non-denominational form of the original *dīn Ibrāhīm*. See G. R. Hawting, *The Idea of Idolatry and the Emergence of Islam: From Polemic to History* (Cambridge: Cambridge University Press, 1999), 21.
145. See Uri Rubin, 'Hanifiyya and Kaʿb – An Inquiry into the Arabian Pre-Islamic Background of the *dīn 'Ibrāhīm*', *Jerusalem Studies in Arabic and Islam* 13 (1990), 85–112. Montgomery Watt has suggested that the original name for the movement founded by Muḥammad was not *Islam*, but rather *tazakkī*, or 'righteousness'. It is after the *Hijra* that the most numerous references to a community of *muʾminūn* begin to occur. It appears that in the early terminology of 'believers', Jews would have been included under this general rubric. During the period of the Prophet's break with the Jews of Medina, he claimed to have been following the religion of Abraham – the *ḥanīfiyya* – and the Prophet's religion may have been called exactly that for some time afterward. See Montgomery Watt, *Muhammad at Medina* (Oxford: Clarendon Press, 1977), 301–2.
146. Julius Wellhausen, *Reste arabischen Heidentums* (Berlin: Walter de Gruyter, 1961), 234. Cf. Hawting, *The Idea of Idolatry*, 27.
147. Ibn Hishām, *al-Sīra al-nabawiyya*, vol. I, ed. Mustafa al-Saqqa *et al.* (Beirut: Dar al-Khayr, 1997), 186.
148. Rubin, *The Eye of the Beholder*, 21–2.
149. See Roggema, *The Legend of Sergius/Baḥīrā*.

150. Ibn Saʿd, *Kitāb al-ṭabaqāt al-kabīr*, vol. 4 (Cairo: Maktabat al-Khānjī, 2001), 69–79. The similarity in narrative is not altogether surprising given that both al-Ṭabarī and Ibn Saʿd owed much of their *maghāzī* material, or 'exploits of the Prophet', as well as the *mubtadaʾ*, or 'beginnings', to Ibn Isḥāq via his student Salamah. See Schoeler, *The Biography of Muḥammad: Nature and Authenticity*, 32. Abū Nuʿaym al-Iṣfahānī, *Ḥilyat al-awliyāʾ*, vol. 1 (Beirut: Dār al-Fikr, 1967–8), 190–5.
151. Ibn Hishām, *al-Sīra* I, 173.
152. Ibid. 174. The precise question uttered by Salmān is: '*man afḍal ahl hādhā al-dīn ʿilman*?
153. Ibid. 174.
154. Newby, *The Making of the Last Prophet*, 2–4. Newby suggests that the exegetical nature of the *Sīra* is particularly concerned with the middle portion of the text. This section, known as the *Kitāb al-mubtadaʾ* or the 'Book of Sending Forth', is 'a commentary on the Bible as well as a commentary on the Quran'.
155. John Wansbrough, *The Sectarian Milieu: Content and Composition of Islamic Salvation History* (Oxford: Oxford University Press, 1978), 2.
156. Ibn Hishām, *al-Sīra* I, 175.
157. Ibid. I, 175.
158. Ibid. I, 175. While the details here clearly serve as an allusion to the eventual *hijra* of Muḥammad, it could also be a foreshadowing of the description of the 'holy man moving between two thickets' that is to come at the end of the narrative. The conclusion of the account will be fully addressed in the final chapter of this book.
159. For the rise of Christianity in Muslim polemics, see Jacob Mann, 'An Early Theologico-Polemical Work', *Hebrew Union College Annual* 12–13 (1968), 417–43. In addition, there is a systematic assessment of medieval Muslim arguments to counter Christianity in Hava Lazarus-Yafeh, 'Some Neglected Aspects of Medieval Muslim Polemics against Christianity', *The Harvard Theological Review* 89:1 (January 1996), 61–84.
160. Hämeen-Anttila, 'The Corruption of Christianity', 118.
161. Ibid. 124.

2

The Changing Fortunes of Christian Holy Places in the Seventh-century Near East

The Precarious Position of Monastic Life on the Eve of Islam

An intriguing Arabic document preserved within the archives of Saint Catherine's Monastery in Sinai, known as the *Achtiname* or 'holy charter',[1] purports to demonstrate an extraordinarily beneficent attitude concerning the security of monastic sites in the early Islamic period. The *Achtiname* document is essentially a deed for liberty and protection for the monastery, which according to the text, was guaranteed by the hand of the Prophet Muhammad himself.[2] It is believed that the original covenant was taken to Istanbul by Sultan Selim I in 1517 during the Ottoman conquest of Egypt, at which time the monks were given a reproduction for their archives.[3] The extant version of this document therefore appears to be a redaction of the stipulations originally composed, at least so the decree itself claims, only a short time following the *hijra* of the Prophet. The precise date that is recorded within the present text identifies the time of its production to be the third of Muharram in the second year of the *hijra*, corresponding to 7 July of the year 623 CE.[4]

Since the late nineteenth century, scholars have challenged the authenticity of this document, in part due to the fact that the *hijri* dating system was not developed until 637 CE, under the caliphate of ʿUmar ibn al-Khaṭṭāb.[5] The date located at the conclusion of the document corresponding to the second year of the *hijra*, therefore, would appear to be a later anachronistic projection. Jean-Michel Mouton has concluded that the *Achtiname* is likely not an original, nor even a recension of an original, document dating from the time of the Prophet, but rather fits into the genre of 'forged' documents that were developed in the ninth century and scattered throughout the Christian communities of the Near East.[6] Whatever the precise historical origins of this particular document, it has clearly served as the archetype for diplomatic arrangements between the monks of Mount Sinai and various Muslim governments over the centuries; several examples of such texts are still preserved within the monastery. In this way, the numerous caliphs and sultans who subsequently reissued or renewed the charter would have been, at least in their perception, explicitly retracing the footsteps of the Prophet with regard to the monastery.[7]

Though the exact provenance of these earliest covenants between Muslims and monastic representatives remain obscure, the circumstances by which monasteries in the Near East were originally brought under Islamic hegemony appear to have been generally favourable. This is especially palpable when considering the fates of such communities, entangled in the struggle between the great powers of Late Antiquity,[8] in the era preceding the arrival of Islam into the Levant and North Africa. In contrast to the widespread

Figure 2.1 St Catherine's Monastery. Courtesy of Omar Attum, 2002.

destruction of this former period, there is virtually no evidence for deliberate attacks against monasteries and churches in the early Islamic era.[9] Even in the period of the seventh-century conquests, where indications of wanton destruction and/or looting of Christian religious sites may be most expected, there are few examples of direct violence against monastic settlements. The disappearance of a number of churches and monasteries that have been connected to the first century of Islam (that is, prior to the year 750 CE) are generally understood to have been the result of gradual abandonment due to socio-economic concerns or natural disasters, owing little to religious issues between Christians and Muslims.[10] Therein lies a significant disparity between the status of eastern monasteries before the advent of Muslim political authority in these regions and after.

The initial decades of the seventh century served as ominous markers for the fragile position of Christian monastic communities throughout the Near East. Escalation in hostilities between the Byzantine and Sassanid Empires at the dawn of the century, resulting in the Persian invasion and occupation of much of Byzantine Syria-Palestine, Mesopotamia and Egypt, triggered a host of devastating effects on the monasteries of those regions. Whether by targeted destruction amidst the military campaign itself, beginning in the year 602 CE, or by indiscriminate raiding activities as a corollary, the conflict resulted in a dramatic close to the previously flourishing era of eastern monastic culture.[11] The ascetic landscape of the Near East had therefore already suffered considerable damage prior to the first waves of Muslim penetration in the third decade of the seventh century. This section will examine the fortunes of monasteries during their initial phases of contact with Islam, demonstrating the fundamental differences of conduct and attitudes concerning the monastic station from the period of the Persian invasion to the early Islamic conquests of the Near East.

To step back, the relationship between the Sasanian monarch Chosroes II (r. 590–628 CE) and the Christians within his realm in the early seventh century is an issue of considerable complexity.[12] A primary challenge to any assessment of Persian religious policy in this period relates to the various confessional divisions within the eastern churches, notably those East Syrian and Miaphysite communities within Persia[13] that were generally dealt with by sectarian-specific strategies. The East Syrian church in particular had been characterised by its clientage to the Sasanian administration since the Council of Seleucia-Ctesiphon in the year 410 CE, resulting in a steadily increasing royal influence upon the ecclesiastical structure. This was not, however, to the detriment of Christian institutions within the realm, which continued to prosper in concert with the Zoroastrian imperial cult.[14] The Sasanian influence over the church was most directly visible over the next two centuries in the nomination and appointment of the catholicos.[15]

A celebrated example for the close connection between imperial authorities and their East Syrian subject populations comes in the year 596 CE, marking the elevation of the monk Sabrīshōʿ to the seat of the catholicos by Shah Chosroes II's own personal initiative.[16] The tenth-century *Chronicle of Seert* provides the details for this consecration of a relatively simple ascetic to the highest ecclesiastical office in the land.[17] A stark contrast should be noted in the image of Sabrīshōʿ, a humble herdsman's son from the village of Fairūzabād,[18] to the preceding catholicoi in terms of educational background and familiarity with state institutions. In this way, he stands as an outsider to the conventional relationship between the church and the government.[19] The details here are revealing in that, initially, the Christian nobles and clergy themselves specifically rejected the idea of an aged Sabrīshōʿ in the highest office, leaving the matter exclusively to the discretion of the shah. Nevertheless, Sabrīshōʿ's fame as a worker of wonders, including exorcising demons and foretelling the future, attracted the favour of the Sasanian king of kings and he was ordained as patriarch with elaborate pageantry and ceremony. At the closing of the ritual, taking place in the palace of Shīrīn[20] (the Christian wife of the king), we glimpse the intimate regard between catholicos and shah. Chosroes II, in the presence of his wife, announces to Sabrīshōʿ that 'the ones who came before you were slaves to my fathers and forbearers, but I am now your son and this woman is now your daughter'.[21]

Such is the manner in which the *Chronicle of Seert* depicts the kindred spirit between the crown and this ecclesiastical figure. For Richard Payne, the narrative has far-reaching consequences for the development of an East Syrian political theology within the Sasanian realm. The consecration ceremony exemplified a sense of fulfilment in the process of integration for the community vis-à-vis the established Zoroastrian political system. It was a narrative of culmination, serving to reinforce the cooperative nature of the Sasanian state, despite obvious sectarian divisions. As Payne states,

> the authority of the patriarchs of Seleucia-Ctesiphon depended on the support of the Zoroastrian king of kings no less than the authority of the patriarchs of Rome, Alexandria, Antioch, Jerusalem, and Constantinople depended on the support of Christian Roman emperors.[22]

When the Miaphysite populations of the empire began to rise exponentially, as a consequence of the persecutions along the Byzantine eastern frontier in the late sixth century[23] as well as Sasanian military occupations of the Near East in the early seventh century, it appears that the monarchy embarked on a policy favouring these newly absorbed communities, to the detriment of its indigenous East Syrian populations.[24] Contemporary scholarship has therefore tended toward the view that the Sasanian government manipulated these sectarian groups, demonstrating both patronage and harassment to each respectively, at opportune times. Such steps were taken in an attempt to further their own internal political interests.[25] An alternative interpretation, as least as far as Chosroes II himself is concerned, is that he actually may have favoured a course of genuine tolerance for both the East Syrian and Miaphysite populations. The pragmatic implications of such a policy would have allowed the regime to better utilise the different Christian sects at its disposal, as well as establishing some degree of political equilibrium between the rival confessional groups.[26]

The manner in which this framework would have applied to the Persian invasion of the Levant in the early seventh century, and by extension the policies concerning the multitude of churches and monasteries of that region, is less clear. The explicit devastation of Christian religious sites throughout the theatres of the campaign is chronicled in a variety of ancient sources, yet the question remains concerning the impetus behind such aggressive measures.[27] The twelfth-century *Chronicle of Michael the Syrian* interprets the Persian actions against Christian communities with respect to a specifically confessional agenda, in this case the persecution of Chalcedonian Christians whose lands were being brought under Sasanian suzerainty. This hostile sentiment against the Byzantine Church could have perhaps been founded upon the perception that these groups formed a fifth column within Persian domains.

In other words, it may have been believed that devotion to the Church in Constantinople would have necessarily implied political loyalty to the Byzantine state as well. A sense of retaliation for years of oppression by the Chalcedonians may have also been a factor that prompted other Christian confessional groups within the Sasanian Empire to encourage aggressions against Melkite churches and monasteries. Concerning the occupation of Edessa, for instance, the *Chronicle of Michael the Syrian* claims the following:

> When the Persians had taken control of Mesopotamia and Syria, Chosroes sent bishops to take possession of the towns of Syria. To Edessa, first of all, came the Nestorian Ahīshema, who was not accepted by the faithful. Then arrived a certain Yōnan, an orthodox[28] bishop, and this one was accepted. Then, under the orders of Chosroes, all of the Chalcedonian bishops were pursued throughout the lands of Mesopotamia and Syria. Their churches and monasteries were then granted to the Jacobites.[29]

The mid tenth-century chronicle of Agapius, the Melkite Bishop of Manbij, also provides an account of the oppression of Chalcedonians at Edessa under the Sassanids, claiming:

> Chosroes persecuted the inhabitants of Edessa, those who were adhering to the Melkite doctrine, and he demanded that they profess the faith of the Jacobites . . . They sent to the inhabitants an order stating that they must profess the doctrine of either the Jacobites or the Nestorians, and if they should do this there would be enmity between themselves and the Byzantines (*al-Rūm*), but if they continue to believe as the Byzantines, they will always be partisans of the Byzantines.[30]

In other areas, however, the influence of a confessional bias seems to have been less of a factor in the Persian actions against Christian religious sites. Perhaps the best example of this would be the fate of the Coptic monasteries of Egypt. Of the Sassanid assault against Alexandria, in the course of their occupation of the region beginning in the year 617 CE, the tenth-century Coptic bishop Severus ibn al-Muqaffaʿ tells of the ruinous effects on the monasteries in the midst of the siege. The account begins with a statement claiming that there were 600 monasteries at Henaton, near Alexandria, that were particularly thriving and populated, their physical appearance being likened to the houses of pigeons (*mithl abrāj al-ḥamām*).[31] In the course of the conquest of the city, these monasteries were surrounded by Persian troops and devastated, their inhabitants being put to sword, and all that they possessed, in terms of wealth and furnishings, were taken as spoils.[32]

Whether it was simply that these monasteries were in such close proximity to the fighting – as Alfred J. Butler has suggested, that they would have been 'almost or actually within view of the Persian encampment'[33] – or that they were specifically sought out for destruction is difficult to determine. However, Severus admits that the damage to monasteries in the area, though severe, was not total; he stated that the important Monastery of Canopus (*Dayr Qanūbūs*), to the north-east of the city, was spared the attack because of its distance from the siege.[34] From there the chronicle continues with the Sassanid march into Upper Egypt and their approach to the town of Nikiou (*Niqiyūs*), where there were a host of monks living within the surrounding caves and mountains. According to Severus, the Persian commander[35] had received word that these hermits had amassed riches behind the walls of their enclosures. The order was thereupon given to the troops to camp for the night and prepare for an assault. On the following day, as the sun rose, the Persian troops entered these compounds and killed all of the monks without exception.[36]

In the Levant, conquered prior to the Persian invasion of Egypt, the consequences for monastic settlements appear to have been as severe.[37] This was not solely a result of military engagements in the region, but also due to the breakdown in the administrative frontiers and arrangements with the desert tribesmen in the wake of the Persian offensive.[38] The Byzantine Empire, when not actively supporting certain tribes of Arab nomads along the frontier, attempted to maintain order within these outlying regions themselves with the stationing of imperial troops. Among the principal functions of this Roman military presence would have been the monitoring of tribal movements and the prevention of raids on settled areas.[39]

Concerning this situation in the early seventh century, the *Chronicle of Seert* claims that these tribesmen, previously utilised by both the Byzantines and Sasanians as federated clients, rose up in a mutiny against their former allies and began laying waste to the provinces, stating, 'The Ṭayyāyē then increased their power and they did not cease to cause disturbances across the lands until the appearance of the Lawgiver of Islam' (*ṣāḥib sharīʿat al-islām*).[40]

The implication here was that these tribes, when not officially regarded as *foederati* or allies[41] of the great late antique empires, simply moved across the Levant and Mesopotamia wreaking havoc. It is however interesting to note that this East Syrian chronicler seems to suggest that the lawless brigandage of the tribes was remedied in the figure of Muḥammad.

The *Chronicle of Michael the Syrian* likewise reports that the regions conquered by the Persians, such as Mesopotamia, Syria, Cilicia, Palestine and Egypt, were not only subjected to pillaging and the taking of captives by the Sasanian army, but these areas also fell prey to Arab raids. The passage states:

> In this year [610 CE], Heraclius was proclaimed Augustus, and his son Constantine, was placed at the head of the army to fight the Persians, those who had overcome the lands of the Romans located on the eastern shores of the Pontus . . . And this same year, a group of Arabs (*Ṭayyāyē*) climbed out of Arabia and went into Syria; they pillaged and devastated a number of areas; they committed many slaughters amongst the people, and they set places ablaze without pity or mercy.[42]

The desert monasteries of Palestine, in particular, became the focal point of raiding activities that sought to take advantage of the upheaval in the vicinity, as Persian forces advanced across the Levant. Gilbert Dagron characterises the devastation of the area in the statement, 'The entirety of the region around Jerusalem, with its illustrious monasteries, became as fire and blood.'[43] The taking of Jerusalem by the general Shahrbarāz in May of the year 614, after a siege lasting twenty-one days, resulted in heavy civilian casualties. According to an account from the monk Antiochus Strategos, a contemporary witness to the conquest of Palestine, the Persians unleashed the carnage without regard for non-combatants of any kind, stating:

> They listened not to the appeal of supplicants, nor pitied youthful beauty, nor had compassion on old men's age, nor blushed before the humility of the clergy. On the contrary they destroyed persons of every age, massacred them like animals, cut them in pieces, mowed sundry of them down like cabbages, so that all alike had severally to drain the cup full of bitterness.[44]

The ancient sources range in their estimates of the loss of life from 57,000[45] to 90,000,[46] though these figures may have been inflated for apologetical purposes.[47] Many of those who managed to survive the siege were reportedly taken back to Cteisphon as prisoners, including the patriarch Zacharius.[48] Regardless of the exact number of casualties, the devastation of the Holy City, along with the numerous monasteries and churches within its orbit, served as a catalyst for mass movements of refugees into surrounding lands.[49] This was also the occasion that witnessed a host of refugees abandoning the Holy Land entirely and fleeing to the security of the West. That Greek monks founded a number of monasteries in Italy at this time serves as a testament to this exodus, one of these new monasteries being dedicated to St Sabas.[50] The account from Antiochus is particularly concerned with the fate of these holy places, in which case both monasteries and churches throughout the city were utterly plundered. The relevant passages state:

> Lamentation and terror might be seen in Jerusalem. Holy churches were burned with fire, others were demolished, majestic altars fell prone, sacred altars were trampled under foot, life-giving icons were spat upon by the unclean. Then their wrath fell upon the priests and deacons: they slew them in their churches like dumb animals[51] . . . How many priests and monks were slain by the sword! . . . How many fled into the Church of the Anastasis, into that of Sion and other churches, and were therein consumed with fire! Who can count the multitude of the corpses of those who were massacred in Jerusalem!
>
> Listen to me, my brethren, and I will relate to you what happened to the holy mothers. In Jerusalem, on the Mount of Olives, there was a monastery in which lived holy virgins four hundred in number. The enemy entered that monastery and expelled, like doves from their nest, those brides of Christ, blessed, of worthy life and blameless chastity. Having led them out of the monastery, they penned them in like cattle; and they shared them among themselves and led them away each to their own quarters.[52]

The outlying Christian holy sites met with similar disastrous fortunes. Only days prior to the fall of Jerusalem a nomadic raiding party had taken the Monastery of St Sabas by surprise, no doubt utilising the panic and chaos in the area and looted the settlement. While many of the monks fled the monastery after this initial raid, including the *hegoumenos* Nicomedes, some refused to leave the laura. When the Arabs launched a second raid, two days later, forty-four of the remaining monks were tortured, as a means of extracting information about the location of the sacred vessels of the church, and finally executed.[53]

The early seventh-century *Life of George of Choziba*[54] reports a similar encounter between hostile tribesmen, here referred to as *Σαρακηνοὶ*,[55] and the community of the Monastery of the Virgin, near Jericho. In this hagiographical account, composed by the monk's disciple Antonius, the arrival of the marauders is precipitated by the Persian military assault against Palestine. During the attack on their monastery, the residents witnessed the murder of an elderly monk, the taking of several other monks into captivity, as well as the theft of their precious objects.[56] Many of the monks must have abandoned the monastery altogether as a result of the raid and the Persian invasion, as it appears to have been in decline throughout the following years.[57]

Prior to the sacking of the settlement at Choziba in 614, this monastery had been revered for its curative powers and was seen as an important pilgrimage site in the region. Though some recovery is made in the ensuing decades, the Monastery of the Virgin does not seem to have reclaimed its former prestige as a pilgrimage centre.[58] According to the account, George laments the unfortunate state of his community in the wake of the Persian invasion by stating:

> 'I remember before the time of the Persians, when we, the men of the cells, would come to the meeting area for the evening prayers to our Lord, one of the brothers would go to that tree and bring back a full basket of fruit; then, again, on the following afternoon we returned to our cells and he would once again bring more.' And I (Antonius) said to him, 'What happened, Father?' He then said to me, 'At that time there were holy men moving and walking about the land, and they spread blessings upon the land and all that was in it, but now evil men trample upon the land and have murdered the upright within it, and the land has become spoilt. So how then can there be a blessing upon it?'[59]

Even before the major Persian assault into eastern Byzantine lands, the remote and isolated monastic settlements of the Levant and North Africa had been under constant threat of harassment from desert tribesmen in the late antique period. In spite of the fortifications for defence of such communities, commonly including walls and towers, rural monasteries provided ideal targets for raiders in search of food and wealth.[60] Hagiographical records typically identify these types of brigands within tribal categories, including those of the Mazices,[61] Blemmyes[62] and Saracens.[63] According to Cyril of Sythopolis, the threat of attacks from tribesmen were of significant concern to the monasteries of Palestine in the early sixth century, prompting St Sabas himself, upon his visit to Constantinople, to make a specific appeal to the Emperor Anastasius. The request issued by St Sabas was for the construction of a fortification (κάστρον) near his monastic settlement, to provide security for the monks in the event of a raid.[64]

The *Life of Samuel of Qalamūn*, a hagiographical account of a seventh-century monk from the Nitrian Desert of Lower Egypt, illustrates the continuation of this problem even after the Byzantine recovery of Egypt by the year 629 CE.[65] This account depicts the struggles with barbarian marauders in grim language:

> The Berbers descended on the marsh from the west . . . and thereupon went into the church, with their swords drawn and shouting in their language. When the saint saw them in this way, he became very frightened and trembled as he saw their audacious treatment of the church and the altar. He responded to this and said, 'What are you doing, defiled and impious ones? The Lord God will repay you for this.' Thereupon they seized him and said to the saint, 'Where are the vessels that are in this place?' . . . The Berbers then dragged him here and there, searching after the vessels of the church.
>
> A few days later, Berbers happened to come wandering in from the mountains, stealing everything from the villagers whom they would find living in the districts at the foot of the mountain and taking their men as prisoners as well. Now, by Divine Providence, the men of the villages knew that the Berbers were upon them, and they hastily took their wives and children, fleeing, they abandoned their homes and possessions and saved their lives from captivity of the Berbers. When evening came, the Berbers went into the village and took everything they found.[66]

This Samuel (d. c. 695 CE), a monk at Scetis, would have been only too familiar with the problems of aggression against monasteries of the Wadī al-Natrūn. By the time of his ordination as a priest in the Monastery of Abba

Macarius, around the year 621 CE, the monasteries of Scetis had already suffered through four major barbarian attacks.[67] The last and perhaps most devastating of these raids, prior to the arrival of Samuel, took place sometime around the year 570 CE, leaving Scetis virtually abandoned for the next several decades.[68] While it is difficult to determine a precise date for the attack mentioned in the passage above, the text clearly places this scene shortly after the arrival of Kyros, the newly appointed Monothelete patriarch of Alexandria, in the autumn of 631.[69]

In addition to the standard barbarian raids in search of plunder, the hostilities against monasteries in Egypt began to take on a discernibly sectarian dimension as well. The persecution of Coptic monasteries became more acute as a result of the Emperor Heraclius' decision to install Kyros as the Melkite[70] patriarch, acting as religious and temporal authority over the predominantly non-Chalecdonian population. In the words of Severus ibn al-Muqaffaʿ, 'he dispatched a provincial governor (*wālī*) to Egypt, known as Kyros, to be both Patriarch and governor'.[71] The move resulted in great consternation among the Coptic populations; their own patriarch, Benjamin, was forced to flee the sectarian tensions of Alexandria. The episode, as recounted from the Coptic perspective in the *Life of Samuel of Qalamūn*, states:

> It happened at the time of Kyros, the criminal, when he came to the city of Alexandria in pursuit of the holy archbishop Father Benjamin. He sought after him with false charges with the intention of killing him and sitting on his throne, but our God the Christ Jesus, saved the archbishop from the hands of the impious one; hiding him in the south of Egypt.[72]

The *Life* further claims that a *magistrianus* was dispatched to the monasteries of Scetis, accompanied by 200 soldiers, to force the monks to accept the Chalcedonian creed. In the course of resisting, the monk Samuel was severely beaten by the guards and left for dead.[73] The chronicle of Severus ibn al-Muqaffaʿ, once again from the Coptic perspective, reports a similar scene of unrest in Egypt; stating:

> When Kyros came to Alexandria, the angel of the Lord announced his coming to the Father Benjamin and ordered him to take flight. The angel then said to him, 'You, and those with you, Flee from this place! Because

> severe hardships are descending upon you. But, take heart, for these struggles will only last for ten years. And write to all the bishops, those within your diocese, so that they might hide themselves until the wrath of the Lord has passed[74] . . . Then Heraclius appointed bishops throughout the land of Egypt, as far as Antinoe, and he put the people of Egypt through difficult trials, and like a ravenous wolf he consumed the flock and was not then satisfied.[75]

The First Encounters with Arabian Believers

The severity of the devastation throughout the Levant during the period of the Persian conquests seemingly served as the backdrop[76] to the first several verses of *Sūrat al-rūm*, which take an openly sympathetic stance toward the Byzantine cause. The passage states:

> The Romans have been vanquished, in a nearby land, but after their defeat they will again gain victory, after several years. God is the authority before and after. And on that day the believers (*al-mu'minūn*) will rejoice. By the help of God, He aids whom he pleases, He is the Mighty, the Merciful. (*Sūrat al-rūm* 30:2–5)

In some sense this passage may also reflect an attitude of solidarity, embraced by the early Muslim community, toward their fellow monotheistic inhabitants of the region. As discussed by one of the earliest exegetes, Mujāhid ibn Jabr (d. c. 720), the verse indeed demonstrates divine favour towards the Byzantines as members of the *ahl al-kitāb*. In this case it is justified for the 'believers' to celebrate such a triumph over the Persian idolaters, the *ahl al-awthān*.[77] Moreover, the use of the term *al-mu'minūn*, 'believers', could perhaps itself be a demonstration of this commonality between the monotheistic traditions. The passages cited above serve as general indications for the condition of Levantine and Egyptian monastic communities on the eve of their initial contacts with Islam – perhaps more accurately called, at this moment in the seventh century, a movement of Believers.[78]

The terminology here is admittedly problematic. While this period might traditionally be known as the 'era of the Islamic conquests', there is little indication that the movement referred to itself with explicitly sectarian expressions at this early stage. Fred Donner, for his part, sees this as a more ecumenical effort, at least in its earliest vestiges. Montgomery Watt has similarly suggested that the emerging community in Mecca first described itself with the term *tazakkī*, meaning 'righteousness' or 'purity', but their religion was not yet definitively called 'Islam'. The markers of self-identity during the Medina period tend toward the term *mu'minūn*, with the religion itself commonly being referred to as the *ḥanīfiyya*.[79] However we might choose to designate this movement and its constituents,[80] their forces certainly interacted with these same types of monastic settlements, many of which were presumably still in the phases of recovery – yet the interface between them provides a glaring contrast to that of the Sassanid invasion. Furthermore, it does not appear that confessional affiliation played a significant role in the relationship between the conquered communities and those in authority during the early period of expansion.[81]

Based on seventh- and eighth-century Syriac historiography, Sebastian Brock has likewise investigated the early Christian reactions to the rise of Islam and their interpretation of the arrival of Muslim hegemony within the Near East. While the accounts do appear to be aware that there was indeed a religious motivation for the expansion, that spiritual impulse was not categorically understood within the Syriac literature of the period to be distinct from Jewish or more general Abrahamic monotheism. In Brock's own words, 'there was a greater awareness that a new empire had arisen (*malkuta*), than that a new religion had been born'.[82] In his contributions to the study of Syriac literature from the early Islamic period,[83] G. J. Reinink has put forth similar questions in regard to the interpretation of Islam by Christian theologians and chroniclers during their initial phases of interaction with Muslims, between the middle of the seventh and early eighth centuries.

For Reinink, a key issue centres upon precisely when Syriac apologetics appear in defence of Christianity against the doctrines of Islam. The determination of how early these kinds of treatises begin to circulate would be indicative of some level of awareness, on the part of the Christian communities of the Near East, to the differences between the practitioners. Reinink begins the discussion:

> If the answer to the question would simply be shortly after the Arab conquests of Syria and Palestine, then the historical implications of such a state-

> ment would be rather sweeping. It would mean that among the Christians at the very early stage after the Arab invasions there was an awareness not only that a new political power has arisen in the Near East, but that the conquerors had introduced a new religious faith against which it is necessary to define the tenets of Christian belief. And that again would mean that nascent Islam already in the first decade after the Arab invasions manifested itself or was at least recognizable as a religious system which could be clearly distinguished from both Judaism and Christianity, the two other monotheistic religions of the Near East . . . However, there does not seem to be much support for this view in the Christian sources which belong with certainty to the seventh century.[84]

At the time of the Sasanian occupation of Egypt, between 618 and 621 CE, the Christian civilian community at large, regardless of specific sectarian identity, were seemingly uniform in their fear of violent reprisals. However, the atmosphere had shifted in the years following the Byzantine re-conquest, in light of the Chalcedonian oppression of the Copts. As such there is little evidence for a particularly negative view of the Muslim conquest of the region, as far as Miaphysites were concerned,[85] beginning in late 639/early 640 CE. Such a contrast is demonstrated in a passage from the *Khiṭaṭ* of al-Maqrīzī (d. 1442), which depicts the reaction of monasteries in the Wadī al-Natrūn to the arrival of the army. According to al-Maqrīzī, the general responsible for the conquest of Egypt, ʿAmr ibn al-ʿĀṣ, met and held negotiations with an assembly of monks from these monasteries. The passage claims:

> Seventy thousand monks from these monasteries, according to Christian historians, met ʿAmr ibn al-ʿĀṣ, each one with a staff in his hand; after declaring their submission to him, he composed a letter for them, which still exists among them . . . Here is the letter [housed within the Monastery of Saint Macarius], written by ʿAmr ibn al-ʿĀs to the monks of the Wadī al-Ḥabīb, concerning the subject of tribute imposed on the northern lands, as has been related to me by one who had heard it from a man who had seen it there.[86]

It should be taken into consideration that the setting in this account, the monastic communities of the Wadī al-Natrūn, was the same mentioned by

Samuel of Qalamūn as the scene of great plundering by desert marauders merely ten years prior. Though the number of monks assembled for an accord with General ʿAmr in this passage is clearly a greatly exaggerated figure, the proposition that monks and/or priests could act as types of envoys in this capacity does not seem altogether implausible. The role of monks as arbiters of local disputes and village mediators had already been well established in the late antique period.[87] The elite-level ecclesiastical officials frequently occupied secular managerial offices as well. The office of the bishop in the Byzantine tradition had by this time become both a high ecclesiastical and administrative position within the cities of the empire, with bishops at times being appointed to the post of the *defensor civitatis*, equating to the leader or judge over a city.[88]

Given his eminent rank as patriarch, it comes as no surprise that Kyros himself also brokered a settlement with ʿAmr ibn al-ʿĀṣ to end hostilities.[89] As part of the treaty established at the fortress of Babylon in late 641, according to John of Nikiu,[90] the Byzantine defence forces were commanded to cease fighting, while the advancing troops were obligated to abstain from the seizure of churches.[91] Shortly after the Byzantine military withdrawal from Egypt, in autumn of 642, the Coptic patriarch Benjamin returned to Alexandria. A tradition is preserved by Severus ibn al-Muqaffaʿ that he was specifically recalled to his post by ʿAmr,[92] as he had been in hiding from the Byzantine authorities for the last thirteen years. The ninth-century historian Ibn ʿAbd al-Ḥakam also suggests that Benjamin and ʿAmr had exchanged communications concerning the position of the Copts at some point prior to his reinstatement as patriarch.[93] Upon his return, the patriarch inspected the condition of the churches. Presumably Benjamin was seeking to assess the damage done to them under the previous Chalcedonian regime, as well as the extent to which the Muslims had respected the pact. John of Nikiu adds that General ʿAmr had indeed been acting according to the agreement, stating, 'he took none of the property of the churches, and he committed no act of spoliation or plunder, and he preserved them throughout his days'.[94]

C. D. G. Müller has concluded, in a study of Coptic relations with Muslim authorities in this period, that the emergence of Muslim rule in Egypt would have represented a positive change for the Coptic ecclesiastical elite. As he states of the meeting between ʿAmr ibn al-ʿĀṣ and Patriarch Benjamin,

> The Coptic patriarch does not conduct himself, in terms of speaking to this conqueror or the prayer that follows, differently than he would before any Christian authority. As he would there, he admonishes and prays. Theological differences with Islam appear to play no role as of yet.[95]

Müller goes on to suggest that while this regime change does not necessarily reflect a complete liberation from Byzantine religious policy, the less rigid confessional strategies of the early Muslim conquerors would have been understood in optimistic terms. Again, in Müller's words,

> the driving impulse in the struggle against Byzantium was the intervention in matters of faith; the imposition of a foreign Christological doctrine. Now, this danger of an attack on one's own spiritual property and kind was turned away . . . The type of the new authority troubled no one as long as it did not infiltrate into one's own personal life.[96]

It is difficult to determine to what extent Coptic attitudes varied in their understanding of this particular conquest of Egypt. The sources, as in the case of John of Nikiu and Severus ibn al-Muqaffaʿ, clearly contain a strongly anti-Chalcedonian bias and therefore tend to view the arrival of the outside force in promising terms. The account preserved by Ibn al-Muqaffaʿ, in particular, is rather late (tenth century) and may reflect an idealised form of early Muslim and Coptic interaction, in reaction to the hardening of confessional boundaries in his own time. The same caveats apply when approaching the Miaphysite and East Syrian sources of the Levant and Mesopotamia, which typically display a sense of relief with the transition from Byzantine to Muslim authority. Still, the movement's early victories are often viewed by contemporary Syriac, Armenian and Byzantine sources as part of an apocalyptic narrative,[97] as a divinely ordained punishment for sin.[98] Broadly speaking, the texts suggest that God was utilising the 'barbaric nation of the desert'[99] to exact vengeance upon the Christian world, but the interpretation of the cause, or the offence in this case, consistently held a sectarian dimension. John bar Penkāyē, an East Syrian chronicler of the late seventh century, states of the coming of Arab rule to his community in northern Mesopotamia:

> We should not consider their arrival as an ordinary thing, but as an action of the divine. Before he summoned them, God had prepared them to hold

> Christians in honor, also possessing a special ordinance (*pūqdānā maram*) from God concerning our monastic station, that they should hold it in honor . . . God summoned them from the ends of the earth to destroy a sinful kingdom.[100]

Still, the chroniclers do report episodes of violence to towns during the Islamic conquests, and on occasion the aggression relates specifically to ecclesiastical structures. In the notable case of the taking of Alexandria, Severus reports that the churches and monasteries of the city were burned.[101] When this type of aggressive action by Muslims is reported, and it is quite rare, it is generally applied to those cities or towns that would either not capitulate under the terms of a treaty, or had broken a recent pact of capitulation. As Ibn ʿAbd al-Ḥakam states of the submission of Egypt:

> And all of Egypt surrendered by treaty (*ṣulḥ*), with the obligation of two dinars upon each man in terms of the poll-tax (*jizya*), which is not to be increased for them, and those maintaining agricultural plots must give a share of their yield, with the exception of Alexandria which must pay both the land-tax (*kharāj*) and the poll-tax, according to whatever amount the governor sees fit, this is because Alexandria was conquered by force of arms (*ʿanwatan*) instead of by covenant.[102]

Even when considering the partiality of the source material, it seems apparent that the churches and monasteries of the region at the time of the Islamic conquests were spared the gratuitous violence that had plagued them throughout the years of the Sasanian invasion and occupation. In contrast to the earlier periods, which the sources depict as particularly devastating to monasteries, the reports of the Islamic conquests contain scant references to direct action against these entities. Severus concludes this section on the relationship between the Coptic patriarch Benjamin and ʿAmr ibn al-ʿĀs with a statement on the reconstruction programmes for their ecclesiastical structures, reporting, 'By his application [the Patriarch Benjamin], he began the rebuilding of the monasteries of the Wadī Ḥabīb and al-Muna, and the pious works of the orthodox [the Copts] flourished.'[103]

The fortunes of monasteries in the Levant again appear to have been parallel to those of Egypt. One of the crucial features of these conquest accounts, in both eastern Christian and Muslim sources, is the presence of capitulation pacts between towns and Muslim military officials, such as the one cited by Ibn ʿAbd al-Ḥakam for ʻall of Egypt' (*fa-kānat misr kuluhā ṣulḥan*).[104] In several cases, the amnesty for churches and monasteries appear as distinct features within these covenants. It then seems possible that the monks of the Wadī al-Natrūn, if the report from al-Maqrīzī is at least somewhat accurate, could have known that such treaties were being produced in the Levant for the surrender of towns, as areas such as Syria and Palestine had fallen before the incursions into Egypt. Important Christian centres like Aleppo, Antioch, Damascus and Jerusalem had already capitulated by the time the Muslim armies began the assault on Egypt in earnest, in late 639 CE.[105]

If the general conditions of such pacts were becoming known throughout the region, it stands to reason that such a delegation of monks may have been induced to make contact with the leader of the Muslim expedition seeking a similar arrangement for the security of their monasteries. The assertion by al-Maqrīzī that these monks would now emerge in throngs to peacefully confer with a conqueror suggests an entirely different set of parameters in effect for ecclesiastical sites, taking into account the aggressive measures that had previously been undertaken at the Wadī al-Natrūn. The composition of these kinds of pacts, at least theoretically, may be modelled on the treaty between the Prophet Muḥammad and the people of Najrān, a largely Christian town in northern Yemen. This pact, purportedly taking place sometime around the year 631, served as a guarantee for the religious immunity of the Christians of the town and particularly emphasised the amnesty of ecclesiastical figures and their respective offices. The ninth-century historian al-Balādhurī reports the relevant provisions of the document as follows:

> To Najrān and its inhabitants is granted the asylum of God and the protection of Muḥammad the Messenger of God, according to their lives, their creed, their lands, their properties . . . their manners of life shall not be altered from what they had been nor their rights, and a bishop will not be removed from his bishopric, nor will a monk from his monastic position (*rahbāniyya*) . . .[106]

A similar rendering of this agreement also exists in the *Chronicle of Seert* as well as in al-Ṭabarī (d. 923 CE), in which case the latter cites the accord in the context of its renewal by Abū Bakr upon the death of Muḥammad.[107] The version of the covenant utilised in the *Chronicle of Seert* was allegedly discovered – so it is claimed within the chronicle itself – around the year 878–9 CE by a monk known as Ḥabīb, who was the curator of the Bayt al-Ḥikma in Baghdad.[108] The relevant passages from the chronicle are as follows:

> In the name of God, the Merciful, the Compassionate
>
> This is a writ of protection from God and His Messenger to those following the Book, to Christians who belong to the faith of Najrān and all other creeds of Christianity (*min niḥal al-Naṣrāniyya*). It was composed for them by Muḥammad ibn ʿAbd Allah, the Messenger of God, to the people of the *dhimma* on behalf of God and his Messenger, and the pact is binding to the Muslims who come after him, that they should engage it, that they should understand it, believe in it, and preserve it[109] . . . This establishes the protection of their persons, their churches, their chapels, their oratories, the abodes of their monks and the places of their anchorites, wherever they are found – in mountains, valleys, in caves, in settled places, in plains or deserts . . .[110]

Whatever the exact historical provenance of these pacts, the agreement between Muḥammad and the Christians of Najrān would seem to have served as a kind of archetypal arrangement for dealing with other Christian communities in the later eras. This is almost certainly the case with the aforementioned *Achtiname* document of St Catherine's Monastery. The problem is, however, that these texts in their extant form are later recensions of a covenant that collectively trace their origins to the time of the Prophet. Even as such, these pacts may still echo certain sentiments for the amnesty of monasteries that existed by at least the time of the conquest period.

It is perhaps of particular relevance to this point to recall that even as early as the year 688 CE[111] John bar Penkāyē was writing concerning an 'ordinance' held by the Muslims that pertained to the security of monastic sites. As demonstrated by the citation of several different types of source material, there does seem to have been some framework in place for the protection of churches and monasteries within a legal context from an early period. It would also appear that the veneration for holymen, as a remnant from Late

Antiquity crossing the boundaries of confessional affiliation, was a central factor in determining this general amnesty for monasteries in the formative stages of Muslim political dominance.

The matter of the practical enforcement of such attitudes is a more difficult question, concerning the precise interpretation of these kinds of pacts by the central government and the chronology for when these would have been fully embraced by the Muslim state. The evolution of these arrangements is the subject of Tritton's analysis of the so-called covenant of ʿUmar,[112] which – in its various incarnations – would become the primary ideological basis for the legal management of *dhimmīs* under the ʿAbbāsid administration. The basic tract of the agreement traces its origin to an amalgamation of certain capitulation treaties between the towns of the Near East and their Muslim occupiers during the conquest period.[113] Several examples of these terms have been preserved in the Islamic conquest literature. While the details vary to some extent depending on location and manner of surrender, the basic formula involves the guarantee of religious tolerance provided the payment of tribute.

Perhaps the most well known of such agreements is the pact between the Caliph ʿUmar ibn al-Khaṭṭāb and the Christian inhabitants of Jerusalem, essentially promising them the safety of their lives, property and churches in return for the *jizya*.[114] This capitulation agreement also was the result of a direct meeting between the patriarch of the town, Sophronius, and the Caliph. The pact is also recorded by Agapius, in which the patriarch is said to have received an assurance of security for 'Jerusalem and all the villages of Palestine'.[115] Although not explicitly stated, monks and monasteries would have surely figured into such an arrangement.

A charter issued by the ʿAbbāsid caliph al-Muktafī (r. 1136–60) to the Nestorian patriarch ʿAbdīshō III (1138–47) not only includes similar wording in its measures for securing monastic sites, but the document[116] insists that its formulation has a lineage that can be traced to the examples from the early period. Even as this particular charter of protection comes from the twelfth century, it identifies its basis with a standard fashioned by the Prophet and the early caliphs, claiming:

> Praise be to God who invested the Commander of the Faithful with the glory of the Caliphate, the inheritance from his fathers, and clothed him

> with its robes . . . Following the precedent sanctioned by the imams, his predecessors, the Commander of the Faithful does also hereby bestow upon you and your followers the statutory prerogatives: your life and property and those of your people will be protected, great care will be taken in the promotion of your welfare, your ways of interring the dead will be respected, and your churches and monasteries will be secured. In all this we are in conformity with the method adopted by the Orthodox Caliphs with your predecessors, a method followed by the high imams, my predecessors – may God be pleased with them – in their interpretation of the terms of our convention with you.[117]

There is an injunction contained within the *futūḥ* corpus, which perhaps serves as link between the redacted versions of the aforementioned pacts and the conquest period, specifically intended to regulate the conduct of soldiers encountering monks. This statement may also reflect a cross-confessional concept of the inviolate sanctity of ascetics in general. According to al-Ṭabarī, this order, given by Abū Bakr, was directed at the military commanders during the beginning stages of the conquest movement. The passage as it is presented by al-Ṭabarī is as follows:

> O people! There are ten orders I have for you, commit them to heart in my name. Do not deceive and do not be disloyal, do not act treacherously and do not maim people . . . and as you pass along the way you will meet people who occupy themselves in monks' cells (*ṣawāmiʿa*); leave them alone, along with whatever they occupy themselves with![118]

Judging by this reference attributed to Abū Bakr, the cross-confessional respect for ascetics appears to have had an influence on the handling of monastic communities, and/or individual ascetic figures, during the conquest phase. Whether or not such a directive was followed without discrepancy – and if the reports of certain conquest activities are accurate, it would appear that they were not – the singling-out of monks is still an instructive feature. An anonymous Syriac source, known as the *Chronicon ad annum Christi 1234 pertinens*, reports a similar declaration by Abū Bakr prohibiting the targeting of both monks and stylite ascetics, by virtue of their withdrawal from the material world and service to God.[119]

The *Life of Timothy of Kākhushtā*[120] offers an additionally positive assessment for the protection of Christian ascetics within Islam, though from a period far beyond the conquest phase. The *Life of Timothy* recounts the career of a monk and stylite ascetic from northern Syria, in the vicinity of Antioch, active around the years 750–830 CE.[121] In the course of providing information on the local economic and social conditions of the Christian communities of this region, the text also affords a glimpse at the relations between Muslims and Christians within this still predominantly Christian area. There is little sign of enmity amongst the differing religious groups in this work;[122] moreover, the *Life of Timothy* seems to indicate a relatively comfortable coexistence in this region at the beginning of the ʿAbbāsid era as well as perhaps hint at the influence of this particular Christian monk across confessional lines.[123] The text is of interest here because it provides an example of a particular leniency toward ascetics, as part of an encounter between a Muslim commander (generally referred to in the text by the Arabic term *amīr*), conducting raids along the Byzantine frontier, and a stylite monk, whose pillar was near their military encampment. In this episode, the commander, intending to alleviate the fear of the monk, issues the statement, 'you should know that I have forbade the harming of monks (*ruhbān*), priests (*kahana*), and ascetics (*zuhhād*)'.[124]

Though this material on the whole should be understood within a larger hagiographical context – and the episode itself clearly bears apocryphal elements that involve a miraculous set of circumstances – it does perhaps still preserve an echo of the general policies for the treatment of ascetics that transcended religious boundaries within the transitional stage from Umayyad to ʿAbbāsid rule.[125] Once again, unfortunately, there is no further clarification concerning the prohibition against the harming of such figures. When taken in context with other related statements, it would seem that the reason behind the temperate Muslim attitude toward monks stems from an awareness of their piety-driven existence.

There can be little doubt that the Islamic conquests of the Levant and North Africa produced general unrest among the civilian populations in those regions, as documentary sources such as the *Doctrina Jacobi nuper baptizati*[126] and the Christmas Day sermon of the Patriarch Sophronius[127] attest. Yet stability did return to the region in the aftermath of the Islamic invasion and, as the passage from the *Chronicle of Seert* suggests, the conditions of monastic life would also recover as a result of the concord imposed by Muslim authorities. This episode would therefore seem to be emblematic for the general situation: that is, that even in the event that monastic life was interrupted and monasteries torn down or subjected to thievery, it was not long before the community would be restored and their monasteries rebuilt.

The handling of monks, ascetics and monasteries themselves appear in many cases to be designated under special auspices from an early point in the development of the Muslim community, apart from the more general governance of Christian communities, and would continue to be a distinct feature of the administration throughout the early Islamic period. This amnesty for monks and monasteries appears to have been first practically articulated in the conquest period, perhaps ultimately owing the sentiment to an even older tradition concerning the inviolate mystique of the *holy man* in Late Antiquity.

Notes

1. The term *achtiname* is a derivation of a compound Arabic-Persian term used within the Ottoman government. The Arabic component stems from the root for 'pact' or 'covenant' – *'ahd*; while the Persian element – *name* – would be translated as 'document'. The Ottoman term *ahdname* is a general designation used for any type of treaty or capitulation agreement that results in a protective status. See entry for 'ahdname' by Papp in the *Encyclopedia of the Ottoman Empire*, eds G. Ágoston and B. A. Masters (Infobase Publishing, 2009).
2. Aziz Suryal Atiya, *The Arabic Manuscripts of Mount Sinai: A hand-list of the Arabic manuscripts and scrolls microfilmed at the library of the Monastery of St. Catherine, Mount Sinai* (Baltimore, MD: Johns Hopkins Press, 1955), xxix.
3. Ibid. xxix. This original text contained a handprint of the Prophet Muhammad, stamped with ink, in lieu of his signature at the conclusion of the document.
4. Jean-Michel Mouton, 'Les musulmans á Sainte-Catherine au Moyen Âge', in *Le Sinaï durant l'antiquité et le Moyen-Âge; 4000 ans d'histoire pour un desert*, actes du colloque 'Sinaï' qui s'est tenu à l'UNESCO du 19 au 2 (Paris, 1998), 2. A variant pact exists, containing the Arabic text with Latin translation, entitled respectively, *Testamentum et Pactiones Initae Inter Mohamedem et Christianae fidei cultores/al-'ahad wa al-sharūṭ allatī sharaṭahā Muḥammad Rasūl Allāh li-ahl al-milla al-Naṣrāniyya*, ed. and trans. (Latin) Gabriel Sionita (Paris, 1630) – that is often mistaken for the *achtiname*. The document edited

by Gabriel Sionita is a more general set of guidelines between the Prophet Muḥammad and Christian communities but does not specifically apply to Saint Catherine's monastery. It likewise records an alternate date for the agreement. According to this additional covenant, the date was set upon the fourth month of the fourth year of the *hijra*. The first few passages of *Testamentum et Pactiones* state: 'The pact and provisions which Muḥammad, the Messenger of God, has stipulated to the people of the Christian confession. This grants to them a pact of God and a charter of protection, with earnestness, sincere friendship and fidelity between the Believers (*al-mu'minīn*) and the Muslims, from the ancients to those of the present day . . . This pact applies concerning their churches and places of worship and prayer, the places of their monks, and the sites of their pilgrims, and wherever these may be found, such as in mountains or valleys, caves or urban spaces, plains or deserts . . .'

5. Mouton, 'Les musulmans á Sainte-Catherine au Moyen Âge', 2. There also appears to be an inaccuracy within the list of Muslim witnesses to the pact. The text specifically records the names of both Abū Hurayra and Abū al-Dardā as attesting to the pact in Medina, yet Abū al-Dardā did not convert to Islam until after the Battle of Badr in 624 CE, and Abū Hurayra did not join the Prophet in Medina until the year 629.
6. Mouton, 'Les musulmans', 2. Tritton has also remarked on such documents. See A. J. Tritton, *The Caliphs and Their Non-Muslim Subjects: A Critical Study of the Covenant of 'Umar* (London: Frank Cass & Co., 1970), 7–12. See also L. Massignon, 'La politique islamo-chrétienne des scribes nestorienes de Deir Qunna à la cour de Bagdad au IXe siècle de notre ère', *Revue Biblique* 2 (1942), 7–14. These types of documents were coming into circulation at this point due to the increasing tension between the Christian communities and their 'Abbāsid overlords.
7. Atiya, *The Arabic Manuscripts of Mount Sinai*, xxix. The oldest extant originals date from the Fatimid period.
8. This is not to say, however, that monastic communities within Sasanian Persia proper were under any duress at all throughout this period. To the contrary, monasticism had already enjoyed a distinguished legacy in Persia and was flourishing across the region in the sixth and seventh centuries. Shah Chosroes II himself was reported to have aided in the construction of the Monophysite monastery of Qaṣr Serīj, north-west of Mosul. See Chase Robinson, *Empire and Elites after the Muslim Conquest: The Transformation of Northern Mesopotamia* (Cambridge: Cambridge University Press, 2000), 64–5.

9. Robert L. Wilkin, 'Byzantine Palestine: A Christian Holy Land', *The Biblical Archaeologist* 51:4 (December 1988), 214–17, 233–7. John Lamoreaux goes so far as to say of the conquest period that 'archaeological evidence for church destruction is almost non-existent'. See 'Early Eastern Christian Responses to Islam', in *Medieval Christian Perceptions of Islam*, ed. J. V. Tolan (New York, NY: Garland Publishing, 1996), 3–31 at 6.
10. Ibid. 6.
11. Lorenzo Perrone, 'Monasticism in the Holy Land: From the Beginnings to the Crusades', in *Proche-Orient Chrétien* 45 (1995), 53–4. The disruption of pilgrim traffic in the Holy Land as a consequence of the wars also seems to have had a significant effect on monastic sustainability in certain areas prior to the Islamic conquest. This phenomenon can be witnessed in the archaeological surveys of monastic sites in the region. The late fifth-century Monastery of Kursi in Galilee, for example, was apparently abandoned during this period because of the lack of pilgrim accessibility. See Tzaferis, 'Excavations at Kursi', *Atiqot* 16 (1983), 55–65.
12. See J. Labourt, *Le christianisme dans l'empire perse sous le dynastie sassanide* (Paris, 1904), 208. For the status of Christian communities in Iran preceding this era, see Kyle Smith, *Constantine and the Captive Christians of Persia: Martyrdom and Religious Identity in Late Antiquity* (Berkeley, CA: University of California Press, 2016).
13. Sebastian Brock has favoured the identifying terms of East Syrian/Assyrian Church of the East, along with Miaphysite, over the more antiquated 'Nestorian' and 'Monophysite' when discussing the non-Chalcedonian Christian communities in the Levant, Iraq and Persia. See Brock, 'The "Nestorian" Church: A Lamentable Misnomer', *Bulletin of the John Rylands Library* 78 (1996), 23–35. The terms traditionally employed by medieval Muslim writers to describe the Christians within the realm were 'Nestorians', 'Jacobites' and 'Melkites'. See Sidney Griffith, *The Church in the Shadow of the Mosque: Christians and Muslims in the World of Islam* (Princeton, NJ: Princeton University Press, 2008), 8–9.
14. Richard Payne, *A State of Mixture: Christians, Zoroastrians, and Iranian Political Culture in Late Antiquity* (Berkeley, CA: University of California Press, 2015), 3–4.
15. Geoffrey Greatrex, 'Khusro II and the Christians of His Empire', *Journal of the Canadian Society for Syriac Studies* 3 (2003), 78–88.
16. For Chosroes II and his alleged direct involvement in Christian religious ceremonies, as well as his interest in Christian relics, see Beate Dignas and

Engelbert Winter, *Rome and Persia in Late Antiquity: Neighbors and Rivals* (Cambridge: Cambridge University Press, 2007), 227–31.

17. *The Chronicle of Se'ert*, ed. and French trans. A. Scher and R. Griveau, *Patrologia Orientalis* 13 (Paris, 1919), 474–98. For a detailed analysis of the text, see Philip Wood, *The Chronicle of Seert: Christian Historical Imagination in Late Antique Iraq* (Oxford: Oxford University Press, 2013).
18. *The Chronicle of Se'ert*, 474.
19. Wood, *The Chronicle of Seert*, 188–9.
20. On the construction of Christian shrines by Khusrū II, in honour of Shīrīn, see Dignas and Winter, *Rome and Persia in Late Antiquity*, 229.
21. *The Chronicle of Se'ert*, 490–1. Cf. Wood, *The Chronicle of Seert*, 191.
22. Payne, *A State of Mixture*, 3. An analogous collective enterprise situating ecclesiastical structures within the government would have applied to other Christian groups as well as Jewish communities, all of whom were bound together by overlapping concepts of law in the Iranian political sphere. East Syrian and Talmudic literature demonstrate a high degree of familiarity with Zoroastrian court and juridical procedure, often suggesting that the episcopal and rabbinic courts acted in a complementary capacity for the higher, state apparatus. See Payne, 104–5.
23. W. H. C. Frend, *The Rise of the Monophysite Movement* (Cambridge: Cambridge University Press, 1972), 333–4.
24. Greatrex, 'Khusro II and the Christians of His Empire', 78–9.
25. J. M. Fiey, *Jalons pour une histoire de l'église en Iraq* (Louvain: Peeters Publications, 1977), 136; Michael Morony, 'Sasanids', *EI*[2] X (1995), 79; Greatrex, 'Khusro II and the Christians of His Empire', 79.
26. G. J. Reinink, 'Babai the Great's *Life of George* and the Propagation of Doctrine in the Late Sasanian Empire', in *Portraits of Spiritual Authority: Religious Power in Early Christianity, Byzantium and the Christian Orient*, eds J.-W. Drijvers and John W. Watt (Leiden: Brill, 1999), 171–93 at 189; Greatrex, 'Khusro II and the Christians of His Empire', 79.
27. For a comprehensive overview, see Clive Foss, 'The Persians in the Roman Near East', *The Journal of the Royal Asiatic Society* 13:2 (July 2003), 149–70, and 'The Persians in Asia Minor and the End of Antiquity', *The English Historical Review* 90:357 (October 1975), 721–47.
28. *Chronique de Michel Le Syrien, Patriarche Jacobite D'Antioche (1166–1199)*, tome II, ed. and French trans. J.-B. Chabot (Paris, 1901), 379. Here the term 'orthodox' refers to the Miaphysite/Jacobite Church.

29. *Chronique de Michel Le Syrien*, 379.
30. Agapius of Manbij, *Kitāb al-unwān*, ed. A. A. Vasiliev, *Patrologia Orientalis*, tome 8, fasc. 3 (1912), part II, 458–9.
31. Severus ibn al-Muqaffa', *History of the Patriarchs of the Coptic Church of Alexandria*, ed. and trans. B. Evetts, *Patrologia Orientalis*, tome 1, fasc. 4, part 2 (Paris: Firmin-Didot, 1904–15), 485. For a discussion on the precise authorship of the chronicle, consult D. W. Johnson, 'Further Remarks on the Arabic History of the Patriarchs of Alexandria', *Oriens Christianus* 61 (1977), 3–16; and J. Den Heijer, *Mawhūb ibn Manṣūr ibn Mufarriğ et l'historiographie copto-arabe. Étude sur la composition de l'Histoire des Patriarches d'Alexandrie*, Corpus Scriptorum Christianorum Orientalium Subsidia 83 (Louvain, 1989).
32. Severus ibn al-Muqaffa', *History of the Patriarchs*, 485.
33. A. J. Butler, *The Arab Conquest of Egypt and the Last Thirty Years of the Roman Dominion*, ed. P. M. Fraser (Oxford: Clarendon Press, 1978), 75.
34. Severus ibn al-Muqaffa', *History of the Patriarchs*, 487.
35. Ibid. 486. The term for 'commander' being taken here from the Persian word *salār*. In this case the Persian commander, according to Butler, would have likely been Shahîn. See Butler, *The Arab Conquest of Egypt*, 75.
36. Ibid. 75.
37. See section on 'The Persian offensive' in Bernard Flusin, *Saint Anastase Le Perse et l'Histoire de la Palestine au Début du VIIe Siècle*, tome II (Paris: Éditions du CNRS, 1992), 151–61, and Foss, 'The Persians in the Roman Near East', 152–3.
38. See Geoffrey Greatrex and Samuel N. C. Lieu, eds, *The Roman Eastern Frontier and the Persian Wars, part II: AD 363–630* (London and New York: Routledge, 2002), 190–1.
39. Walter Kaegi, *Byzantium and the Early Islamic Conquests* (Cambridge: Cambridge University Press, 1992), 54.
40. *Chronical of Se'ert*, 539–40. According to the chronicle, the original source of trouble between the Persians and the Arabs was the murder, by means of poisoning, of al-Nu'mān, the King of the Lakhmids, by order of Chosroes II. For the problematic term *Ṭayyāyē*, see Michael C. A. Macdonald, 'Arabs and Empires before the Sixth Century', in *Arabs and Empires before Islam*, ed. Greg Fisher (Oxford: Oxford University Press, 2015), 11–89, especially 76–9 – the term being most commonly translated now as 'tent-dwellers' or 'nomads'.
41. On *foederati*, see Walter Kaegi, *Heraclius, Emperor of Byzantium* (Cambridge: Cambridge University Press, 2003), 242, and Fred Donner, *The Early Islamic*

Conquests (Princeton, NJ: Princeton University Press, 1981), 98–101, 105–8.

42. Michael the Syrian, *Chronique de Michel Le Syrien*, 401.
43. Gilbert Dagron, 'L'Église Byzantine au VIIe siècle', in *Évêques, Moines, Et Empereurs (610–1054), Histoire du Christianisme des Origines à Nos Jours*, tome 4, eds Gilbert Dagron, Pierre Riché and Andre Vauchez (Paris: Desclee, 1993), 15.
44. F. C. Conybeare, 'Antiochus Strategos, the Capture of Jerusalem by the Persians in 614 A.D.', *English Historical Review* 25 (1910), 502–17 at 507; Antiochus Strategos, *La prise de Jérusalem par les Perses en 614*, ed. and Latin trans. G. Garitte (Corpus Scriptorum Christianorum Orientalium, Scriptores Iberici 11 and 12).
45. Sebeos, *The Armenian Chronicle Attributed to Sebeos*, trans. R. W. Thompson (Liverpool: Liverpool University Press, 1999), 69. Butler makes a note that in one of the manuscripts of Sebeos' chronicle, the number of casualties is listed as 17,000. See Butler, *The Arab Conquest of Egypt*, 60, footnote 2.
46. Theophanes, *Chronographia*, vol. I, ed. C. De Boor (Leipzig, 1883), 237–8.
47. Kaegi, *Heraclius, Emperor of Byzantium*, 78.
48. Conybeare, 'Antiochus Strategos', 509–10.
49. The Christian towns of Arabia, to the south, and Egypt (particularly Alexandria) appear to have been the most common destinations for such refugees. See Butler, *The Arab Conquest of Egypt*, 62.
50. H. Chadwick, 'John Moschus and his Friend Sophronius the Sophist', *The Journal of Theological Studies* 25 (1974), 41–74.
51. Conybeare, 'Antiochus Strategos', 507.
52. Ibid. 509.
53. Joseph Patrich, *Sabas, Leader of Palestinian Monasticism: A Comparative Study in Eastern Monasticism, Fourth to Seventh Centuries* (Washington, DC: Dumbarton Oaks Research Library and Collections, 1995), 326.
54. David Olster, 'The Construction of a Byzantine Saint: George of Choziba, Holiness, and the Pilgrimage Trade in Seventh-Century Palestine', *Greek Orthodox Theological Review* 38 (1993), 309–22 at 309. The exact date of production is uncertain, but the *Life* concludes by stating that peace was eventually restored to the monastery and it gives no reference to the Arab/Islamic conquests. This would suggest an *ante quem* date of around the year 630.
55. *Life of George of Choziba*, 'Sancti Georgii Chozebitae: Confessoris et Monachi

Vita Auctore Antonio ejus discipulo', ed. and Latin trans. C. Houze, *Analecta Bollandiana* 7 (1888), 129.

56. Ibid. 129–30.
57. Joseph Patrich, 'The Cells of Choziba, Wadi el-Qilt', in *Christian Archaeology in the Holy Land, New Discoveries: Archaeological Essays in Honour of Virgilio C. Corbo OFM*, eds G. Claudio Bottini, Leah Di Segni and Eugenio Alliata, Studium Biblicum Franciscanum Collectio Maior 36 (Jerusalem, 1990), 205–25.
58. Olster, 'The Construction of a Byzantine Saint', 317–18. This monastery was renowned for its miraculous oil that seeped from the tombs of the founders of the settlement.
59. *Life of George of Choziba*, 143–4.
60. Ewa Wipszycka, *Moines et Communautés Monastiques en Égypte (IVe–VIIIe Siècles)*, The Journal of Juristic Papyrology, Supplement XI (Warsaw, 2009), 613–15.
61. For Mazices, or Maziques, see D. Roques, *Synésios de Cyréne et la Cyrénaïque au Bas Empire* (Paris: Éditions du CNRS, 1987), 270–3.
62. For Blemmyes, see J. Desanges, *Catalogue des tribus africaines de l'antiquité classique à l'ouest du Nil*, Publications de la section d'histoire no. 4 (Dakar, 1962), 184–7, as well as *The History of the Peoples of the Eastern Desert*, eds Hans Barnard and Kim Duistermaat, Monograph 73 Cotsen Institute of Archaeology (Los Angeles, CA: University of California Press, 2012).
63. It moreover appears that the raiding was not always directed at the largest and most important monastic centres in the region, as even the loosely organised eremitic communities suffered such trials as well. In an analysis of the *Ammonius*, λόγος/διηγημα, a narrative concerning a fourth-century Bedouin attack on the monks of St Catherine's in the Sinai, Mayerson discusses the account of the preceding destruction of an ascetic community at Raithou by the Blemmyes. This settlement at Raithou was apparently just a simple outpost of communal monks, perhaps not even maintaining a 'superior'. The few who managed to escape Raithou sought refuge with the other monks at St Catherine's Monastery. See Philip Mayerson, 'The Ammonius Narrative: Bedouin and Blemmye Attacks in the Sinai', in *The Bible World, Essays in Honor of Cyrus H. Gordon* (1980), 113–48.
64. Alexander Vasiliev, 'Notes on Some Episodes Concerning the Relations between the Arabs and the Byzantine Empire from the Fourth to the Sixth Century', *Dumbarton Oaks Papers* 9 (1956), 306–16. Vasiliev mentions here that the Emperor granted the request and ordered the construction of a castle

near the monastery, with a military detachment as well. The imperial command, however, was not carried out.

65. Following the agreement between Heraclius and Shahrbarāz at Arabissos. See Kaegi, *Heraclius*, 187–8.
66. *Vie de Samuel de Kalamoun*, ed. A. Alcock, *The Life of Samuel of Kalamoun by Isaac the Presbyter* (Warminster: Aris & Phillips, 1983), 12–14 original text, 87–90 translation. The term 'Berber' here is a translation of the original Coptic text's usage of *Mazices*.
67. Hugh G. Evelyn White, *The Monasteries of the Wâdi'n Natrun, Part II: The History of the Monasteries of Nitria and Scetis* (New York: Metropolitan Museum of Art Egyptian Expedition, 1932), 249–54.
68. Ibid. 257.
69. Walter E. Kaegi, 'Egypt on the Eve of the Muslim Conquest', in *The Cambridge History of Egypt*, vol. 1, *Islamic Egypt, 640–1517*, ed. Carl F. Petry (Cambridge: Cambridge University Press, 1998), 34–61 at 44. Prior to this, Kyrus had been the Bishop of Phasis. See also Kaegi, *Heraclius*, 216.
70. The theological position of the Byzantine court at this time being Monotheletism. For details of the success of Monotheletism as a theological position, see D. Larison, dissertation: 'Return to Authority: The Monothelete Controversy and the Role of Text, Emperor, and Council at the Sixth Ecumenical Council', University of Chicago, 2009, 44–82.
71. Severus ibn al-Muqaffaʿ, *History of the Patriarchs*, 490.
72. *Vie de Samuel de Kalamoun*, 79.
73. Ibid. 80–1.
74. Severus ibn al-Muqaffaʿ, *History of the Patriarchs*, 491.
75. Ibid. 492.
76. The specific event that is reflected in this passage may be related to the Byzantine loss at Adhriʿāt in 614. See Kaegi, *Heraclius*, 78, and Robert Schick, 'Jordan on the Eve of the Muslim Conquest, A.D. 602–634', in *La Syrie de Byzance à l'Islam VII–VIII Siècles*, eds P. Cavinet and J.-P. Rey-Coquais (Damascus: Institute Français de Damas, 1992), 107–19.
77. Mujāhid ibn Jabr al-Tābiʿī, *Tafsīr Mujāhid*, vol. II, ed. ʿAbd al-Raḥmān al-Sūratī (Beirut: Manshūrāt al-ʿIlmiyya, 197?), 499. See also Nadia El Cheikh, '*Sūrat al-Rūm:* A Study of the Exegetical Literature', *Journal of the American Oriental Society* 118:3 (1998), 356–64.
78. Fred Donner, *Muhammad and the Believers: At the Origins of Islam* (Cambridge, MA: Belknap Press of Harvard University Press, 2010), 106–10.

79. Montgomery Watt, *Muhammad at Medina* (Oxford: Clarendon Press, 1977), first published in 1956.
80. While a phrase such as *Arabian believers* would seem most appropriate in this section, for the sake of clarity I will continue to employ the more familiar terminology of *Muslim* and *Islam*.
81. Even the Chalcedonians/Melkites, the sectarian group that was apparently most perceived as a threat to Sasanian interests, were able to retain possession of their main churches and monasteries during the Muslim seizure of control. This was clearly the case in the major towns of Syria-Palestine and appears to have been the accepted norm in the surrounding countryside as well. The notable exception to this was the Cathedral of St John the Baptist in Damascus, which was eventually expropriated – though even in this case the structure was not fully converted into a mosque until the early eighth century, well after the conquest period. Nancy Khalek discusses medieval accounts of this event, taking place in the reign of al-Walīd I (r. 705–15), in *Damascus after the Muslim Conquest: Text and Image in Early Islam* (Oxford: Oxford University Press, 2011), especially 45–50. The Melkite Christians of Damascus however, were allowed to maintain custody of the Cathedral of St Mary in the 'Street Called Straight', which would become the primary Melkite church in the city, as it is today as well. Hugh Kennedy, 'The Melkite Church from the Islamic Conquest to the Crusades: Continuity and Adaptation in the Byzantine Legacy', in *The 17th International Byzantine Congress* (New Rochelle, NY: A. D. Caratzas, 1986), 325–43.
82. Sebastian Brock, 'Syriac Views of Emergent Islam', in *Studies on the First Century of Islamic Society*, ed. G. H. A. Joynboll (Carbondale, IL: Southern Illinois University Press, 1982), 13. Brock goes on to speak of those earliest Syriac sources concerning the conquests as interpreting them primarily as 'Arab, and not Muslim', 14.
83. G. J. Reinink, 'The Beginnings of Syriac Apologetical Literature in Response to Islam', in *Syriac Christianity under Late Sasanian and Early Islamic Rule* (Aldershot: Ashgate Variorum, 2005), 165. There are several essays of importance concerning Syriac perspectives on early Islam in this volume, including 'Ps.-Methodius: A Concept in History in Response to the Rise of Islam' and 'The Lamb on the Tree: Syriac Exegesis and anti-Islamic Apologetics'.
84. Reinink, 'The Beginnings of Syriac Apologetical Literature', 165.
85. Terry G. Willfong, 'The Non-Muslim communities: Christian communities', in *The Cambridge History of Egypt*, vol. I, *Islamic Egypt, 640–1517*, ed. Carl F. Petry (Cambridge: Cambridge University Press, 1998), 175–97 at 178.

86. L. Leroy, 'Les couvents des chrétiens: Traduction de l'Arabe d'al-Makrizi', *Revue de l'Orient chrétien* 13 (1908), 192–204 at 198–9.
87. Robert Kirschner, 'The Vocation of Holiness in Late Antiquity', in *Vigiliae Christianae* 38 (1984), 105–24; Peter Brown, 'The Rise and Function of the Holy Man in Late Antiquity', *The Journal of Roman Studies* 61 (1971), 80–101.
88. Andrew Louth, 'Justinian and His Legacy (500–600)', in *The Cambridge History of the Byzantine Empire, c. 500–1492*, ed. Jonathan Shepard (Cambridge: Cambridge University Press, 2008), 97–129 at 102.
89. There are reports that suggest this was the second attempt of Kyrus to negotiate with the Muslims, the first one occurring at some time in the year 637 CE. The first was apparently an attempt to avoid an invasion altogether, with the agreement to pay 200,000 dinars to the Muslims. Among other places, this appears in the *Kitāb al-unwān* of Agapius of Manbij, 472.
90. The date of composition for this *Chronicle of John of Nikiu* falls some time between 650 and 690 CE. See Robert Hoyland, *Seeing Islam as Others Saw It: A Survey and Evaluation of Christian, Jewish, and Zoroastrian Writings on Early Islam* (Princeton, NJ: Darwin Press, 1997), 153.
91. *The Chronicle of John, Coptic Bishop of Nikiu*, trans. Robert Henry Charles (Amsterdam: Apa-Philo Press, 1981), 193–4.
92. Severus ibn al-Muqaffaʿ, *History of the Patriarchs*, 496.
93. Ibn ʿAbd al-Ḥakam, *Futūḥ Miṣr wa-akhbāruhā*, ed. Charles Torrey (New Haven, CT: Yale University Press, 1922), 58.
94. *The Chronicle of John*, 200.
95. C. D. G. Müller, 'Stellung und Haltung der koptischen Patriarchen des 7. Jahrhunderts gegenüber islamischer Obrigkeit und Islam', in *Acts of the Second International Congress of Coptic Studies: Roma, 22–26 September* (1985), 203–13 at 204. See also Harald Suermann, 'Copts and the Islam of the Seventh Century', in *The Encounter of Eastern Christianity with Early Islam*, eds E. Grypeou, M. N. Swanson and D. Thomas (Leiden: Brill, 2006), 95–109.
96. Müller, 'Stellung und Haltung der koptischen', 204–5; see also Suermann, 'Copts and the Islam of the Seventh Century', 99.
97. See Amir Harrak, 'Syriac Views of History after the Advent of Islam', *Redefining Christian Identity: Cultural Interaction in the Middle East since the Rise of Islam*, eds J. J. Van Ginkel, H. L. Murre-Van Den Berg and T. M. Van Lint (Leuven: Uitgeverij Peeters en Departement Oosterse Studies, 2005), 45–66.
98. S. P. Brock, 'Syriac Views of Emergent Islam', in *Studies on the First Century of*

Islamic Society, ed. G. H. A. Joynboll (Carbondale, IL: Southern Illinois Press, 1982), 9–22.

99. Maximus the Confessor uses this phrase in a letter dated between 634 and 640. See Brock, 'Syriac Views of Emergent Islam', 9–10.
100. Book XV of the *Rīsh Mellē* in *Sources Syriaques*, ed. A. Mingana (Leipzig: Otto Harrassowitz, 1908), 141.
101. Severus ibn al-Muqaffaʿ, *History of the Patriarchs*, 494.
102. Ibn ʿAbd al-Ḥakam, *Futūḥ Miṣr wa-akhbāruhā*, 84.
103. Severus ibn al-Muqaffaʿ, *History of the Patriarchs* 500.
104. Ibn ʿAbd al-Ḥakam, *Futūḥ Miṣr wa-akhbāruhā*, 84.
105. See Donner, *The Early Islamic Conquests*, 128–55; Walter Kaegi, *Byzantium and the Early Islamic Conquests* (Cambridge: Cambridge University Press, 1992), 147–80.
106. Al-Balādhurī, *Futūḥ al-buldān* (Beirut: Dar al-Kutub al-ʿIlmiyya, 1983), 76.
107. Al-Ṭabarī, *Taʾrīkh al-rusul waʾl mulūk*, vol. 2 (Beirut: Dar al-Kutub al-ʿIlmiyya, 1987) 294–5.
108. *Chronicle of Seʿert*, 601. See also M. Benedicte Landron, 'Les Relations Originelles entre Chretiens de l'est (Nestoriens) et Musulmans', *Parole de l'Orient* 10 (1981–2), 193.
109. *Chronicle of Seʿert*, 602.
110. Ibid. 611.
111. See Sebastian Brock, 'North Mesopotamia in the Late Seventh Century: Book XV of Bar Penkāye's *Ris Melle*', *Jerusalem Studies in Arabic and Islam* 9 (1987), 51–75 at 52.
112. See Tritton, *The Caliphs and Their Non-Muslim Subjects*, opening chapter.
113. Ibid. The main conclusion to Tritton's analysis is that there was no universally recognised set of statutes for the treatment of *dhimmīs*, as manifest in the covenant of ʿUmar, until the ʿAbbāsid period. It was only in this later era that such a pact was produced and then projected backwards in time to the initial conquest phase. The document is actually based on a mixture of the various independent treaties reached between towns and conquerors, then developed into a single theoretical set of guidelines under the later jurists. For the complicated interpretation of the so-called 'pact of ʿUmar', see also Milka Levy-Rubin, 'Shurūṭ ʿUmar: From Harbingers to Systematic Enforcement', *Beyond Religious Borders: Interaction and Intellectual Exchange in the Medieval Islamic World*, eds D. M. Freidenreich and M. Goldestein (Philadelphia, PA: University of Pennsylvania Press, 2012), 30–43.

114. Al-Ṭabarī, *Ta'rīkh al-rusul wa'l-muluk* 2, 448–51, and also al-Balādhurī, *Futūḥ al-buldān*, 134–5.
115. Agapius of Manbij, *Kitāb al-unwān*, 471.
116. The earliest extant version of this document is found within the Ryland's Library, under the designation *Rylands MS. Arabic 694*, and dates from around the year 1200 CE. See 'A Charter of Protection Granted to the Nestorian Church in AD 1138, by Muktafi II, Caliph of Baghdad', ed. and trans. A. Mingana, *Bulletin of the John Rylands Library* X (1926). Arabic manuscript included as a facsimile.
117. 'A Charter of Protection Granted to the Nestorian Church in AD 1138', manuscript pp. 6–7.
118. Al-Ṭabarī, *Ta'rīkh al-rusul wa'l-muluk* 2, 246.
119. *Chronicon ad annum Christi 1234 pertinens*, vol. I, ed. J. B. Chabot, Corpus Scriptorum Christianorum Orientalium vol. 109, *scriptores syri*, tome 56 (Paris, 1937), 240.
120. *Life of Timothy of Kākhushtā*, ed. and trans. J. Lamoreaux and C. Cairala, *Patrologia Orientalis*, tome 48, fasc. 4, no. 216 (Turnhout: Brepols, 2000).
121. The approximate chronology for the composition of this hagiography is discussed by Clive Foss in 'Byzantine Saints in Early Islamic Syria', *Analecta Bolliandiana* 125 (2007).
122. To the exclusion of this statement is the account of the exile of Theodoret, the Patriarch of Antioch, by Caliph Harun al-Rashid. See *Life of Timothy*, episode between Patriarch and Caliph, 27 (Paris manuscript edition of J. Lamoreaux). There are several other references to Muslims in this text and, while they do not portray hostility, it should be cautioned that the text itself is an example of hagiography and is not necessarily focused on social relationships as such, but more on the extraordinary and often miraculous details of this particular ascetic's life. The types of wondrous activities in this hagiography include the story of the conversion of a Muslim to Christianity at the hands of Timothy and the saint's condemnation of a Muslim villager guilty of adultery.
123. Foss, 'Byzantine Saints in Early Islamic Syria', 69.
124. *Life of Timothy of Kākhushtā*, 66–7.
125. Such lenient attitudes were of course not always uniformly adopted and there do exist several martyrologies relating to Christian monks in this early period of Islamic rule. By and large however, these texts, as concluded in an analysis by Griffith, are mainly focused on problems of religious conversion (in this case the apostasy from Islam to Christianity) and therefore do not necessarily insinuate a growing hostility toward monks in general. Moreover, even though

as accounts some of these are presented in an Umayyad context, Griffith suggests that they may actually belong to a later period. See Sidney Griffith, 'Christians, Monks, and Neo-Martyrs: Saints' Lives and Holy Land History', *Sharing the Sacred: Religious Contacts and Conflicts in the Holy Land, first to thirteenth centuries*, eds Arieh Kofsky and Guy G. Stroumsa (Jerusalem: Yad Izhak Ben Zvi, 1998), 163–207.

126. *Doctrina Jacobi nuper baptizati*, ed. and German trans. by G. N. Bonwetsch, Abhandlungen der Königlichen Gesellschaft der Wissenschaften zu Göttingen, Philologisch-historische Klasse (Berlin: Weidmann, 1910); also, edited and updated commentary provided of *Doctrina Jacobi* in *Juifs et Chrétiens Dans L'Orient du VIIe Siècle*, G. Dagron and V. Déroche (Paris: Bilans de Recherche, 2010), 17–273.

127. Sophronius, *Christmas Sermon*, ed. H. Usener, 'Weihnachspredigt des Sophronios', *Rheinisches Museum für Philologie* 41 (1886); *Patrologia Graeca* 87, 3201–12.

3

Monastic Life under Caliphal Rule in the Early Centuries

A Shifting Political Landscape

Depite being confronted with decades of sectarian discord and social upheaval following the Persian military campaigns within the Levant and Egypt in the early seventh century,[1] the fact persists that a host of monasteries survived these turbulent periods to become subject entities under the emerging Muslim administration. The restoration of political stability under Islamic dynasties, as well as the evolution of a system for religious toleration, had significant implications for the fortunes of these monastic communities. The goal here will be to determine the nature of the dynamic between the government and monasteries that facilitated this continuation of Christian monastic life under the early Islamic state.

The research presented here will reveal a relatively benign political situation for monasteries throughout the early Islamic period. The contention that the monastic communities in question were in some manner connected to the Muslim state administration and therefore to some degree regulated by imperial policies, as had been the established norm prior to the coming of Islam,[2] can be made with relative certainty. Even though these eastern monasteries had a long legacy of fervent support from their local religious communities, it was indeed ultimately the position of the monastery vis-à-vis the administration that would ensure its long-term fortune, or not. The cohesion of the Islamic state, as well as its administrative strategies dictating the terms for religious tolerance, was of pivotal importance to the security and degree of prosperity for monasteries under its jurisdiction. To this may be added the proposal that when monasteries did suffer the most egregious harm while under the early Muslim government, the factors yielding to violence against monasteries generally has more do to with an interruption in the balance of civil authority than with any detrimental policies directed specifically against them.

This chapter will therefore be dedicated to the examination of the correlation between the state and monasteries, focusing on the discrepancies between Christian and Muslim regimes pertaining to the state attitudes and administrative measures enforced upon monastic communities – including matters relating to the imperial protection and conservation of monasteries, the position of the monastery in the economic framework of the state, and regulations for the lives of monks therein. The issues of fundamental import here relate more specifically to the particular measure or weight of imperial pressure exerted upon monastic communities, which illustrate a divergence in policy that is conspicuous from either the earlier Byzantine or later ʿAbbāsid eras.

Though being severed from a degree of direct assistance or patronage from the imperial Church at Constantinople as in previous eras, at least as far as Chalcedonian communities were concerned,[3] many of these monasteries, as well as those associated with rival confessional traditions, remained in operation much as before on the eve of Islamic political domination. The *Spiritual Meadow* of John Moschus, composed in the early decades of the seventh century,[4] stands as a key witness to this transitional period and illustrates the enduring contacts between monastic communities across the Levant, even amidst precarious times.[5] Though the regime change that accompanied the Islamic conquests in the following years would create a new set of challenges for Christians of the region, the policies governing the junction between the state and monasteries generally appear to have remained sufficiently accommodating. Even in light of temporary impediments brought about as a result of the conquest period, there is no doubt that monasticism continued to thrive under Muslim governance and there is even evidence of new foundations and restorations to monasteries throughout the early Islamic period.[6] This period therefore represents a discernible contrast, in terms relating to the fate of Christian ecclesiastical entities, to both the period of the Sassanid invasions and the later ʿAbbāsid era.[7]

It can therefore be affirmed that the paradigm of Levantine monasticism that emerges in the post-conquest era generally tends toward the continuance of intellectually thriving[8] and economically viable[9] communities within a newly established Muslim political context. The Great Laura of Mar Saba in Palestine serves as an important testament to this continuance, having principally remained in operation from its establishment in the late fifth century into modern times. Even in the wake of the sacking of the monastery in the year 813 CE by Arab raiders,[10] coinciding with the eruption of civil war within the ʿAbbāsid caliphate, Mar Saba was able to retain its prominent standing as a spiritual and theological bastion until at least the end of the millennium.[11]

While the precise nature of this relationship was appreciably complex and the delineation of official administrative strategies is somewhat obscure, there was clearly a level of forbearance afforded to these entities, which appears to be a distinct feature of the early Islamic period. The interpretation of the meaning of this administrative stance, taken in conjunction with the local-level policies and popular views on monasteries to be discussed in the later chapters, may yield further insight into the nature of confessional relationships in this period. The underlying assertion here, to be more fully developed in the coming sections of this research, is that the emphasis on piety within early Islam, in many ways still exemplified by the monastic ideal, may have been instrumental in the formation of an inter-confessional community of 'Believers'[12] The remnants of this relative ecumenism, based on a respect for individual piety present from the earliest stages in the formation of the Muslim community, would play a significant role in the later imperial policies on monasteries. The management of Christian monasteries throughout the regions under Muslim control can therefore be understood as corroboration for this special ecumenical attitude within Islam during its formative period.

While in some instances this tolerant outlook can be witnessed in policies toward non-Muslims in general, there are likewise cases in which the institution of monasticism itself has been specifically identified for a particular set of administrative parameters. The fact that such discrepancies exist enables the argument to be set forth that monasteries still held an important socio-religious position within the state, regardless of confessional affiliation. As demonstrated in the previous chapter, there is little evidence for widespread,

Figure 3.1 Mar Saba Monastery. Credit: Sean Leatherbury/Manar al-Athar Photo-Archive, Oxford 2013.

and moreover deliberate, aggression against Christian monasteries during the initial stages of political consolidation over the region and it appears that some measure of security for ecclesiastical property had begun to be negotiated in the conquest era.[13]

The Byzantine Sphere

Even during the most flourishing phase of monasticism in the East, the growth of the monastery and its membership was not always viewed in a positive manner by the imperial government in Constantinople, because such communities could at times present a challenge to the official policies of the state according to both sanctioned religious practices and doctrine. Particularly in relation to the East, the increasing prominence of monasticism was frequently connected to popular ascetic movements that were largely self-directed and distinct from the mainstream religious authority. This independence was of little concern to civil or ecclesiastical authorities in the early stages of monastic expansion, as they were typically situated in isolated and remote areas. Tensions began to intensify, however, during the reign of Theodosius II in the fifth century, involving the movement of ascetics and monasteries into more urbanised locations.[14] Efforts to temper the growing influence of monks over towns and villages as a result of monastic urbanisation trends can be witnessed in the following statute of the Theodosian Code: 'If any persons should be found in the profession of monks, they shall be ordered to seek out and to inhabit desert places and desolate solitudes.'[15]

Additionally, the crucial role of monasteries within the economic and social structure of the Byzantine state cannot be overstated, a fact which prompted H.-G. Beck to make the assertion that as early as the sixth century the empire had indeed 'become monasticized'.[16] The growth of monastic establishments was such a widespread phenomenon that it has been estimated that by the end of the seventh century nearly one-third of serviceable land throughout the empire was in the possession of churches and/or monasteries.[17] Ecclesiastical officials had by this time become recognised as *dynatoi*, or 'elites', within the Byzantine social strata, due to these vast territorial acquisitions and the socio-economic influence that accompanied such holdings.[18] The intimate connection between the government and monastic communities is therefore a product of this multifaceted influence and can be witnessed in the copious legislative measures and church canons directed at monasteries throughout this period, either in the attempt to buttress or to restrict their impact upon society.

This situation is mirrored to a point with the Islamic conquest and its aftermath, which cannot only be viewed as a religious venture but also as a politico-economic undertaking,[19] particularly with respect to the emphasis on the extraction of tribute from subject populations. The implementation of a taxation policy for non-Muslims, as will be shown, generally maintained special privileges toward monks and, at times, their monasteries. On the converse side, throughout this period it can be argued that the most severe episodes of direct oppression to monasteries lie primarily within this economic realm.

Although monasteries typically owed their foundation to pious individual endowment, it was their legal standing under the state that would ultimately guarantee the measure of prosperity for a monastic institution.[20] The first examples of legal interaction between the imperial establishment and ecclesiastical offices, with respect to monks as an extension of the clergy, come from the time of Constantine[21] and extend into the Islamic period. However, the bulk of the ecclesiastical legislative provisions of the middle period in Byzantine history specifically relate to monastic property, as opposed to ecclesiastical holdings in general, due to the fact that by this period the monasteries had accrued the majority of the assets.[22]

In his study of monastic communities in sixth-century Anatolia, Trombley asserts that the monastery was an integral component to the local village economy of that region, by means of both sensible management of their estates and the fostering of cooperation with the rural inhabitants involved with monastic lands, either in terms of agricultural productivity or building projects. Whereas previous scholarship had traditionally focused on urban decline of this region during the sixth century,[23] Trombley alternatively characterises this as a phenomenon of demographic and economic ruralisation, in which monasteries played a crucial role in the economic development of the hinterland. With this capacity for economic productivity, monasteries became hubs of opportunity for labourers throughout the countryside seeking employment as stonemasons, carpenters, mosaicists and so forth. In this particular case, it seems that in addition to their reputation for medical and spiritual healing, monasteries of that region were often renown for their accretion of wealth – at times at the expense of the local temporal authorities and ecclesiastical officials.[24]

The situation in late antique Palestine was virtually analogous in terms of the economic influence of monastic communities, albeit the factors contributing to this heightened role in the local economic system and its results tended to differ. According to Avi-Yonah,[25] in the case of Palestine the economy of the region was concentrated upon the influx of imperial donations and private patronage for churches and monasteries. This capital in turn served the basis for employment of various kinds throughout the area, initially falling to those responsible for the erection of ecclesiastical structures and then trickling into the larger economic network. The study of Avi-Yonah is, in contrast, largely concerned with the negative long-term effects of such funding by concentrating investments in the 'unproductive hands' of clergymen,[26] creating an 'artificially high level of economic life'.[27] The Byzantine government recognised this type of untenable financial condition, particularly as it applied to monasteries, and subsequently promulgated legislation in an attempt to correct it.

Insofar as this relationship in the early Islamic period can be characterised as one concerning an 'official' level of interaction, thereby relating to state policies on matters associated with monasteries, a necessity arises of defining the precise condition of these monasteries under a preceding Byzantine administration. In other words, the subsequent procedures relating to monasteries enacted by Muslim authorities were in some ways a legacy from the previous Byzantine codes,[28] albeit with several interesting disparities. In order to construct a model for the status of Christian monasteries under a Muslim administration, the investigation must attempt to delineate the nature of this official relationship prior to their governance under an Islamic regime.

This phase of the examination presents a measure of difficulty however: namely, that the relationship between the imperial government in Constantinople and the widespread monastic communities was not static, but rather it was subject to change depending on the social and political pressures upon a given administration.[29] The attitude of the Byzantine state toward monasteries, as will be demonstrated in terms of this relationship in the early Islamic period, was therefore sufficiently complex and dynamic depending on the particular era to be examined. As previously mentioned, the patterns of monastic life in the East themselves varied according to region and even within individual monasteries, including different incarnations of the ascetic existence such as the *laura* and *coenobium*. There likewise were no monastic orders in the East, so the interpretation of regulations tended to apply to specific communities.[30]

In addition to the episodic struggle for uniformity concerning dogmatic elements, issues emerged with regard to how tightly the imperial government would be able to control the expansion of the monastery and its environs, which would have serious implications for the provincial economy and local religious hierarchy.[31] It should be underscored here that the monastery in this legal context was not necessarily confined to the monastic church and living quarters for monks in residence, but often included substantial rural estates as well. Typically, these tracts of property could have included the surrounding arable lands, groves and vineyards, livestock, as well as additional buildings designated for monastic utilisation.[32] Studies focusing on Byzantine *typika* documents – though the majority of the existing foundational charters for monasteries come from a later period – illustrate this concern for the administration of ecclesiastical estates in their entirety. In the case of the *typika*, the issues relating to the management of monastic lands apply to the manner in which the abbot (*hegoumenos*) and/or the head treasurer (*oikonomos*) would exercise authority over certain fiscal aspects of monastic life.[33] Generally, the responsibilities for management would have included a host of structures related to the monastery, such as the adjacent churches, residences for workers, kitchens, storehouses, stables, agricultural lands, fields rented to the local peasantry, and fortifications.[34]

The monasteries, in a similar fashion to churches, could legally possess property under the earlier Byzantine codes, which was generally either endowed by private benefactors or by grants of wealth from the imperial government – and it appears that legislation aimed at regulation on the provincial level was more successful in theory than in practice. As Meyendorff has stated, 'the new power of the Church was, first of all, economic';[35] therefore, the perception of competition between the churches, backed by the imperial bureaucracy, and monasteries, from time to time falling outside the realm of conventional ecclesiastical authority, was clearly a cause for trepidation. Evidence for concern over the legal status of church and monastic properties is visible throughout various stages of rulings from the imperial government in conjunction with the ecclesiastical authorities, beginning in the era of Constantine[36] and proceeding throughout the ecumenical councils of the fifth century, before concluding with the reign of Manuel I Komnenos in the mid-twelfth century.[37] The first 400 years of these proceedings, according to Frazee, 'marks the first and normative period of legislation dealing with monastic life'.[38]

The initial policies concerning the legal status of ecclesiastical bodies and their properties date from the time of Constantine, which permitted local churches to be classified as 'corporations' possessing the right to inherit property and to accept grants of land as gifts. This guarantee for the legal entitlement to ecclesiastical organisations was clearly designed to promote Christianity, and stands as one of the first examples in Byzantine history of such direct privileges to religious groups.[39] Additionally, Constantine included the Christian clergy among the privileged classes of Byzantine society to receive immunity from public duties (*omnibus omnino publicis functionibus*) because of their contributions to the public welfare of the state.[40] This ordinance was specifically formulated with the goal of relieving clerics of any and all secular duties, thus allowing them to concentrate solely on their divine functions.[41] Within this class of state obligations, broadly defined under the term *munera*, would have been included liability for public works projects, municipal services, and support for the military. Even as the church clearly realised some measure of economic privilege from such grants and reaped benefits from sanctions on holdings,[42] the exception from obligations did not, however, directly include the repeal of all forms of taxation on ecclesiastical property, but rather seemed to focus on exemptions for the clergy itself.[43] The early taxation benefits to church officials is evident in the removal of the *capitatio* (head tax) on the rural clergy as well as the exemption of the urban clergy regarding the *collatio lustralis* (the taxes upon urban craftsmen).[44]

These types of regulations were later expanded by the emperors Constantius and Constans to include the immunity of clerics and their acolytes, as well as the tradesmen among their ranks, from all tax payments.[45] The assumption here was that all such profits would ultimately benefit the poor and also serve to increase the number of people in ecclesiastical organisations.[46] It was additionally under Constantius that church lands were eliminated from paying the *iuga* (land tax); however, the stipulation stated that the individual land-owning members of the clergy must still be subject to land tax and *munera* as it related to their personal property.[47]

These measures were likewise not fixed but subject to manipulation by imperial authorities according to the necessities of the time, as the development of the Theodosian Code bears witness to. In this example, some of the aforementioned exemptions from the *munera* were revoked in the middle of the fifth century under the Novels of the Sainted Valentinian, stating:

> the building and repair of military roads, the manufacture of arms, restoration of walls, the provision of the annona (capitation/land tax?), and the rest of the public works through which we achieve the greatest splendor of public defense, without which no success for the greatest affairs results, by whose aid We guard alike the safety and glory of the Empire, and not to proceed without details, without which services no necessary work can be

> accomplished . . . By a repetition of the regulation of Our Clemency, we sanction that all privileges shall be abolished which were either bestowed upon dignitaries or were obtained by the guilds of various branches of the imperial service or which were acquired in the name of venerable religion.[48]

The first regulations for the relationships between monks and their bishops were formulated in the Fourth Canon of the Council of Chalcedon in AD 451, stating:

> Those who lead a true and genuine monastic existence shall receive due honor. As, however, some assuming the monastic state for a pretext, confuse the affairs of the Church and State, and go about in the cities indiscriminately, and at the same time wish to found monasteries for themselves, the Synod decrees that no one shall anywhere build or set up a monastery or a poorhouse without the consent of the bishop of the city; that the monks of each neighborhood and city shall be subject to the bishop, that they love quiet, and give themselves only to fasting and prayer, stopping in the places to which they are assigned; that they do not encumber themselves with ecclesiastical and secular affairs or take part in them, leaving their monasteries, except when, in the case of necessity, they are required to do so by the bishop of the city; that no slave shall be received into the monasteries to become a monk without the permission of his master. Whosoever transgresses this ordinance shall be excommunicated, that the name of God shall not be blasphemed. The bishop of the city ought to take careful oversight of the monasteries.[49]

As shown, this canon stipulated that monks of the country and of the town are under the jurisdiction of the bishop, although the extent of this control is somewhat vaguely defined in terms of the rights to interfere with internal administrative policies.[50] Within this statute as well can be found the proscription for monks to engage in travel between towns and a ban on the erection of new monasteries without the direct consent of the bishop. The canons that follow instruct that monks should not involve themselves with matters of church or state,[51] nor should they accept civil duties (as in the case of military service),[52] engage in secret societies or otherwise become subversive to the bishops of their diocese,[53] nor disturb the public order.[54] Regulations of this kind were clearly designed to restrict the influence of monks within the larger social networks of their increasingly urbanised settlements, intending to harness their spiritual and political impact on public opinion. As such they also serve as a reflection of the contemporary anxieties regarding sectarian tensions, particularly in the East, and the susceptibility of ascetics to resist the authority of local bishoprics.[55] The role of the monk was, therefore, at least from the viewpoint of the ecclesiastical authorities, to be confined to penitential activities within the monastery proper, to 'apply themselves only to fasting and prayer'.[56]

These assessments were further developed in the legal codes of Justinian from the sixth century, which contain a number of specific references to the regulation of monastic life by the central government. Of particular relevance are the statutes that place the monastic communities under the direct supervision of the local bishop, or exarch, reinforcing the previous traditions dictated at Chalcedon. The measures included that new monasteries must only be founded with the consent of the village bishop,[57] who would in turn personally appoint the abbot to preside over the monastery. In terms of its obligations to the local ecclesiastical authorities, monasteries were subject to the regular *canonicum*, or episcopal tax, and would be required to commemorate the local bishop in its liturgy.[58] Rulings of this kind clearly indicate the perceived necessity for the central government, along with the imperial Church, to manage and restrict the independence of monasteries and their acquisitions of property.[59]

Controversies over the management of church and monastic property extended into the Sasanian realm as well, where the Nestorian clergy was compelled to issue several canonical rules throughout the sixth century to deal with the increasing wealth of the Church of the East through lay donations. According to the proceedings of the *Synod of 554*, the donations were to be solely under the charge of whatever institution, either church or monastery, was receiving the endowment. They were therefore not subject to control by the local bishop or presiding abbot, in the interest of restricting any potential complications involving issues of inheritance and the alienation of church property.[60] Given the fact that this type of legislation needed to be pronounced, as it simply reflects the standard practices of religious property rights of the time, would seem to suggest that ecclesiastical authorities in that region had been previously noncompliant to normative procedure.[61]

In addition to revisiting issues of misappropriation of ecclesiastical grants, the *Synod of 585* announced new legislation that specifically applied to monasteries and the disparity of wealth among monastic communities in Persian lands. The records of this council indicate that while a number of rural monasteries had fallen into ruin or become abandoned due to the lack of sustainable donation funds, others in the larger metropolitan areas had been flourishing.[62] In an effort to limit this phenomenon, *canon 11* prohibited the foundation of new monasteries, or repair to older ones, unless there was a guarantee of appropriate levels of donation for the continued maintenance.[63] The ensuing canon further attempted to redistribute the grants to monasteries, in both rural and urban settings, in a more equitable manner.[64]

The regulation of daily life in monasteries also extended into the economic sphere, in the context of disputes concerning the legality of professions for monks which lay outside the confines of their spiritual duties. Members of the clergy and monks had long been allowed entry into a variety of occupations, with the traditional caveat that they be prohibited from certain public functions, particularly ones involving finances, that could have placed them into the category of state official, thereby compromising their standing under ecclesiastical supervision. This type of restriction focused as well on the more morally questionable occupations,[65] such as tavern or innkeeping, dealing in perfumes, working in bath houses, money-handling and lending, tenant-farming land, and so on.[66]

A Synthesis of Policy under Muslim Hegemony

Whereas the important station of monastic institutions can scarcely be doubted as it applies to the Christian world of Late Antiquity,[67] the position of monasteries under Muslim political hegemony during the early Islamic period is understood with substantially less clarity. The most prolific phase for the formation of eastern monastic centres had already come to a close prior to the arrival of Islam into the Near East, reaching its zenith between the early fifth and late sixth century CE.[68] Following the upheaval of the early to mid-seventh century, the restoration of political stability under Islamic dynasties, as well as the evolution of a system for religious liberality, had significant implications for the fortunes of these monastic communities. Though it appears that the construction of new monasteries stagnated during this period, in contrast to the previously intense phases of Christian building activity under Byzantine suzerainty, archaeological data suggests that many of the pre-existing monasteries continued to function and prosper under Muslim authority.[69]

The question nonetheless remains as to the definitive articulation between the Islamic state and monastic institutions over which they held political jurisdiction, particularly with regard to the extent of governmental involvement and interest in monastic affairs. The picture that emerges, when dealing with an administrative stance toward monasteries, is generally one of a tempered policy offering considerable latitude for monastic life. On a certain level this period represents a departure from the previous Byzantine reality concerning the condition of monasteries, which had been characterised by strict attention to the details of sanctioned monastic life as well as episodic state interference in internal monastic issues.[70]

In the early period, the developing Muslim administration was typically less invested in ecclesiastical matters such as these. As far as the eastern churches are concerned, the first vestiges of official involvement by the Islamic state within internal church affairs do not begin until the ʿAbbāsid era. The initial example of this Muslim administrative interest comes in the form of the election of the catholicos Ḥenanishō II in the year 775 CE by a synod held at the behest of the caliph al-Mahdī.[71] The appointment of the Nestorian catholicos had also historically been subject to the state jurisdiction of the Sassanid court, suggestive of a Sasanian political remnant being transferred into an Islamic context. This device would remain an administrative fixture at certain points during the ʿAbbāsid period, with several later appointments of catholicoi also being imposed by Muslim rulers.[72] Apart from the bureaucratic impositions in the selection of major church officials, the eastern monasteries themselves appear to have largely retained their internal autonomy under the early Islamic dynasties.

Through his study of Syriac legal documents concerning ascetic practices, Arthur Vööbus has shown that internal monastic legislation and independent rules of conduct continued to be formulated without interruption from imperial authorities.[73] Among several that stand out in this respect are the *Rules of Jacob of Edessa* – composed in the late seventh century; the *Rules of Gīwargī* of Antioch – composed in the late seventh to early eighth century;

and the *Canons of Qūriaqos* – composed in the late eighth to early ninth century. These documents are included in the vast legislative corpus of the *Synodicon* of the Jacobite Church,[74] comprised of canonical documents from the beginnings of the organised church to the high medieval period. The classes of laws dating from the Islamic period within the *Synodicon* demonstrate a remarkable continuity of administrative procedure over centuries, in essence managing ecclesiastical issues under a Muslim regime in much the same way as they handled like matters in the Sasanian or Byzantine era.[75] The opening statement of the *Canons of Patriarch Gīwargī* demonstrate this point:

> By the strength of Our Lord Jesus Christ we have begun to write the book which contains all the new canons of the later patriarchs, I mean those of Gīwargī, Qūriaqōs, the two cycles, and of Dīonūsiōs, of Jōḥannān, of Ignātiōs, and of all the laws, judgments, ordinances and inheritances and the rest (of the administrative affairs[76]) of all the Greek kings, as well as all of the judgments, laws, ordinances, inheritances regarding the liberation of slaves, and of all the properties and the rest of the affairs by the rulers of the Arabs under whose ordinances the believers [*mhaīmōnē*] behave and whose laws they accept.[77]

While the continued development of internal monastic legislation demonstrates a degree of autonomy for monasteries under various Muslims regimes, it should be noted here that the *Canonical Rules of Jacob of Edessa* contain references to their status as subjects under Islamic authority and the allowances that must be necessarily assumed under these conditions. One of the rules stipulates that 'when an emir invites the abbot to eat with him this must be understood as an emergency situation'.[78] There is unfortunately no additional commentary on this point, but the presence of such a statement in an official canonical document suggests that meetings of this kind between local Muslim officials and monastic overseers would not have been uncommon. As well it reinforces the idea that while monasteries could conduct their own affairs, in terms of liturgical rites and social procedures, they were ultimately beholden to the will of the local administration. In this situation, the superior of a monastery could hardly have rejected the overtures of a high official within the Muslim state.

While the cultural and spiritual significance of monasteries continued unabated into the Islamic period, even across various confessional lines, it was the connection between the monastery and the imperial government that provided the requisite framework for monastic stability. The main obstacle for an inquiry into such features – as can so often be the difficulty when dealing with the early Islamic period – is the relative shortage of documentary source material for definitive administrative policies.[79] To some extent this Umayyad imperial development can be viewed as a process of incorporation, or inheritance, of pre-existing Byzantine and Sasanian administrative models.[80]

Just as monasteries continued to be ubiquitous elements of the socio-political and religious landscape of the Levant, to which now the Muslims had been made the imperial heirs, it would seem to have been obligatory that the emerging Islamic state in Damascus should devise some formalised methods of dealing with these institutions. The policies would therefore heavily lean toward the system embraced by its imperial predecessors. While the Umayyads in particular had engaged in the practice of determining legal procedures by administrative rescript, modelling Byzantine usage,[81] this was still a time in which the codification of Islamic law was in its foundational stages and there appears to have been a degree of fluidity in jurisprudence.[82]

The management of monastic estates under Muslim authorities, particularly with regard to fiscal matters, represents a fusion of the earlier Byzantine model with the basic principles for dealing with religious minorities in an early Islamic context. While there does seem to have been a roughly defined policy, it too was subject to change as required by local economic and social conditions. As will be demonstrated, monks and monasteries had frequently become segregated from the more broadly defined, inclusive category of 'non-Muslim subjects' – principally as it related to issues of protection and sanctuary for ascetics. At least that would seem to be the case on an ideological level. In terms of how this exclusive category of *dhimmīs* were then to be situated within the socio-economic apparatus of the state, it is appropriate to call attention here to the fact that according to the *Kitāb al-kharāj* of Abū Yūsuf (d. 798 CE), monks (*al-mutarahibūn fī al-diyārāt*) and ascetics (*ahl al-sawāmiʿa*) were theoretically recognised as one of the certain categories of *dhimmīs* that would have been exonerated from the *jizya*,[83] most commonly interpreted in this context to mean 'poll-tax'.[84] The celebrated eighth-century

Muslim ascetic Ḥasan al-Baṣrī stated that this exemption existed because monks were inherently bound to personal poverty and that they had resigned from the secular world.[85]

The *Life of Gabriel of Qartmin*, a hagiographical text concerning the life of the abbot of the monastery at Qartmin (as well as the metropolitan of Dara) in the early to middle seventh century, reports a meeting between Mâr Gabriel and the caliph ʿUmar ibn al-Khaṭṭāb shortly after the conquest period. During this encounter there is a discussion of terms relating to the fiscal responsibilities of monks. The text states that the abbot

> received his [ʿUmar bar Khaṭṭāb] signature to the statutes and laws, orders and prohibitions, judgments and precepts pertaining to Christians, to churches and monasteries, and to priests and deacons that they do not give poll tax, and to monks that they be freed from any tax.[86]

Robert Hoyland has questioned the authenticity of such a meeting between Gabriel and the caliph, though he affirms the plausibility that Gabriel would have been in a position to negotiate with Muslim officials.[87]

The one theoretical caveat to such a proposal seems to be in connection to the independent wealth of the monastic membership itself. Abū Yūsuf stipulates that under certain conditions monks could be expected to pay taxes: that being if the monastery possessed properties that contributed to an exceptionally profitable sustenance, by virtue of properties personally owned by the monks in residence.[88] These taxes would then be categorised under the classification of *jizya*. In this case the abbot (*ṣāḥib al-dayr*) bore the responsibility for the collection of the money for the state – although apparently a plea of poverty, taken by the swearing of an oath under God, could nullify the taxation measures.[89]

It is unclear whether the technical term *jizya*, as employed here by Abū Yūsuf, is to be defined as 'tribute payment' or simply 'poll-tax'.[90] Donner has suggested that, in the earliest period of Islam, the term likely was a general designation for tribute of some kind and may not only reflect a 'poll-tax' in the strictest sense.[91] In any case, as a general rule it can be understood that monks, as well as priests at times, were exempted from this particular form of taxation at an early stage in Muslim governance. Based on studies of surviving papyri from Egypt in this period, particularly the *Aphrodito* collection, Simonsen concludes that the earlier Byzantine *diagrafe* tax was often translated into Arabic by the term *jizya*; furthermore, he states that monks and monasteries were excluded from this poll-tax, just as they had been under a Byzantine administration.[92]

Fluctuations did however occur in the practical implementation of this policy, as they did in its theoretical composition.[93] These divergences though seem to be relatively rare. One documented case to the contrary, supplied by Severus ibn al-Muqaffaʿ, discusses the rising tensions between Christians and Muslims in Egypt after the governorship had passed from ʿAbd al-Azīz ibn Marwān (d. 704 CE) to his son, al-Aṣbagh. The new governor is described in the text as 'having a hatred of Christians, a shedder of their blood, a wicked man, like a lion'.[94] In particular, as it applies to monasteries, al-Aṣbagh conducted a census of the monks throughout the land and demanded that a poll-tax of one dinar be placed on each of them, here referred to as the *jizya* (*wā-jaʿala ʿalayhim jizya dināran wāḥidan*).[95] In addition, the governor also forbade that any new monks should be ordained after the tax assessment had been concluded. As Severus claims, 'this was the first *jizya* paid by monks'.[96] Furthermore, this appears to be one of the few records of an episode in which monks were required to pay the poll-tax in the early Islamic period.[97]

The example therefore depicts an extraordinary measure of *jizya* application to monks, worthy of citation by Severus within the text because of its infrequency. As well, this type of legal redaction illustrates the flexibility of policy on the local level, not necessarily indicating a shift in imperial attitudes. As it applied to the governorate of Egypt, there were two possible motivations behind this departure from the standard financial policies toward monks – the first, as explicitly mentioned in the text, had to do with the malicious nature of al-Aṣbagh toward non-Muslims. Severus further relates of the governor that 'he did not forgo any hardships that he might inflict on the Christians'.[98] The imposition of a poll-tax on monks, where there had been none before, is clearly perceived by the chronicler as an extension of this economic burden visited upon the *dhimmīs* of Egypt.

Monastic estates themselves, to the contrary, had been generally obligated to pay the *kharāj*, or land tax.[99] Whereas the *jizya* firmly held a confessional dimension, the *kharāj* was less explicit in this respect and presumably, under the straightforward meaning of taxation on land, could have applied to converts to Islam as well.[100] In this way, there seems to have been little possibility of exemption from the *kharāj*. This was a rather similar method of dealing with the financial aspects of monastic regulation as had existed under the Byzantine government, noted above. Tritton's citation of a tax inventory from Egyptian papyri dating to the first century of Islam, illustrates that monasteries were required to pay various levels of land taxes to the central government. Judging from the register, some of the monasteries appear to have been quite wealthy during this period, with the taxes being adjusted according to their prosperity from year to year.[101]

The *kharāj* moreover applied to all church lands, not just monasteries. Severus demonstrates this point by stating that 'afterwards, al-Aṣbagh required that the bishops of the territories should provide two thousand dinars in addition to the regular taxes on their lands, to be paid yearly'.[102] The insufferable burdens of this land tax are later highlighted in connection to the governorship of Qurra ibn Shārik (r. 709–15 CE), stating explicitly that the severe rates of the *kharāj* produced a devastating effect on the monasteries and churches. As the text explains, this episode too was a result of both the acutely hostile attitude toward Christians on the local level and the money-lust of the governor Qurra.[103] The account relates a meeting between a Christian administrative official and the governor, in which the former appeals for a reduction in the monastic land tax. This passage states:

> And there was a man called Yūnus (John), a notable man, to whom had been granted by God the favor of the governors. So, he went to Qurra and said to him, 'you should be informed that as to the monks and bishops in all areas, the land tax weighs heavily upon them. Here is a simple matter, because some of them have a great deal, while others do not even have the means of survival. And we know the condition of all the Christians, so if you see me as suitable to be in charge over their affairs, I will extract the taxes (*kharājāt*).' So, then he [Qurra] placed him over the monks and bishops.[104]

This brings about the second possible motivation behind al-Aṣbagh's modification of policy; that is, while monasteries under the early Islamic government had been required to pay the traditional taxes on land, the freedom of monks from the *jizya* may have induced those wishing to escape such taxes to join the monastic fold. The basic premise being that all non-Muslims throughout Islamic domains were subject to the *jizya*, apart from the category of monastics alone having no other financial requirement to the state. In the event then that the monasteries may have at times been subjected to heavy economic obligations, as the above passage suggests, the monks therein would have remained personally and individually immune. The moratorium placed on the initiation of novices into monastic life, prompted by al-Aṣbagh, could therefore have been a measure to remove such a stimulus.[105]

Tax registers from Egypt, in the form of papyri, have demonstrated the problem of monasteries as bastions for those wishing to escape taxes; some of these dating from the eighth century denote persons attempting to evade such burdens as φυγόντες.[106] The imposition of the *jizya* on monks was, however, repealed after the rule of al-Aṣbagh.[107] Upon the succession to the caliphate of ʿUmar ibn ʿAbd al-Azīz (r. 717–20 CE), the ecclesiastical policy was further altered to prohibit the *kharāj* from being extracted from church lands and their bishoprics (inferring that monasteries would be included), though this redaction only lasted one year.[108] While this type of legislative restriction appears to have been unique in the early Islamic period, it does perhaps preserve an echo of Byzantine statutes concerning issues of apprenticeship and motivations for entering the monastic station.[109]

A hagiographical text concerning the martyrdom of the ninth-century Palestinian monk ʿAbd al-Masīḥ al-Najrānī al-Ghassānī provides another illustration of the burdens of the *kharāj* tax on monasteries, as well as the role of monks in such fiscal responsibilities.[110] There are two passages in the text that specifically mention economic issues. The first discusses the appointment of ʿAbd al-Masīḥ to the position of *oeconome* (*aqnūm* in the Arabic text) of a monastery in Sinai as a result of his vigilance concerning financial affairs.[111] The passage reports that he often was sent to deal with the local authorities in Aylah concerning the taxation (*kharāj*) of the village of Qaṣr al-Ṭūr[112] and the Christian communities of Fārān and Rāʾyah.[113] The second mention of financial issues also highlights the role of monks in the intercession of taxation disputes. The passage claims that upon the death of the superior of the monastery, the monks elevated ʿAbd al-Masīḥ to the highest position (*rāʾs al-dayr*), at which time he was forced to contend with burdensome taxation levies from the local collection official. The text states that 'the manager of the tax had been unjust with the mountain (*fa-taḥāmala ṣāḥib al-kharāj ʿala al-Ṭūr*), and in those days their *kharāj* went to Palestine, so he and a group of monks headed out for al-Ramlah'.[114] As the account further explains the group was never able to plead their case before the officials at Ramlah due to extenuating circumstances, yet it is worthwhile noting that the land tax in this case was apparently particularly heavy on the monastery and that the superior himself had intended to lead a delegation to request that the sum be reduced.

These features in the economic policies toward monks and monasteries clearly resonate with the earlier Byzantine legislation, as can be said in general concerning the connection between the Byzantine *capitatio* and *iugatio* and the evolution of the *kharāj* system under Muslim administrations.[115] Though there are recorded instances of physical violence against monastic communities, rare as they may be, it seems to be the stress of utilising the wealth of monasteries as a contributor to the tax base that forms the majority of what might be termed 'oppressive policies' toward monasteries in this period. In some ways these administrative attitudes can be understood as a natural extension of Byzantine procedure and, aside from the aforementioned cases of particularly avaricious local officials, Christian monasteries appear to have been absorbed into the Islamic socio-economic context with little adversity.

Apart from the more practical interests of economic directives for the state – which were, in some measure, imitations of the Byzantine codes – these policies may also have had a grounding in the particular reverence toward ascetics, and the monasteries connected to them, within the late antique and early Islamic traditions. This would be especially crucial for the measures of safeguarding monasteries. The chronicle of John bar Penkāyē, the *Ktābā d-Rīsh Mellē*,[116] deserves attention here because it specifically addresses the issue of monasticism as part of a larger historical/theological context concerning the establishment of Muslim rule over the Near East. John bar Penkāyē, also known as John of Fenek,[117] appears to have composed his chronicle not long after the year 688 CE[118] and is therefore considered an important witness to the first three decades of Umayyad rule in the borderlands of Mesopotamia and Syria. Even as the coming of Islam is couched in apocalyptic terms, as a consequence of corruption and scandal within the

Church,[119] Bar Penkāyē clearly presents a positive appraisal of religious tolerance in the early Umayyad dynasty.

Though the overall theme of this passage appears to be as much an indictment of the abuses levied against the Nestorian church by the Byzantine government as it is a testimony for the beneficence of Islamic rule, its direct reference to monasticism being a privileged institution under the Muslims still deserves consideration. In particular, the ambiguous reference to an 'ordinance' found in the passage below, in some manner applied to the institution of monasticism, will be more fully examined. The passage states,

> There came a man, known as M'away,[120] and he became king controlling the two kingdoms, of the Persians and of the Byzantines. Justice flourished under his reign, and there was great peace in the regions under his control, for he permitted everyone to live as they wanted. For they held an ordinance coming from the man who had been their guide (*mhaddyānā*), concerning the people of the Christians and the monastic station.[121]

In terms of the legal protection afforded to monasteries, the reference to an 'ordinance'[122] by John bar Penkāyē and its possible historical origins is worthy of some additional explanation. This passage from the *Rīsh Mellē* not only seeks to reaffirm a standing connection between the people of this agreement – specifically the Nestorian communities of northern Mesopotamia and the Umayyad authorities – but clearly attempts to contextualise the policy with a cryptic reference to the Prophet Muhammad, here designated by the term *mhaddyānā*.[123] It was, after all, during this period that the Prophet Muḥammad and his Companions were becoming recognised as the ultimate form of sanction and authority for governance.[124]

To be certain, bonding the origins of such a pact to the Prophet would have been a convention to further validate the contemporary position of religious minorities within the state, perhaps even by virtue of an anachronistic projection. It may, however, have some historical precedent as well. According to al-Balādhurī (d. 892 CE), the first example of an agreement of this kind is the settlement (*ṣulḥ*) between Muḥammad and the Christians of Najrān and was provided as a written document for the town. In this episode, reportedly taking place around the year 631 CE, the pact essentially guarantees religious freedom and way of life to this group of Christians, provided they make a consistent tribute payment. In the pact transmitted by al-Balādhurī, monks are specifically referenced in the text as 'not being removed from their monastic station' (*rahbāniyya*).[125]

The ideological framework for the general amnesty of Christian holy places was further clarified by Abū Yūsuf in the era of Hārūn al-Rashīd (d. 809 CE), with the stipulation that no new churches be constructed.[126] Later in the text of Abū Yūsuf, however, on the authority of Ibn ʿAbbās, the prohibition is somewhat redacted to assert that

> as far as a town that has been founded by Arabs goes, it is not permitted that Christians may construct new churches, nor beat the *nāqūs*, nor publicly display wine or pigs therein, but in the towns established by non-Arabs (*al-ʿajam*), though it has been conquered by the Arabs, they may do these things.[127]

Fattal concludes that the jurists of the ʿAbbāsid period did indeed permit repairs to be conducted to damaged churches, but major construction was considered illegal.[128] Whether such prohibitions actually stem from a later date, at some point in the early ʿAbbāsid era as suggested by Tritton, or they were simply disregarded on the local level from the initial stages of Muslim rule, the textual and archaeological evidence confirms this important point – churches and monasteries continued to be founded and renovations to existing monasteries were made throughout the Umayyad period.[129] The system which actually seems to have been in place related more to the requisite sanction of church or monastery foundation on the part of the Muslim administration. If this should be the case, then the policies for new construction would have further mirrored the Byzantine procedure concerning the connection between the local bishop and new monastery construction within his jurisdiction.[130]

The *Ktābā d-rīshānē*, or *Book of Governors*, composed in the middle of the ninth century by Thomas of Marga, records that around the year 743 CE the abbot of the Nestorian Monastery of Bēth ʿĀbhē, located in northeastern Iraq between Mosul and Arbela, pulled down the old monastic church and constructed a new one in its place. The abbot, Mār Īshōʾyahb, was apparently under some pressure from the monks in residence due to the expense required and difficulty of the project, given that the region was undergoing difficult times.[131] Judging from the account, the provincial Muslim officials at Mosul likewise felt this was an extravagant use of funds, so the congregation was fined 15,000 dirhams (*kispē*, literally meaning 'pieces of silver') upon completion of the project.[132] Again, the text depicts the penalty in part as a result of the character of the local governor, 'a greedy and impudent man'.[133] Though the passage does not directly mention that government approval was part of the issue, it might be suggested that such a fine would have been levied, taken in the context of the failing local economic conditions, because the construction had not been approved in the first place by the Muslim authorities. In this sense, the legality of the issue would seem to have had some flexibility, implicitly hinging upon whether or not the case had been ratified by local administrators before commencing construction.

As an illustration of this proposed requisite sanctioning, there is an account claiming that the caliph Muʿāwiya (d. 680 CE) explicitly gave permission that a church at Edessa be restored after its damage by an earthquake.[134] That the authorisation to rebuild was enforced by the caliph himself would appear to indicate that there had been some prohibition on church construction, which thereby necessitated administrative intervention. The *Life of Saint Simeon of the Olives*, referring to events in the early eighth century, contains a passage claiming the monk specifically appealed to the 'king of the Arabs' for permission to build churches and monasteries at Nisibis. As Simeon was held in high regard by the Muslim officials, the authority was granted for construction and restoration projects in the area. In return for their acquiescence, the text reports that the saint constructed a large mosque next to the Church of Mar Theodore inside the eastern gate to the city.[135]

A more detailed example of an arrangement between monks and temporal authorities comes from the Syriac *Life of John of Dailam*, which recounts the career of an East Syrian monk of the seventh to eighth century. According to the text, John of Dailam received special permission to build churches and monasteries from the ruling caliph ʿAbd al-Malik (r. 685–705 CE) as a reward for a miraculous healing of the caliph's daughter. The text states,

> He visited the Arab king ʿAbd al-Malik ibn Marwān, who was residing in Damascus at the time; he greeted him and was received with great honour. The king asked him to pray for his daughter who was trialed by demons.

> She was healed, and the king, delighted, gave him royal gifts, which, however he refused, asking the king instead for peace and calm for the Christian people, and for permission to build churches and monasteries wherever they wanted.
>
> He wrote a royal missive to the governor who resided at Bēth Aramayē and Persayē: 'Let this holy man build churches and monasteries throughout our entire empire wherever he wishes; furthermore, let the expense be provided to him from our royal treasury.' He wrote another document to the effect that 'tribute [*medaṭṭē*] should not be exacted from any of the priests, monks, teachers or leaders of the Christians throughout our entire empire; but let the Christians be honored in their laws and customs, as it befits them'.[136]

The claim in the text that ʿAbd al-Malik allotted treasury funds for the construction of monasteries, to the amount of 12,000 silver pieces according to a variant account,[137] is a more difficult matter for historical interpretation. The legacy of non-Christian imperial patronage of the church may be another illustration of the residual policies from the pre-Islamic era, tracing its origins to the Sasanian period.[138] The late ninth-century *Chronicle of Seert* reports, for instance, that the Sasanian monarch Chosroes II (d. 628 CE) bestowed a golden cross to the monastery of Saint Sergius at Ruṣāfa, in addition to constructing churches for his Christian wives.[139] There are also scattered examples of similar patronage for Christian ecclesiastical institutions by Muslim elites,[140] though typically on a more modest scale from what the *Life of John of Dailam* suggests.

Another crucial aspect of this relationship between imperial authorities, either Byzantine or Muslim, and monasteries is the issue of sectarianism and its influence upon official policies. When applied specifically to the Byzantine state, the question concerns the manner in which the administrative strategies of a Chalcedonian government managed both the formally orthodox monastic communities and non-Chalcedonian monasteries of the region. It is this confessional divide that most distinguishes the ecclesiastical policies between the periods of Byzantine and early Islamic rule over the Levant. It should be kept in mind that the Chalcedonian populations of the region have been generally viewed as being more burdened than their sectarian counterparts as a consequence of Muslim domination.[141] While such an assessment appears to be accurate, this had less to do with any policies directed specifically against Melkite/Chalcedonian communities or favouritism to Miaphysites on the part of the new regime; rather, it was the result of a breakdown in contacts between the imperial Church and its members residing within Muslim domains, making assistance to these communities more difficult.[142]

The polarisation between the statuses of confessional communities in the East had been established well before the coming of Islamic rule, primarily existing in the form of Miaphysite struggles against Chalcedonian authorities.[143]. The most heavy-handed policies against such Levantine and Mesopotamian communities had come in the early decades of the sixth century as their bishops faced exile from their sees or imprisonment for their rejection of imperial Church theological principles; the discrimination reached its pinnacle under the direction of the Byzantine Emperor Justin around the year 519 CE.[144] The persecution was extended to Miaphysite monasteries a few years later when monks were forcibly expelled from their residences.[145]

Although many of these intolerances were relieved under the reign of Justinian (527–65 CE) and monks throughout the East were permitted to return to their respective monasteries, the partition between the imperial Church and the Miaphysite communities of Syria and Mesopotamia had by this time extended beyond the confines of doctrine. As a result of previous Chalcedonian restrictions, the foundation had been laid for the development of an indigenous canon law for the standardisation of liturgy and worship that was distinct from the imperial Church.[146] By the early seventh century, a similar break had taken place along confessional lines in Iraq, between adherents of the Jacobite Church of Syria and Nestorian communities; their congregations and monasteries were transformed into formally distinct entities in terms of both their particular legal and theological traditions.[147]

This trend toward the regulation of Miaphysite Church order as well as the strengthening of organised monasticism continued to thrive under various Muslim administrations.[148] The phenomenon of relative Muslim tolerance and religious universalism can therefore be witnessed through the lens of monasteries: these sectarian institutions at times seem to have enjoyed greater prosperity in the absence of Byzantine rule. In other words, this can be understood as a virtual 'levelling of the playing field' as it relates to monasteries throughout the Levant, without sectarian biases influencing administrative policies. Again, the evidence suggests that the various Christian confessional groups within the region were afforded equal toleration by the Muslim government, and their respective monasteries persisted as before as an extension of this policy of moderation. The writings of the late seventh-century Anastasius of Sinai would appear to testify for such restraint as it also applied to the Chalcedonian community in Palestine, where they were able to retain their holy places.[149]

Cyril Mango has stated in reference to this point that, 'even under Arab rule Orthodox monks were able to retain their principal establishments in Palestine as well as Mount Sinai . . . Unexpectedly, it was the Byzantine Empire rather than under the infidel that monasticism was dealt its severest blow.'[150] While Mango is alluding to the severity of the eighth- and ninth-century iconoclastic controversies in the Byzantine realm, at which time iconophile monks were systematically targeted for religious persecution,[151] the statement still reveals a measure of religious toleration for varying types of monastic tenets that differentiates the early Islamic period from both the Byzantine and the ensuing ʿAbbāsid era in this respect. It should be underscored that even though there existed in Islam the basic prohibition against the use of images, or icons, this proscription generally seems to have been applied solely to Muslim religious sites in the early Islamic period.[152] With the exception of the Umayyad caliph Yazīd II (d. 724 CE) and his iconoclastic edict, there is no evidence of any serious enforcement of such an issue relating to Christian holy sites over the course of the period.[153]

This is not, however, to insist that the harmony between the early Muslim administration and monasteries was unyielding, as there have been examples provided to the contrary, but it does generally illustrate the divergence of religious toleration exhibited within the initial phases of the Caliphate, prior to the year 750 CE, and the subsequent advent of the ʿAbbāsid regime, characterised by the hardening of confessional boundaries and more restrictive management of non-Muslim populations. It is as early as the year 751 CE that, according to the *Chronicle of Dionysius of Tell-Mahre*, monasteries and Christian ascetics became specifically targeted for violence.[154] During the caliphate of al-Manṣūr (r. 754–75 CE), a governor was appointed over the district of Mosul who had a particularly hostile attitude toward the monasteries of the region. This governor, Mūsa ibn Musʿab, was apparently so publicly disparaging of the local monks and bishops that they would not even dare to walk the streets from fear of inciting a riot among the Muslims.[155] The *Chronicle of Dionysius* further contextualises this attitude by stating that the monasteries were perceived by the local population as being exceedingly wealthy, having in their possession livestock, tracts of land and vineyards – all of which were coveted by the urban masses. It was the contempt of this regime against Christians, along with the avarice of the common people, which led to further harassment of monasteries.[156] The trend toward aggression against monasteries was therefore not just a matter of official endorsement by governors or caliphs, as it appeared on the popular level as well in the form of mob activity.[157]

These types of threats against monasteries due to their purported wealth, aside from representing the rising tide of sectarian intolerances, appear to be operating on a much older tradition of depicting monasteries as potential bastions of greed. In its origins such a characterisation of monasteries comes from early Christian ascetics themselves, denouncing the increasing popularity of the coenobitic life to the detriment of the solitary ideal. Criticism from these late antique ascetic circles, exemplified in figures like Isḥaq of Antioch, hinged upon the perceived rejection of the fundamental principle of poverty. The rise of the large communal monastery and the possessions that necessarily accompanied its growth, including these aforementioned gardens, flocks and vineyards, could be then interpreted as an absolute contradiction to the intended existence of the ascetic – the 'purposely poor life of prayer and contemplation'.[158]

Aside from variations in the interpretation of administrative policies in the ensuing periods, it generally appears to be temporary breakdowns in civil authority that most adversely affected monastic communities under the early Islamic state. The Syriac chronicle of John bar Penkāyē, the *Ktābā d-Rīsh Mellē*, demonstrates this crucial interface between political stability and the fate of monasteries. Even while stating that monasteries had been afforded a special status under Muslim regimes,[159] Bar Penkāyē demonstrates how the absence of effective civil authority could prove to be disastrous for monastic life.[160]

In this case, Book XV of the chronicle references the civil unrest under the caliphate of ʿAbd al-Malik (r. 685–705 CE), stemming from the opposition movement of Mukhtār ibn Abī ʿUbayd. In the course of the conflict, as the chronicle reports, the people of the borderlands between Mesopotamia and the Levant were subjected to all manners of hardships, due to the increasing waves of brigands and looters that moved freely across the territories because caliphal attention had been diverted elsewhere. The monasteries of the region were also targeted for violence during the disruption, though certainly not as a result of any official order on the part of the state but rather from the lack of governmental control. The proposition that monasteries would have become primary targets for raiding, especially during lawless times, had been well established throughout the late antique period.[161] The following selection from the *Rīsh Mellē* describes the tragic fate of these communities entangled in the civil conflict, both with respect to the general population and their local ecclesiastical structures. The passage states:

> Our priests and guardians have perished, the churches have become deserted, the places of our saints have been defiled, the villages have been engulfed by flames, our towns have been razed to the ground, and fear has overtaken the roads . . . our convents and monasteries have been destroyed, and the monks wander about in all directions.[162]

Severus ibn al-Muqaffaʿ provides additional information concerning the fate of monastic communities in times of political crises for the Umayyad caliphate.[163] In the course of recounting the events of the ʿAbbāsid revolution against the Umayyads, the text discusses the flight of Marwān II (r. 744–50 CE) across the Levant into Egypt. While being pursued by an ʿAbbāsid military detachment, the forces of Marwān II laid waste to the provinces in their retreat and, as the account indicates, monasteries of the region became prime targets for looting.[164] The monastery of Dayr Mūt in Palestine, evidently a particularly large and prosperous monastic community,[165] was plundered and robbed by the caliph himself, killing the head of the monastery and his chief assistant in the process.[166]

The struggle for control over Syria between the *ashrāf*, or tribal nobility, and the ʿAbbāsid government, engulfed in civil war following the death of Caliph Harūn al-Rashīd in the year 809 CE, likewise served as a catalyst for unchecked banditry throughout the Levant.[167] These Arab raiders, known as the Zawāqīl,[168] took advantage of the political vacuum and ravaged the monasteries of Palestine. According to Theophanes, the incompetent administration and the lack of order throughout the region allowed for a five-year period of 'slaughter, rapine, and various misdeeds among themselves and against their Christian subjects'.[169] During this time, the churches of the Holy City, as well as the major monasteries of Sts Chariton, Kyriakos, Sabas, Euthymius and Theodosius were made desolate.[170] It was only with the eventual emergence of al-Ma'mūn as caliph and the restoration of order in 813 CE that the lawlessness within the provinces came to an end.[171] Taking such reports into account, it seems that direct violence against monasteries was relatively limited in scope and most specifically applies to periods of political unrest.

Isolated incidents from the Umayyad period notwithstanding, it does indeed appear to be with the administrative transition of the ʿAbbāsid revolution that Christian monasticism in the Near East begins to receive its most systematic interference from the state.[172] There is a discernible shift in the attitude towards monasteries that goes hand-in-hand with an increasingly sectarian stance on the part of the ʿAbbāsid regime. As Tritton has stated concerning the hardening of confessional boundaries in connection to the waning of Umayyad rule and the advent of the ʿAbbāsid dynasties, 'As the antithesis between Arab and non-Arab disappeared, so that between Muslim and non-Muslim was sharpened.'[173] The monasteries, taking into account their continued social and religious importance as symbols for a rival religious affiliation, would have become natural targets for sectarian hostilities over time. By contrast to the increasingly rigid delineation of confessional lines in the mid-eighth century and beyond, it is clearly this former spirit of relative ecumenism within emergent Islam that prompted Īshō'yahb III, the Catholicos of the Church of the East (r. 650–8 CE), to issue this statement in a letter to one of his bishops, only a short time following the Islamic conquests of the Near East:

> And as it concerns the Arabs (*Ṭayyāyē*), whom God has now granted this authority over the world, behold you shall know how they behave toward us. For not only are they not in opposition to Christianity, rather they extol

the virtues of our faith, respect the priests and saints of our Lord, and they provide aid (*ma'edrānā*) to the churches and monasteries.[174]

Notes

1. Philip Mayerson, 'The First Muslim Attacks on Southern Palestine', in *Monks, Martyrs, Soldiers and Saracens: Papers on the Near East in Late Antiquity*, ed. P. Mayerson (Jerusalem: Israel Exploration Society, 1994), 53–98. There are numerous reports of monks being forced to flee their monasteries at the time of the Sassanian invasion of Palestine (beginning in 614 CE), seeking refuge either from the Persians or the menacing Bedouin tribes left unchecked as a result of the hostilities. See Robert Schick, 'Jordan on the Eve of the Muslim Conquest', *La Syrie de Byzance à L'Islam, VIIe–VIIIe Siècles* (Damascus: Institut Français De Damas, 1992).
2. In the case of Sassanid Persia, for example, the establishment of churches and monasteries were permitted only with requisite royal approval. See Michael Morony, 'Religious Communities in Late Sasanian and Early Islamic Iraq', *Journal of the Economic and Social History of the Orient* 17:2 (May 1974), 113–35. This theory regarding the obligatory direct state approval appears to have been maintained into the Islamic period, although the practical policies for the construction of churches and monasteries on the local level were not necessarily fixed according to such principles.
3. Hugh Kennedy, 'The Melkite Church from the Islamic Conquest to the Crusades: Continuity and Adaptation in the Byzantine Legacy', in *17th International Byzantine Studies Congress* (New Rochelle, NY: A. D. Caratzas, 1986), 325–43 at 328–9.
4. Lorenzo Perrone, 'Monasticism in the Holy Land: From the Beginnings to the Crusades', *Proche-Orient Chrétien* 45 (1995), 53–4.
5. See John Moschus, *Pratum Spirituale, Patrologia Orientalis* 87, fasc. 3, 2851–3112. Also, *Pratum Spirituale*, translation and commentary by John Wortley (Kalamazoo, MI: Cistercian Publications, 1992).
6. For an example of this, see *Chronique de Michel le Syrien, Patriarche Jacobite D'Antioche*, tome II, ed. and trans. J. B. Chabot (Paris, 1901), 481. The account here speaks of a monastery founded by Eustathius of Dara, marking the location of the martyrdom of the chief of the tribe of Taghlib, who had refused to accept Islam. Although the precise date of foundation is not mentioned in the text, the persecution of the Taghlibids cited here occurred in the early eighth

century, under the reign of Caliph Walid I. It therefore seems likely that the monastery would have been established shortly afterwards, presumably some time in the early eighth century. This is not the only evidence for monastic foundations under Muslim rule, and others will be cited in the course of this chapter. On the basis of archaeological records, see Andrew Palmer, *Monk and Mason on the Tigris Frontier: The Early History of Tur ʿAbdin* (Cambridge: Cambridge University Press, 1990), 184–6.

7. Robert Schick, *The Christian Communities of Palestine from Byzantine to Islamic Rule: A Historical and Archaeological Study*, Studies in Late Antiquity and Early Islam II (Princeton, NJ: Darwin Press, 1995), 129.
8. Various works by Sidney Griffith illustrate the importance of monasteries as intellectual centres into the ʿAbbāsid period. Notably: 'The Monks of Palestine and the Growth of Christian Literature in Arabic' and 'Greek into Arabic: life and letters in the monasteries of Palestine in the 9th Century: the example of the *Summa Theologicae Arabica*', in *Arabic Christianity in the Monasteries of Ninth-Century Palestine*, Variorum Collected Studies Series 380 (Aldershot: Ashgate, 1992); 'Comparative Religion in the Apologetics of the First Christian Arabic Theologians', in *Proceedings of the Patristic, Medieval and Renaissance Conference 4* (Philadelphia: Villanova University, 1979); 'Images, Islam and Christian Icons: a Moment in the Christian/Muslim Encounter in Early Islamic Times', in *Syrie de Byzance à l'Islam, VIIe–VIIIe siècles: actes du Colloque international 'De Byzance à l'Islam', Lyon, Maison de l'Orient méditerranéen, Paris, Institut du monde arabe, 11–15 septembre 1990*, eds Pierre Canivet and J.-P. Rey-Coquais (Damascus: Institut français de Damas, 1992), 121–38.
9. Yizhar Hirschfeld, *The Early Byzantine Monastery at Khirbet Ed-Deir in the Judean Desert: The Excavations in 1981–1987*, QEDEM 38 (Jerusalem: The Hebrew University of Jerusalem, 1999), 155. The *Vita of Saint Stephen the Sabaite* (d. 794) makes it clear that monasticism was flourishing throughout the Judean desert even into the ʿAbbāsid period, see Gérard Garitte, 'Le début de la Saint Étienne le Sabaite retrouvé en arabe au Sinaï', *Analecta Bollandiana* 77 (1959).
10. *The Chronicle of Theophanes*, ed. and trans. C. Mango and R. Scott (Oxford: Clarendon Press, 1997), 665–6.
11. Sebastian Brock, 'Syriac into Greek at Mar Saba: The Translation of St. Isaac the Syrian', in *The Sabaite Heritage in the Orthodox Church from the Fifth Century to the Present*, Orientalia Lovaniensia Analecta, ed. J. Patrich (Leuven: Uitgeverij Peeters rn Departement Oosterse Studies, 2001), 201–8.

12. See Fred Donner, 'From Believers to Muslims: Confessional Self-Identity in the Early Islamic Community', *al-Abhath* 50–1 (2002–3), 19–21.
13. There are numerous examples in the primary source material which illustrate impromptu compromises between Muslims and church/monastic officials for the amnesty of holy places; direct references to this kind of arrangement exist across the classical Muslim chronicles. Arrangements of this sort also appear in Christian histories such as that of Bar Hebraeus, who specifically mentions a pact between the Caliph ʿUmar and the people of Damascus – with respect to their safety. See Bar Hebraeus, *The Chronography of Gregory Abu al-Faraj, commonly known as Bar Hebraeus, being the first part of his political history of the world*, vol. I, ed. and /trans. E. A. Wallis Budge (London, 1932), 94.
14. Charles Frazee, 'Late Roman and Byzantine Legislation on the Monastic Life from the Fourth to the Eighth Centuries', *Church History* 51:3 (September 1982), 263.
15. Clyde Pharr, *The Theodosian Code and Novels and the Sirmondian Constitutions: A Translation with Commentary, Glossary, and Bibliography* (Princeton, NJ: Princeton University Press, 1952), 449: Emperors Valentinian, Theodosius and Arcadius Augustuses to Tatianus, Praetorian Prefect, 2 September 390, *Theodosian Code* 16.3.
16. Hans-Georg Beck, *Das byzantinische Jahrtausend* (Munich: C. H. Beck, 1978), p. 207. See also Eleutheria Papagianni, 'Legal Institutions and Practice in Matters of Ecclesiastical Property', in *The Economic History of Byzantium, from the Seventh through the Fifteenth Century*, vol. 3, ed. Angeliki E. Laiou (Washington, DC: Dumbarton Oaks Research Library and Collection, 2009), 1059–69.
17. Peter Charanis, 'The Monastic Properties and the State in the Byzantine Empire', *Dumbarton Oaks Papers* 4 (1948).
18. Papagianni, 'Legal Institutions', 1059–69.
19. Arthur Vööbus, *A History of Asceticism in the Syrian Orient: A Contribution to the History of Culture in the Near East*, vol. III, *Corpus Scriptorum Christianorum Orientalium*, vol. 500, tome 81 (Louvain, 1988), 296–7.
20. Rosemary Morris, *Monks and Laymen in Byzantium, 843–1118* (Cambridge: Cambridge University Press, 1995), 145.
21. Clémence Dupont, 'Les Privilèges des clercs sous Constantin', *Revue d'histoire ecclesiastique* 62 (1967), 729–52.
22. Papagianni, 'Legal Institutions', 1059.
23. Specifically, reference is made to John B. Bury, *A History of the Late Roman*

Empire from the death of Theodosius I to the death of Justinian (395–565), vol. 2 (New York: Dover Publications, 1958); E. Stein, *Histoire du Bas-Empire II. De la disparition de l'Empire d'Occident à la mort de Justinien (476–565)* (Bruges/Paris: Desclée de Brouwer, 1949–59); and A. H. M. Jones, *The Later Roman Empire 284–602, a Social Economic and Administrative Survey* (Norman, OK: University of Oklahoma Press, 1964).

24. Frank R. Trombley, 'Monastic Foundations in Sixth-Century Anatolia and their Role in the Social and Economic Life of the Countryside', *Greek Orthodox Theological Review* 30:1 (1985), 45–59 at 58–9.
25. See M. Avi-Yonah, 'The Economics of Byzantine Palestine', *The Israel Exploration Journal* 8 (1958), 39–52.
26. Ibid. 47. He claims in this passage that the effects of indiscriminate funding for charitable institutions, which particularly attracted monks and beggars, was economically unsustainable – notwithstanding the benefits for the soul.
27. Ibid. 51.
28. Daniel C. Dennett, *Conversion and the Poll Tax in Early Islam* (Cambridge, MA: Harvard University Press, 1950), 49–51. Dennett here states that the tax administration in Syria should be viewed through the lens of not only the circumstances of the Islamic conquests but also with respect to the existing Byzantine fiscal and legal arrangements.
29. J. F. Haldon, *Byzantium in the Seventh Century: The Transformation of a Culture* (Cambridge: Cambridge University Press, 1997), 296.
30. Philip Rousseau, 'Monasticism', in *The Cambridge Ancient History, vol. XIV, Late Antiquity: Empire and Successors.* A.D. *425–600*, eds Averil Cameron *et al.* (Cambridge: Cambridge University Press, 2000), 745–80 at 750.
31. See Trombley, 'Monastic Foundations in Sixth-Century Anatolia', 45–59.
32. Alice-Mary Talbot, 'A Monastic World', in *A Social History of Byzantium*, ed. John Haldon (Chichester: Wiley-Blackwell, 2009), 268–9.
33. Konstantinos Smyrlis, 'The Management of Monastic Estates: The Evidence of the Typika', *Dumbarton Oaks Papers* 56 (2002), 245–61. Though this is not the exclusive purpose of the *typika*, which were more intended to be regulatory texts for monks, wills, and liturgical documents.
34. Ibid. 248.
35. John Meyendorff, *Imperial Unity and Christian Divisions: The Church 450–680* AD (Crestwood, NY: St Vladimir's Seminary Press, 1989), 13.
36. This specifically relates to the issue of legal status of property possessed by both churches and monasteries, in which case Constantine declared that local

churches would be considered legal corporations with the right to inherit property as a gift. See Frazee, 'Late Roman and Byzantine Legislation', 267.

37. Talbot, 'A Monastic World', 268–9. Haldon additionally claims that, over the course of several centuries, there were actually some 300 monasteries in Constantinople alone. See Haldon, *Byzantium in the Seventh Century*, 294.
38. Frazee, 'Late Roman and Byzantine Legislation', 263.
39. Ibid. 267. Boyd argues that the policy actually antedates the reign of Constantine, citing several individual cases of litigation ruling in favour of church properties from the time of Galerius and Maxentius in the late third and early fourth century. In these cases, it seems that Christian churches, prior to Constantine, were understood to be a class within the *collegia tenuiorum* and were thus able to secure their corporate possessions as legal interests; see William K. Boyd, *The Ecclesiastical Edicts of the Theodosian Code*, Studies in History, Economics and Public Law 24:2 (New York: Columbia University Press, 1905), 79.
40. Other groups such as teachers, rhetoricians and physicians had been excluded from state burdens on behalf of previous emperors; see Boyd, *The Ecclesiastical Edicts of the Theodosian Code*, 73.
41. Pharr, *The Theodosian Code*, 441: Emperor Constantine Augustus to the People, *Title 2: De Episcopis, Ecclesiis, et Clericis*, recorded in Book XVI of the *Theodosian Code*.
42. See Michel Kaplan, *Les Hommes et la terre à Byzance du VIe au XIe siècle: Propriété et exploitation du sol* (Paris: Publications de la Sorbonne, 1992).
43. Boyd, *The Ecclesiastical Edicts of the Theodosian Code*, 84.
44. John Philip Thomas, *Private Religious Foundations in the Byzantine Empire* (Washington, DC: Dumbarton Oaks Research Library and Collection, 1987), 24–5.
45. Pharr, *The Theodosian Code*, 442: Emperors Constantius and Constans Augustuses to all the bishops throughout the various provinces, 26 May 353 (or possibly 320?), *Theodosian Code* 16.2.10.
46. T. G. Elliott, 'The Tax Exemptions Granted to Clerics by Constantine and Constantius II', *Phoenix* 32:4 (1978), 326–36.
47. Thomas, *Private Religious Foundations*, 26.
48. Pharr, *The Theodosian Code*, 525: Emperors Theodosius and Valentinian Augustuses to Maximus, Praetorian Prefect, 14 March 441, *Novels of the Sainted Valentinian Augustus* 10.2.
49. Fifteenth Session Canons, Canon 4 of the Fourth Ecumenical Synod. See

Charles Joseph Hefele, *A History of the Councils of the Church from the Original Documents*, vol. III (Edinburgh, 1883), 389–90.

50. Helen Robbins Bittermann, 'The Council of Chalcedon and Episcopal Jurisdiction', *Speculum* 13:2 (April 1938), 198–203. The question of the local bishop's spiritual authority over his diocese was not in question, rather the extent to which he might control the internal economy and elections within the monasteries.
51. Hefele, *A History of the Councils of the Church*, 389.
52. Ibid. 789, Canon 7.
53. Ibid. 806, Canon 18.
54. Ibid. 809, Canon 23.
55. Bittermann, 'The Council of Chalcedon and Episcopal Jurisdiction', 198. Canon 4 was specifically formulated in reference to the fifth-century movement of Barsauma, leading his fellow Monophysite monks to withdraw from the authority of their bishop in Mesopotamia. See W. H. C. Frend, *The Rise of the Monophysite Movement: Chapters in the History of the Church in the Fifth and Sixth Centuries* (Cambridge: Cambridge University Press, 1972), 91–5.
56. Hefele, *A History of the Councils of the Church*, 779.
57. These types of local bishops appear to have been quite widespread, particularly in the East during the early Byzantine period, where the common practice seems to have been to appoint a bishop to each city, regardless of the size of its Christian population, and also occasionally even to smaller villages attached to larger provincial cities. See Jones, *The Later Roman Empire 284–602*, 875.
58. Haldon, *Byzantium in the Seventh Century*, 294.
59. For the later developments, see Charanis, 'Monastic Properties and the State in the Byzantine Empire', 54–60. The aristocracy of the provinces also effectively included the high ecclesiastical and monastic officials, which are collectively referred to as δυνατοι in tenth-century legal digests. It was within this tenth-century setting that the Byzantine government sought to restrict the ecclesiastical holdings within the empire, hoping to alleviate the struggles between the rural peasantry and the landed elite. The novel issued by the Emperor Nicephorus Phocas in the year 964 is one of several examples of such measures, essentially stating that gifts to monasteries in the form of land property would henceforth be prohibited. Even so, this promulgation was directed primarily against the foundation of new monastic establishments and their accompanying stations (such as hostels and churches), and not necessarily against the ideal or the right to monasticism itself. As such, there is no claim in the novel of

Nicephorus against the foundation of individual monastic cells or the collective *laurae*, with the stipulation that they would not seek to further acquire more land than was vital to their existence. Furthermore, particular admonition is demonstrated in the novel for the cessation of founding new monasteries at the expense of allowing those which are struggling to continue without due assistance – in essence stating that there were already too many monasteries which held too much of the land property within the state.

60. J. B. Chabot, *Synodicon Orientale* (Piscataway, NJ: Gorgias Press, 2010), Canon 35, 560.
61. Victoria Erhart, 'The Development of Syriac Christian Canon Law in the Sasanian Empire', in *Law, Society, and Authority in Late Antiquity*, ed. Ralph W. Mathisen (Oxford: Oxford University Press, 2001), 115–29 at 124.
62. Ibid. 126.
63. Chabot, *Synodicon Orientale*, 405–9.
64. Ibid. 408–9.
65. Gilbert Dagron, 'The Urban Economy, Seventh–Twelfth Centuries', in *The Economic History of Byzantium: from the Seventh through the Fifteenth Century*, vol. 2, ed. Angeliki Laiou (Washington, DC: Dumbarton Oaks Research Center, 2002), 393–461 at 426.
66. Gilbert Dagron, 'Remarques sur le statut des clercs', *Jahrbuch der Osterreichischen Byzantinistik* 44 (1944), 33–48.
67. Significant contributions to this field include Peter Brown, 'The Rise and Function of the Holy Man in Late Antiquity', *The Journal of Roman Studies* 61 (1971), 80–101; Derwis Chitty, *The Desert a City: An Introduction to the Study of Egyptian and Palestinian Monasticism under the Christian Empire* (Crestwood, NY: St Vladimir's Seminary Press, 1995); S. P. Brock, 'Early Syrian Asceticism', *Numen* 20:1 (April 1973); Robert Kirschner, 'The Vocation of Holiness in Late Antiquity', *Vigiliae Christianae* 38 (1984), 105–24; Arthur Vööbus, *A History of Asceticism in the Syrian Orient: A Contribution to the History of Culture in the Near East, Corpus Scriptorum Christianorum Orientalium* vol. 184, tome 197 (Louvain, 1958–). For monasticism in its specifically Byzantine context, see Peter Charanis, 'The Monk as an Element of Byzantine Society', *Dumbarton Oaks Papers* 25 (1971), as well as 'Monastic Properties and the State in the Byzantine Empire', *Dumbarton Oaks Papers* 4 (1948). The crucial role of monasteries within the economic and social structure of the Christian East cannot be overstated, a fact which prompted H.-G. Beck to make the assertion that as early as the sixth century the Byzantine empire had indeed

'become monasticized'. See Hans-Georg Beck, *Das byzantinische Jahrtausend* (Munich: C. H. Beck, 1978), 207.

68. Lorenzo Perrone, 'Monasticism in the Holy Land: From the Beginnings to the Crusades', *Proche-Orient Chrétien* 45 (1995), 39.
69. Hirschfeld, *The Early Byzantine Monastery at Khirbet Ed-Deir in the Judean Desert*, 155.
70. Papagianni, 'Legal Institutions', 1059.
71. C. Villagomez and M. G. Morony, 'Ecclesiastical Wealth in the East Syrian Church from Late Antiquity to Early Islam', in *Orientalia Lovaniensia Analecta, After Bardaisan: Studies on Continuity and Change in Syriac Christianity in Honour of Professor J.W. Drijvers*, eds G. J. Reinink and A. C. Klugkist (Louvain: Peeters Publishing, 1999), 307.
72. See Wilhelm Baum and Dietmar W. Winkler, *The Church of the East* (London: Routledge, 2011), 43.
73. See Arthur Vööbus, *Syriac and Arabic Documents Regarding Legislation Relative to Syrian Asceticism* (Stockholm: Estonian Theological Society in Exile, 1960).
74. *The Synodicon in the West Syrian Tradition*, part I, ed. Arthur Vööbus, *Corpus Scriptorum Christianorum Orientalium* vol. 367, Scriptores Syri tome 161.
75. *The Synodicon in the West Syrian Tradition*, 23; part of the editor's introduction for 'Civil Laws of the Islamic Period'.
76. *The Synodicon in the West Syrian Tradition*, part II, *Corpus Scriptorum Christianorum Orientalium* vol. 375, Scriptores Syri tome 164. The footnote denotes an edition to the text made by Vööbus in his translation, 1.
77. Ibid. Scriptores Syri tome 163. Canon 54: Canons of Patriarch Gīwargī. Introductory Letter, fol. 109b.
78. Vööbus, *A History of Asceticism in the Syrian Orient* III, 354.
79. Fred Donner, 'The Emergence of the Islamic State', *Journal of the American Oriental Society* 106:2 (1986), 283–96. The article makes the distinction between the literary sources, mainly coming from the ʿAbbāsid period, and the existence of contemporary papyri from the late first century AH which provide evidence of an early state formation.
80. Petra M. Sijpesteijn makes this clear in the post-conquest administrative system of Egypt, where even Christian officials remained in authority into the Islamic period. See *Shaping a Muslim State: The World of a Mid-Eighth-Century Egyptian Official* (Oxford: Oxford University Press, 2013), 64. See also H. I. Bell, 'The Administration of Egypt under the Umayyad Khalifs', *The Articulation of Early Islamic State Structures*, ed. Fred Donner, The Formation

of the Classical Islamic World vol. 6 (New York: Routledge Press, 2016), 217–26. This is also the case throughout the administration taking shape in Syria-Palestine and Iraq. See Andrew Louth, 'Palestine under the Arabs 650–750: The Crucible of Byzantine Orthodoxy', in *Holy Land, Holy Lands and Christian History*, ed. R. N. Swanson (Ecclesiastical History Society, 1998); Daniel J. Sahas, 'Cultural Interaction during the Umayyad Period. The "Circle" of John of Damascus', *ARAM* 6:1 (1994); Hugh Kennedy, 'The Last Century of Byzantine Syria: a Reinterpretation', *Byzantinische Forshungen* 10 (1985); and Faliḥ Ḥusayn, 'The Participation of Non-Arab Elements in the Umayyad Army and Adminstration', in *The Articulation of Early Islamic State Structures*, ed. Fred Donner (New York: Routledge Press, 2016), 265–90.

81. Hamilton A. R. Gibb, 'Arab-Byzantine Relationships Under the Umayyad Caliphate', *Dumbarton Oaks Papers* 12 (1958), 224. Though as Gibb points out few of these rescripts are extant, they may be discerned from later legal rulings that decide either to uphold or reject the earlier Umayyad opinions.
82. See J. Schacht, *The Origins of Muhammadan Jurisprudence* (Oxford: Clarendon Press, 1950).
83. Abū Yūsuf, *Kitāb al-kharāj* (Cairo: al-Maṭbaʿah al-Salafiyya wa-Maktabatuhā, 1962), 122 – although the Muslim jurist al-Shāfiʿī (d. 820 CE) challenged this exclusion in his *Kitāb al-umm*; see A. J. Tritton, *The Caliphs and Their Non-Muslim Subjects: A Critical Study of the Covenant of ʿUmar* (London: Frank Cass & Co., 1970), 217. Others would have included women, adolescents, hermaphrodites, slaves and the physically infirm. See Antoine Fattal, *Le Statut Légal des Non-Musulmans en Pays D'Islam* (Beirut: Recherches Publiées sous la Direction de l'Institut de Lettres Orientales de Beyrouth, 1958), 270.
84. The difficulties of interpretation for this term, in addition to its connection to the *kharāj* (or land tax), has been commented upon at length by Frede Lokkegaard in *Islamic Taxation in the Classical Period, with Special Reference to Circumstances in Iraq* (Copenhagen: Branner and Korch, 1950) and more recently by Kosei Morimoto in *The Fiscal Administration of Egypt in the Early Islamic Period* (Kyoto: Dohosha, 1981).
85. Muḥammad ibn Yaḥya al-Sūlī, *Adab al-kuttāb* (Baghdād: al-Maktabah al-ʿArabiyya, 1922–3), 216.
86. Gabriel of Qartmin, *Life* XII, 72, as a microfiche supplement to Palmer, *Monk and Mason*; this section is translated in Robert Hoyland, *Seeing Islam as Others Saw It: A Survey and Evaluation of Christian, Jewish, and Zoroastrian Writings on Early Islam* (Princeton, NJ: Darwin Press, 1997), 123.

87. Hoyland, *Seeing Islam*, 123.
88. Judging from the study of early Syriac monastic canons by Vööbus, the renunciation of personal property for admittance into monastic life was flexible in the East. This is in contrast to the more rigid Pachomian and Basilian statutes concerning the rights of property. See specifically the *Canons of the Monastery of Mar Mattai* in Vööbus, *Syriac and Arabic Documents Regarding Legislation Relative to Syrian Asceticism*.
89. Abū Yūsuf, *Kitāb al-kharāj*, 122.
90. See *The Fiscal Administration of Egypt*, 32–3, where Morimoto offers a sound assessment for the development of the term by stating, 'At the time of the Prophet the word *kharāj* did not exist, and the taxes paid by the people of the book (*ahl al-kitāb*) were called *jizya*. This jizya was used in a broad sense but included the meaning of "capitation tax". Thus, if one uses the Muslim sources to formulate a hypothesis, one may argue that earliest standard of taxation was a poll tax of one dinar and a conceptually unclear land tax, which was probably assigned to villages and communities as units.'
91. Donner, 'The Formation of the Islamic State', 287.
92. Jorgen Baek Simonsen, *Studies in the Genesis and Early Development of the Caliphal Taxation System, with Special References to Circumstances in the Arab Peninsula, Egypt, and Palestine* (Copenhagen: Akademisk Forlag, 1988), 98–9.
93. Tritton references the fact that the Muslim jurist al-Shāfiʿī, in his *Kitāb al-umm*, suggests that monks would have indeed been subject to the *jizya*. See Tritton, *The Caliphs and Their Non-Muslim Subjects*, 217.
94. Severus ibn al-Muqaffaʿ, *History of the Patriarchs of the Coptic Church of Alexandria*, ed. and trans. B. Evetts, *Patrologia Orientalis*, tome 5, fasc. 1, part 3 (Paris: Firmin-Didot, 1907), 50.
95. Ibid. 51.
96. Ibid. 51.
97. Tritton exclusively states that while the poll-tax varied from time to time in its application to priests, there is no indication in the surviving papyri (one of the main sources of information on the subject) that monks were ever obligated to pay. See Tritton, *The Caliphs and Their Non-Muslim Subjects*, 198.
98. Severus ibn al-Muqaffaʿ, *History of the Patriarchs*, 51.
99. Daniel C. Dennett, *Conversion and the Poll Tax in Early Islam* (Cambridge, MA: Harvard University Press, 1950), 79.
100. ʿAbd al-Aziz Duri, 'Notes on Taxation in Early Islam', *Journal of the Economic and Social History of the Orient* 17:2 (May 1974), 136–44. For Muslims, it

seems to have been only a certain measure of the yield of their land as a tithe, presented as either a *ṣadaqāt* or *ʿushr*. See H. A. R. Gibb, 'The Fiscal Rescript of ʿUmar II', *Arabica* 2 (1955), 1–16 at 13.

101. Tritton, *The Caliphs and Their Non-Muslim Subjects*, 200. The desert Monastery of Mary, for example, apparently had eight estates attached to it in AH 98.
102. Severus ibn al-Muqaffaʿ, *History of the Patriarchs*, 51.
103. Ibid. 64. Certain official letters from Qurra ibn Shārik to Flavius Basilius, the pagarch of Aphrodito, may however suggest an alternative explanation for the increased financial burdens. It seems that in the years of his governorship, between 709 and 711, there had been a persistent tardiness on the collection of taxes from the district. The arrears prompted the governor to scold his pagarch in an effort to claim the overdue amounts. This may perhaps also account for the perception of a tax increase. See Lionel Casson, 'Tax Collection Problems in Early Islamic Egypt', *Transactions and Proceedings for the American Philological Association* 69 (1938), 274–91 at 286.
104. Severus ibn al-Muqaffaʿ, *History of the Patriarchs*, 62.
105. Dennett, *Conversion and the Poll Tax in Early Islam*, 79.
106. Nikolaos Gonis, 'Arabs, Monks and Taxes: Notes on Documents from Deir Balaʾizah', *Zeitschrift für Papyrologie und Epigraphik* 148 (2004), 213–24 at 220.
107. The only further occurrence of it being reported by Severus under the governorship of al-Qāsim, at which time the measures of al-Aṣbagh were reinstated for a short time. See Severus ibn al-Muqaffaʿ, *History of the Patriarchs*, 92–4.
108. Ibid. 71–2.
109. Pharr, *The Theodosian Code*, 546: Emperor Valentinian Augustus to Firminus, Praetorian Prefect and Patrician, *Novels of the Sainted Valentinian Augustus* 35.1.
110. Sidney Griffith, 'The Arabic Account of ʿAbd al-Masīḥ al-Najrānī al-Ghassānī', *Le Muséon: revue d'études orientales* 98 (1985), 331–74. It should be pointed out that the precise dating of this episode is somewhat elusive. One of the existing versions of the text bears a scribal note that the martyrdom of ʿAbd al-Masīh occurred in the Umayyad era, but based on certain details within the text, Griffith concludes that this story corresponds to events in the middle to late ninth century.
111. Ibid. 365. The Arabic text appears to be somewhat corrupted in this passage. The text actually states that 'the monks took notice of him as a result of his *ḥaraṣ* and made him oecumene over them', which I have substituted for the

more appropriate word *ḥaras*, which has the meaning of 'superintendence' or 'administration'.

112. Ibid. 365. Presumably the village connected with his monastery in Sinai.
113. Ibid. 365.
114. Ibid. 367. Founded by Caliph Suleiman ibn 'Abd al-Malik in 716 CE, Ramlah was the capital of Jund Filistin in the Umayyad and 'Abbāsid period.
115. Fattal, *Le Statut Légal des Non-Musulmans*, 323.
116. A. Mingana (ed.), Book XV of the *Rīsh Mellē* in *Sources Syriaques* (Leipzig, 1908), 172–97.
117. Little is known about his life, except that he was a monk from the town of Fenek in north-western Mesopotamia, near the border of Syria, and lived in the monastery of John Kamul. See entry in Robert Hoyland, *Seeing Islam as Others Saw It: A Survey and Evaluation of Christian, Jewish, and Zoroastrian Writings on Early Islam* (Princeton, NJ: Darwin Press, 1997), 194–200.
118. Brock concludes that the text of John bar Penkāyē was completed at some point before 693/694 CE. See Sebastian Brock, 'North Mesopotamia in the Late Seventh Century: Book XV of Bar Penkāyē's *Ris Melle*', *Jerusalem Studies in Arabic and Islam* 9 (1987), 51–2.
119. Mingana (ed.), Book XV of the *Rīsh Mellē*, in *Sources Syriaques*, 172–3. In particular, such accusations are directed at the Byzantine Church and its ecumenical councils. The eschatological theme is a common convention in Syriac writings from this period. See S. Brock, 'Syriac Views of Emergent Islam', in *Studies on the First Century of Islamic Society*, ed. G. H. A. Joynboll (Carbondale, IL: Southern Illinois Press, 1982).
120. It is clear that Mu'āwiya is being referred to here, although the specific ordinance as it relates to the Prophet Muhammad is subject to interpretation.
121. Mingana (ed.), Book XV of the *Rīsh Mellē*, in *Sources Syriaques*, 175.
122. Ibid. 175.
123. Ibid. 175.
124. Robert Hoyland, 'Arabic, Syriac and Greek Historiography in the First Abbasid Century: An Inquiry into Inter-Cultrual Traffic', *ARAM* 3:1&2 (1991), 211–33.
125. Al-Balādhurī, *Futūḥ al-buldān* (Beirut: Dar al-Kutub al-'Ilmiyya, 1983), 76.
126. Abū Yūsuf, *Kitāb al-kharāj*, 141.
127. Abū Yūsuf, *Kitāb al-kharāj*, 149.
128. Fattal, *Le Statut Légal des Non-Musulmans*, 175–8.
129. For a list of new church constructions, some of which had monastic settlements

attached to them, see Schick, *The Christian Communities of Palestine*, the chapter entitled 'Churches in the Early Islamic Period'.

130. See Frazee, 'Late Roman and Byzantine Legislation', 263; Boyd, *The Ecclesiastical Edicts of the Theodosian Code*, 79.
131. Thomas of Marga, *The Book of Governors* (2 vols), ed. and trans. E. A. Wallis Budge (London: Kegan Paul, Trench, Trübner & Co., 1893), vol. I, 203–6.
132. Ibid. 207.
133. Ibid. 207.
134. *Chronicon anonymum ad annum Christi 1234 pertinens* I, 288.
135. Sebastian Brock, 'The Fenqitho of the Monastery of Mar Gabriel in Tur ʿAbdin', *Ostkirchliche Studien* 28 (1979), 168–82 at 176.
136. Sebastian Brock, 'A Syriac Life of John of Dailam', *Parole de l'Orient* 10 (1981), 123–189 at 139, paragraphs 27–8; translation of text on 165–6.
137. Ibid. 123–89.
138. C. Villagomez and M. G. Morony, 'Ecclesiastical Wealth in the East Syrian Church from Late Antiquity to Early Islam', in *Orientalia Lovaniensia Analecta, After Bardaisan: Studies on Continuity and Change in Syriac Christianity in Honour of Professor J. W. Drijvers*, eds G. J. Reinink and A. C. Klugkist (Louvain: Peeters Publishing, 1999), 305.
139. *The Chronicle of Seʾert*, ed. Addai Scher, *Patrologia Orientalis*, tome 13, fasc. 2, no. 65 (Paris, 1918), 466–7. See also *The Book of Governors*, book I, chapter XXIII, which states that Khusrū constructed a monastery/convent for his wife, Shīrīn, at Beleshphār/Hulwān.
140. Al-Shābushtī cites this phenomenon even into the Tulunid period in the *Kitāb al-diyārāt*, ed. Kūrkīs ʿAwwād (Beirut: Dār al-Rāʾid al-ʿArabī, 1986), 284. As well, Hārūn al-Rashīd was a benefactor for the monastery of Mâr Pethion at Baghdad. See Johannes Pahlitzsch, 'Christian Pious Foundations as an Element of Continuity between Late Antiquity and Islam', in *Charity and Giving in Monotheistic Religions*, eds Miriam Frenkel and Yaacov Lev (Berlin: Walter de Gruyter, 2009), 125–51 at147.
141. Kennedy, 'The Melkite Church', 328.
142. Ibid. 328–9.
143. However, conflict is not simply confined to these broad categories, as Morony demonstrates in 'Religious Communities in Late Sasanian and Early Islamic Iraq'.
144. *Chronicon anonymum ad A.D. 846 pertinens*, ed. E. W. Brooks, *Corpus Scriptorum Christianorum Orientalium, Syri* (Louvain, 1904), 255. See also Arthur Vööbus,

'The Origin of the Monophysite Church in Syria and Mesopotamia', *Church History* 42:1 (March 1973).

145. *Incerti auctoris chronicon anonymum Pseudo-Dionysianum vulgo dictum*, ed. J. B. Chabot, *Corpus Scriptorum Christianorum Orientalium, Syri* 53 (Louvain, 1933), 27.
146. Vööbus, 'The Origin of the Monophysite Church', 20.
147. Morony emphasises that after this point villages tended to be either all Nestorian or all Jacobite, though prior to this break there was a higher degree of mutability for these sectarian groups and intermixing was frequent. Presumably this was likewise the case with monastic communities in the region which had not been officially stratified by confessional distinction. See Morony, 'Religious Communities', 115–16.
148. The publication of Syriac texts by Vööbus concerning ascetic principles demonstrates the continued cultivation of monastic rules in the East that extends into the ʿAbbāsid period. See Vööbus, *Syriac and Arabic Documents Regarding Legislation Relative to Syrian Asceticism*.
149. Anastasius of Sinai, *Questions and Answers*, ed. and trans. Joseph A. Munitiz, Corpus Christianorum in Translation 7 (Turnhout: Brepols, 2011); see John Haldon for the authorship and collected materials of Anastasius in 'The Works of Anastasius of Sinai: A Key Source for the History of Seventh-Century East Mediterranean Society and Belief', in *The Byzantine and Early Islamic Near East*, ed. A. Cameron and L. I. Conrad (Princeton, NJ: Darwin Press, 1992), 107–47.
150. Cyril Mango, *Byzantium: The Empire of New Rome* (New York: Charles Scribner's Sons, 1980), 114.
151. Paul J. Alexander, 'Religious Persecution and Resistance in the Byzantine Empire of the Eighth and Ninth Centuries: Methods and Justifications', *Speculum* 52:2 (April 1977), 238–64.
152. G. R. D. King, 'Islam, Iconoclasm, and the Declaration of Doctrine', *Bulletin of the School of Oriental and African Studies* 48:2 (London: University of London, 1985), 267–77.
153. A. A. Vasiliev, 'The Iconoclastic Edict of Caliph Yazid II, A.D. 721', *Dumbarton Oaks Papers* 9 (1956), 25.
154. *Chronique de Denys de Tell-Mahre*, ed. J. B. Chabot (Paris, 1895), 49–51. It is worth noting here that the text places the responsibility for the desecration of monasteries on the outbreak of sectarian discord within the caliphate, specifically referring to the destruction caused in the region of Edessa at this time as

a result of conflict between civil authorities and Kharajite revolutionaries. The Syriac text here reads *Harourīthā*, which is to be understood as Kharajites. The chronicle levels particular blame on a certain Bar (*Ibn*) Bokhtarī, as a leader in this insurgence, for the 'seizure of wealth, and the killing or captivity of a great number of the inhabitants. He devastated the monasteries in the region of Edessa, of the Harran, and of Tela, stealing their books and bringing about the death of their overseers.' The text is silent as to how the imperial government dealt with the targeting of monasteries.

155. *Chronique de Denys de Tell-Mahre*, 91.
156. Ibid. 98–9.
157. The *Book of Governors* from Thomas of Marga centres upon the Monastery of Bēth ʿĀbhē, and in the course of detailing the history of the monastery, the author makes several explicit references to problems between the heads of the monastery and their local Muslim officials. One particularly antagonistic encounter, referring to events of the late eighth century, relates to a regional 'Ishmaelite' overlord, ʿAmran bar Muḥammad, attempting to force the abbot Mār Cyriacus and his monks to sign a deed that would sell him the monastery and its estates. See *The Book of Governors*, 450–1.
158. Arthur Vööbus, *A History of Asceticism in the Syrian Orient* II, *Corpus Scriptorum Christianorum Orientalium* vol. 197, tome 17, 147–9.
159. A. Mingana (ed.), Book XV of the *Rīsh Mellē*, in *Sources Syriaques* (Leipzig: Otto Harrassowitz, 1908), 175.
160. Ibid. 182–6.
161. During and just prior to the Persian invasion of Palestine in 614 CE there were two attacks on the Monastery of Mar Sabas by Saracen marauders; the first assault sent many of the monks fleeing for their lives across the Jordan, and the second involved the martyrdom of some forty-four monks who had remained at the laura. A similar situation occurred at the Monastery of Choziba, in which the monks were taken captive by Arab tribesmen. See Joseph Patrich, *Sabas, Leader of Palestinian Monasticism: A Comparative Study in Eastern Monasticism, Fourth to Seventh Centuries* (Washington, DC: Dumbarton Oaks Research Library, 1995), 326.
162. Mingana, Book XV of the *Rīsh Mellē*, *Sources Syriaques*, 189–91.
163. Severus ibn al-Muqaffaʿ, *History of the Patriarchs of the Coptic Church of Alexandria*, ed. and trans. B. Evetts, *Patrologia Orientalis*, tome 5, fasc. 3, part 3 (Paris, 1910), 150–5.
164. Ibid. 154.

165. Ibid. 154. The text states that it was 'a clean and decent monastery, which entertained thousands of visitors and contained a thousand monks'.
166. Ibid. 154.
167. *Chronique de Michel le Syrien, Patriarche Jacobite D'Antioche*, ed. and trans. J. B. Chabot (Paris, 1901), tome III, 21.
168. Paul M. Cobb, *White Banners, Contention in 'Abbāsid Syria, 750–880* (Albany, NY: State University of New York Press, 2001), 91–5.
169. Theophanes, *Chronographia, The Chronicle of Theophanes*, trans. C. Mango and R. S. Scott (Oxford: Clarendon Press, 1997), 665.
170. Ibid. 665.
171. Cobb, *White Banners, Contention in 'Abbāsid Syria*, 95.
172. Vööbus, *A History of Asceticism in the Syrian Orient*, vol. 500, tome 81, 360–2.
173. Tritton, *The Caliphs and Their Non-Muslim Subjects*, 3.
174. Īshō'yahb III, *Liber Epistularum*, ed. R. Duval, *Corpus Scriptorum Christianorum Orientalium, Scriptores Syri*, tome 11 (Louvain, 1904), 251. The letter does not further elaborate as to precisely what kind of assistance was offered to monasteries, but it seems reasonable to infer that Īshō'yahb III is here alluding to the measure of security for ecclesiastical structures offered by the Muslims.

4

Between Temples and Taverns: The Case for Confessional Flexibility at Monasteries

The Complexities of Muslim Visitation to Christian Shrines

The brief but influential reign of the Umayyad caliph ʿUmar ibn ʿAbd al-Azīz came to an end with his passing in the month of Rajab, 720 CE, the result of an illness lasting several weeks.[1] According to al-Ṭabarī, the caliph died and was buried at Dayr Simʿān in northern Syria.[2] It is worthy of attention here that ʿUmar ibn ʿAbd al-Azīz, generally depicted in the later Muslim tradition as the most pious ruler of the Umayyad dynasty and sometimes referred to as the 'fifth member of the Rashīdūn',[3] would have been staying at a Christian monastery during his last days. The account additionally claims that the caliph ordered his men to deal with the resident monks in securing a personal burial plot within the monastic grounds.[4] The report does not, however, expressly clarify the purpose for his visit to Dayr Simʿān, providing some opportunity for speculation.

Contemporary scholarship has demonstrated certain connections between monastic communities and the emerging Muslim populations between the seventh and ninth centuries,[5] making it plausible that the caliph's destination was simply emblematic of a fundamental Muslim curiosity for such locales. The research here will attempt to go beyond reinforcing this relative certainty for Muslim interest in monasteries, but rather propose that this fascination with Christian monastic life was articulated through a fluid, piety-centred movement at the rise of Islam that did not rigidly distinguish between sectarian groups.[6] The canon necessitated for inclusion into such a movement was

Figure 4.1 St Simeon (Qalaat Simaan) – Sacred Way. Credit: Christian Sahner/ Manar al- Athar Photo-Archive, Oxford 2008.

a relatively simple formula that involved self-definition as 'a separate group of righteous, God-fearing monotheists, separate in their strict observance of righteousness from those around them'.[7] Ultimately this would suggest an overlapping of confessional affiliation at the dawning of Islam, revealing a relatively amorphous religious context that closely reflected the flexible identifications within late antique Christianity. Such ambiguity would echo throughout the following centuries of the Islamic period, manifesting itself in Muslim appreciation, interest, and at times, participation, in Christian monastic life.

While considering the possible motives behind the caliph's sojourn at Dayr Simʿān, this essay will attempt to more broadly explain the multifaceted popular interest in monasteries during this formative period for Islam. With respect to ʿUmar ibn ʿAbd al-Azīz in particular, his unwavering dedication to a serious, pietistic life will perhaps serve as some indication: the ninth-century biographer Ibn Saʿd refers to the caliph's austere nature as 'reminiscent of monks' (*yamshī mishya al-ruhbān*).[8] The celebrated early Muslim ascetic Malik ibn Dīnār of Baṣra (d. 749) stated of the devout character of ʿUmar ibn ʿAbd al-Azīz, 'people say that I am an ascetic (*zāhid*), but in truth, the real ascetic is ʿUmar ibn ʿAbd al-Azīz; as the whole world has been laid before him but he has rejected it'.[9] Fāṭima bint ʿAbd al-Malik, the wife of ʿUmar ibn ʿAbd al-Azīz, is additionally credited with the statement, 'There were those who surpassed him in prayer and fasting, but I have never seen anyone more fearful of his Lord than ʿUmar.'[10]

It may also be possible to suggest, continuing on the tradition of Ibn Saʿd, that the caliph himself subscribed to a rather flexible policy of confessional division during worship, as well as an open-minded attitude toward churches.[11] Upon his succession to the caliphate, he is said to have led the people in prayer within a church.[12] If such characteristics do imply an inclusive outlook between the worlds of Christian and Muslim religious devotion, at least among the most piety-minded individuals, this may serve as a further explanation for a cross-confessional interest in monastic life on a broader level. The proposal for a fluid religious movement at the dawn of Islam based on individual piety, transcending the bonds of any particularly strict confessional stance,[13] could then have far-reaching implications for an interpretation of Muslim interest in monasteries. Given the absolute weight accorded to piety and righteous action within the sacred scripture,[14] would there have been a more appropriate setting for the distillation of these principles amongst early Muslims than Christian monasteries?

This is not to suggest that the case of ʿUmar ibn ʿAbd al-Azīz is entirely unique, as other Umayyad caliphs as well had some connection to monasteries. Yazīd ibn Muʿāwiya (r. 680–3),[15] for instance, is credited with the initiation of this imperial interest in visitation to monasteries, as a corollary to the movement on the part of early Umayyad elites to withdraw into the Syrian limitrophe.[16] The 'high culture' trend of travelling to outlying areas, in the company of courtly entourages, constituted an effort to mitigate the gravity of urban existence. In remote venues, the elites of the early Islamic period could engage in their favoured pastimes such as hunting, games, parties and listening to the songs of poets.[17] In this case, rural monasteries would have been regarded as places of relaxation, well removed from the activity and political life of Damascus. They were apparently such pleasant locations – often containing beautiful orchards, carefully tended gardens and flowing springs – that several of the later Umayyad *quṣūr*, or desert palaces, were constructed adjacent to existing monasteries or above the ruins of monastic sites.[18] In addition, both al-Walīd I (r. 705–15)[19] and

Hishām (r. 724–43)[20] are reported to have undertaken visits to monasteries for health reasons.

The case of ʿUmar ibn ʿAbd al-Azīz may, however, present an alternative to these motivations for visiting monasteries; one that is perhaps centred upon an abiding interest in ascetic practices as a core component to a pietistic life. Admittedly, there is an absence of documentary evidence as to the precise reason that this caliph would have visited Dayr Simʿān. It certainly could have been for health concerns, as al-Ṭabarī claims that the caliph was ill for some time; this would make sense considering the association between monasteries and hospices for the sick.[21] Yet the inclination towards ascetic practices, which seems to have been a feature of the caliph's personal religious convictions, could provide a different interpretation. Should such a pursuit have been a concern, there would have been few better places in the early Islamic period for the observation of its merits than an abode of Christian monks.

An appreciation for the wisdom and mystical knowledge of monks was a well-established literary device in sources from the classical Islamic period,[22] which indicates that the association of monasteries with places for religious instruction would have been widely acknowledged across confessional boundaries. There has likewise been suggested a continuity between the emergence of early Islamic asceticism (*zuhd*) and the Syriac and Byzantine monastic heritage.[23] In support of this claim, there are accounts of Muslim ascetics (*zāhid*/ pl. *zuhhād*) interacting with monks throughout the medieval Islamic period and at times purportedly receiving ascetic training under the direction of Christian hermits. For this reason, the ancient typology of the *Apopthegmata Patrum*, or 'sayings of the desert fathers', has frequently occurred in Islamic mystical texts and hagiographies.[24] In many cases, the accounts picture a Muslim mystic pursuing spiritual advice from a monk, in this context being a fellow ascetic as well as a seeker of wisdom.[25]

Both Louis Massignon[26] and Tor Andrae[27] attempted to explain the potential connection between the development of early Islamic mysticism and Christian asceticism. For Andrae especially, the legacy of monasticism was instrumental in the formulation of Muslim ascetic practices, largely through the process of direct contact between sectarian groups. Though the image of the Christian hermit was that of a misanthropic outsider to society, clearly acknowledged as such within the late antique Christian tradition itself, there was still much esoteric knowledge to be gained from their experience; thus, forming a model for the transmission of spiritual wisdom that transcended any rigid boundaries between confessional groups. Accounts of Muslim mystics visiting Christian ascetics therefore actually conform to more ancient Mediterranean patterns for the diffusion of knowledge.[28]

This paradigm proposes that even one recognised as a sage, regardless of a particular philosophical orientation, could benefit considerably from discussions with other enlightened personalities.[29] Strictly speaking, in matters of theology and ritual observance, Muslims would have, of course, turned to their own holy scripture. However, those particular individuals that were seeking knowledge regarding ascetic piety and its methods of praxis, would appear to have been naturally drawn to practitioners from other religious backgrounds. As Andrae definitively asserted,

> Such conversations between Muslims and Christian monks obviously are not without a basis in reality. In any case they bear witness to the fact that Islam, during the first centuries, dared to learn, and in fact did learn, from Christian ascetic piety.[30]

Muslim fascination with Christian monastic life was not, however, strictly confined to mystical impulses. Medieval Arabic literature, including accounts from historical and geographical sources as well as the extant remnants of the *diyārāt*[31] corpus, sought to explain this monastic allure in a variety of ways. Popular Muslim interest in monastic life and Christian ceremonies at monasteries engendered an entire sub-field of medieval *khamriyya* poetry, or wine-songs,[32] with monasteries often serving as the backdrop to drunken escapades and amorous encounters. These places would have been especially celebratory and welcoming for the local laity during religious festivals, and this revelry could have, in turn, facilitated a rare degree of interaction between the sexes.[33]

However, the image of monasteries that emerges from the source material is often a dynamic one, as they are able to play the role of both taverns for all manner of licentious behaviour – referred to in this context as *ḥānāt*[34] by Muslim commentators – as well as devotional shrines for ardent pilgrims, including in either case both Christians and non-Christians. The popular interest in monasteries, at least as interpreted by Muslim accounts, therefore fluctuates between decadent curiosity and genuine pietistic observance. By virtue of such seemingly incompatible extremes of explanation, it is clear that early Muslim attraction to these settlements and interest in the monastic way of life is a complex issue. Undoubtedly, the allegations that Muslim visitation to monasteries included occasional improprieties cannot be dismissed.

Monastic settlements, especially those of the desert and wilderness areas, would have represented ideal places for Muslim elites to avail themselves of alcohol and other vices.[35] Monastic estates throughout the Bilād al-Shām, Mesopotamia and Egypt commonly included vineyards and presses among their agricultural grounds,[36] with some of their regional vintages even attaining popularity within western Christendom during the late antique period.[37] The concern for tending such vineyards figures prominently in the *Life* of the fourth-century Palestinian monk Hilarion; the venerable holy man himself would, on occasion, travel throughout the region to bless the vintages produced by various monastic establishments.[38] The importance of wine-production for the monastic economies of the region did not come to an end with the advent of Islamic rule. In fact, monasteries would have naturally remained the largest producers of wine throughout Muslim lands.[39]

If the availability of wine should have been a concern on the part of the Muslim elite, monasteries would have surely provided a steady means of access. The tenth-century *Kitāb al-diyārāt* of al-Shābushtī[40] references Muslim visitation to monasteries and obtaining wine in a number of passages. In many instances, monasteries are reported to have contained these *ḥānāt*, or taverns, within their grounds. Dayr Sābur,[41] Dayr Mar Jurjīs,[42] and Dayr Qūṭā[43] are all mentioned as possessing taverns and wine-shops within the estates. Of Dayr Ishmūnī, near the village of Quṭrabul on the western banks of the Tigris, al-Shābushtī writes:

> This monastery has a religious festival on the third day of Tishrīn, which is one of the most celebrated days in all of Baghdad. The people gather together at the monastery as a great host for this festival, not a single person being left behind to miss the merry-making and enjoyment. They are all witnesses to its majesty . . . and while there they admire the things that this monastery possesses and take part in its good cheer. Then they assemble

along the banks of the river, forming a circle around the monastery and its taverns.[44]

If certain pleasure-seeking individuals of the Muslim court were in search of forbidden indulgences, it would seem that monastic settlements would have been an appropriate venue. A specific example of this enduring wine culture amongst the Muslim elite can be identified in the archaeological remains of al-Muʿtaṣim's palace at Sāmarrā', which included a great number of wine jars. Based on the labelling of these vessels, David Rice concluded that many of such containers had been procured from the neighbouring monasteries. Rice further commented, 'Throughout the golden age of the Abbasid caliphate, the best wines were to be sampled in taverns attached to monasteries',[45] a quote based on archaeological analysis that would surely buttress the numerous reports of caliphal visits to monasteries found in al-Shābushtī's work. Particularly in the earliest period of Islam, the continued fascination with wine culture might be viewed as an appropriation of the Hellenistic traditions that had been politically supplanted in the region – a phenomenon that tends to characterise the Umayyad regime.[46]

Simply being recognised as ideal locations for debauchery does not, however, provide a suitable explanation for Muslim interest in monasteries as a whole, as there are reports that suggest a greater religious dimension to this fascination. Visitation to monasteries strictly on the basis of convenience for illicit behaviours would, after all, hardly justify the presence of ʿUmar ibn ʿAbd al-Azīz at Dayr Simʿān, considering the caliph has been universally recognised as a paragon of morality in the Umayyad period.[47]. It should also here be noted that the consumption of wine was itself controversial even within the monastic communities of Late Antiquity.[48] The pursuit of relaxation and revelry is then clearly not a sufficient answer to the overall question of Muslim visitation to monasteries. The comforts of wine and isolation could certainly be sought after, yet it seems that there was much more to such encounters that assumes a religious nature. The following example from al-Shābushtī, concerning a religious celebration held at the shrine (*qubba*) of al-Shatīq, one of the ancient churches of al-Ḥīra, lends itself to this interpretation. In his discussion on various rituals of the local Christian community during this particular holy day, the author makes reference to the fact that Muslims too were present during the festivities. The passage states:

> On the day of their religious festival, all of the Christians go out in procession from the monastery of al-Shakūra to the shrine, wearing their most beautiful garments, marching alongside a cross and holding palms in their hands. Their liturgical cantors and priests walk among them, worshipping aloud with a chant, and it has a pleasing melody. And a large throng of cheerful Muslims follow them (*wa-yatbaʿuhum khalq kathīr min mutaṭarbī al-muslimīn*), until they reach the qubba al-Shatīq. There they receive communion and baptisms are performed, then they return in the same manner as they came. It is a pleasant sight.[49]

The crowd here, composed of both Christians and Muslims, revels in the hymnody and spectacle of the scene. Chanting and music like this would have been, no doubt, an essential part of the festival atmosphere and thus also part of the attraction to Muslim onlookers.[50] Having little in the way of 'nourishment for the senses' regarding holy days in their own tradition,[51] a Christian religious service that included such merriment would have appeared all the more charming to local Muslims.[52] There is, of course, no mention of any type of shameful behaviour in the accounts like the one demonstrated above. Nor does the author al-Shābushtī offer any further qualification of these scenarios, rather, merely pointing out that Muslims were among those involved in the proceedings at some level. That such inter-confessional relations were not expounded upon may suggest that these types of occurrences were not altogether unusual at other Christian shrines throughout the medieval Near East. Accounts like these would then seem to simply offer a glimpse of reverent Muslim visitation, or perhaps *ziyāra*, to Christian holy places.

The implication for this type of visitation to monasteries and Christian shrines may be either that the boundaries of a distinct Muslim confessional identity had yet to be fully articulated, or that such parameters were not particularly applicable among the rural populations of mixed Muslim and Christian communities.[53] At the very least it can be proposed that these confessional lines were apparently still quite pliable well into the Islamic period, even at the time, for instance, when al-Shābushtī was compiling his information. These manifestations of a religious *ziyāra*, without an overtly specific confessional identity, lend further support for a nebulous confessional context: a movement in which active participation in a broader, piety-centred community, including votive attendance at religious ceremonies and visitation to holy places, transcended rigid categories. Though such flexibility would have necessarily reached its zenith in the formative periods of Islam,[54] the continuing Muslim interest in Christian rites and fascination with monastic life may perhaps be seen as a trace of this early piety-driven movement.

The Hospitable Sacred

The accounts concerning inter-confessional visitation to monasteries was likewise facilitated by one of the central monastic tenets: the emphasis on hospitality.[55] As a result of this drive toward service for mankind, monasteries began to be associated with hospitality for wayfarers, places for care of the sick, and centres for almsgiving. In addition to the life of personal contemplation and prayer, one of the primary functions of early monastic life in the East became the care for travellers. As such, the concept of monastic hospitality figures prominently in the patristic literature of the Byzantine period. Foundational charters, or *typika* documents, from virtually every period of Byzantine monasticism serve as a testament to this commitment to hospitality, as they commonly stipulate that monasteries should open their doors to those in need, either the local poor or pilgrims.[56] At times this tenet of hospitality also involved inviting visitors to the settlement, as well as offering food and refreshments to lay travellers along the pilgrim routes.[57] The special area designated for the reception of visitors and care for the sick became known as the *xenodocheion* in some monasteries.[58] The seventh-century *Life of George of Choziba* demonstrates the continuance of this maxim in times of the most severe hardships for monastic communities, for even in the aftermath of the early seventh-century Persian invasion of Palestine, welcome was still extended to visitors who stopped at his Monastery of Choziba, on the road between Jerusalem and Jericho.[59]

This hospitable sentiment also remained a recognisable fixture of monastic life into the Islamic period, certain monasteries even becoming famed for their accommodating nature by later Muslim authors. Al-Shābushtī, for example, reports of the reception of guests at Dayr Mar Yuḥannā at Takrīt: 'There they had constructed, next to the monastery, a building where pilgrims arrived. The monks then offered hospitality to them, as well as offering them lodgings.'[60] In another passage, al-Shābushtī demonstrates an awareness that this monastic geniality not only applied to Christian travellers, but also to strangers of different varieties that happened to pass by monasteries – including in the case of Dayr Mar Mār (Mārī),[61] near Sāmarrā', the reception of a hunting party in the company of caliph al-Mu'tazz (r. 866–9). The passage concerning the welcoming of these figures within the 'Abbāsid court is as follows:

> This monastery is filled with a host of monks and is surrounded by vineyards and orchards. It is an unblemished place, a location of great natural beauty . . . al-Faḍl[62] gave this account that, one day, he went out hunting with al-Mu'tazz; and as he explained: 'we became separated from our entourage; myself, the caliph, and Yūnus ibn Bughā; and the caliph started to become very thirsty'. I then said to him: 'O Commander of the Faithful, there is a settlement of monks around here, and I know one of them. This man possesses wonderful charity (*muwadda ḥasana*) and a charming spirit (*khafif al-rūḥ*), and in [this monastery] there are beautiful dishes' [of food and drink]. Then asking the Commander of the Faithful, I said, 'Should we turn away from it?' And he replied, 'Let us go there.'
>
> So, we set out and we approached the head of the monastery and he wished us welcome and we were received in a gracious manner. We went straight over to the cool water and drank. He [the superior] suggested to us that we should go inside with him, saying, 'you should refresh yourselves here with us and we ourselves will offer you all the things to be found in our monastery, will you come?' And the caliph found the monk to be most pleasant and agreed that we should go inside with him . . . and he subsequently brought us bread and other things to eat, and we enjoyed everything thoroughly . . . eventually our other comrades rejoined us and the superior became alarmed, but the caliph said to him, 'On my life, do not stop what you are doing. For indeed, as for those men over there, I am their master. And as for all those here, I am your friend.'
>
> We rested for a while longer, and then the caliph ordered that the monastery should be granted a hefty sum of money. [The monk] responded:

'By God, I cannot accept it, but on the condition . . . that the *amīr* and his entourage should visit the monastery again.'[63]

In his report on Dayr al-Aʿlā, near Mosul, al-Shābushtī reports that the caliph al-Maʾmūn (r. 813–33) also indulged in the local monastic welcome. The passage begins with a description of the grounds:

> It is a monastery that is full of people . . . in it there are many cells for monks, with carved staircases along the mountain and leading down to the river (the Tigris), there are ladders coming up from the water . . . under the monastery is the large spring that pours into the river. The people head down there to spend time and take baths in it . . . al-Maʾmūn stopping by this monastery when on a trip to Damascus, spent several days there. He arrived during Palm Sunday (*ʿīd al-shaʿānīn*). Aḥmed ibn Ṣadaqa recalled: 'we all went out with al-Maʾmūn, and we went down to Dayr al-Aʿlā at al-Mawṣil for its goodness and purity. Then came Palm Sunday, and al-Maʾmūn reclined there with his entourage along the river, amidst the desert and gardens. He sat watching the people coming into the monastery, the monastery on that day having been adorned with decorations. The monks then came out for the offering, around them were their fine attendants with censers of incense in their hands and wearing crosses around their necks, donning embroidered stoles. al-Maʾmūn took all of this in, and found it pleasing. The people then withdrew to their cells and their offerings.'[64]

The geographer Yāqūt al-Ḥamawī (d. 1229) goes a step further in reporting the activities of al-Walīd ibn Yazīd (d. 744) at Dayr Bawannā, in which case the Umayyad prince actually participated in the Christian religious rites. Yāqūt begins this section with a brief description of the monastery:

> It lies alongside the Ghūṭa of Damascus in the most pleasant location and is one of the oldest of such Christian buildings. It is said that it was constructed in the time of the Masīḥ, peace be upon Him, or shortly thereafter. It is quite small and houses only a few monks. Passing by it, al-Walīd ibn Yazīd looked upon its beauty and stayed for a while, engaging in baffoonery and drink. He said of it:
> 'Cheer for my night at Dayr Bawannā,

> for drinks served and songs sung . . .
> We took their Communion (*qurbānahum*)
> and we kneeled before the crosses of their monastery.'[65]

Given that al-Walīd was well known for his carousing and drinking at monasteries, we may not be able to suggest that this example was indeed an authentic expression of religious observance. The report could perhaps be seen as a literary polemic against a despised ruler, one whot was already understood as 'arguably the most vilified member of the Umayyad dynasty'.[66] Fully aware of his scandalous pursuits in this instance, even al-Walīd himself is said to have proclaimed in verse: 'we have become notorious amongst the people, as they talk about what we did there'.[67] The precise reason that the prince and his entourage would have engaged in the taking of the Eucharist at Dayr Bawannā is simply a matter of conjecture. Still, there does appear to be some level of confessional ambiguity in the report. Steven Judd has likewise persuasively argued that there is more to the legacy of al-Walīd than just moral depravity and licentious behaviour, instead demonstrating his impact on Umayyad religious thought and political theory.[68]

The physical charm and tranquility of these rural settlements is often highlighted in accounts concerning the allure of eastern monasteries.[69] An appreciation for such natural beauty, as well as the renowned hospitable attitude of monks, would have been immediately evident to the nomadic peoples of the Levant and North Africa, particularly when contrasted by the invariably harsh conditions of the surrounding terrain. The non-Christian admiration for monastic gardens, architecture and art – primarily in the form of mosaics and icons – seems to have persisted for several centuries after the arrival of Islam.[70] On this point, Yāqūt provides an illustration of Dayr Murrān:

> This monastery lies close to Damascus, on a hill above fields of saffron and beautiful meadows, with buildings of plaster and its floors decorated with colored tiles. It is a large monastery, containing many monks within, and in its temple church (*haykal*) there is a wonderful image of obscure meaning; there are trees surrounding it.[71]

A further example of Muslim admiration for Christian imagery[72] is recorded in the tenth-century *Kitāb adab al-ghurabā'*.[73] This illustration, presented by Abū al-Faraj al-Iṣfahānī, takes place within the Mukhtār palace of Caliph al-Wāthiq (d. 847) at Sāmarrā'. While enjoying the luxury of the court there, the caliph pondered a moment and asked one of the attendants if he had ever seen a place as lovely as the Mukhtār. The attendant responded with affirmation for the magnificence of the palace: 'May God grant the *amīr al-mu'minīn* life-long pleasure in it!' According to the text, a striking feature of its beauty was the many wonderful images lining the palace walls, the most notable of which depicted monks performing nightly prayers in a church (*aḥsanuhā ṣūrat shahār/sahār al-bī'a*). The beauty of the image prompted the caliph to inscribe a verse on the wall during one his feasts, stating: 'We have never seen anything like the elegance of al-Mukhtār. No! Nor anything such as the painting of the night prayer.'[74]

The *Kitāb al-diyārāt* also demonstrates that the fascination with monasteries was in part due to the admiration of the natural beauty of the monastic environment – invariably going into some detail concerning the topography of each monastery within the compilation, including their precise locations, the scale of the constructions, when the celebrations and feast days are observed in each location, and the aesthetic quality of their agricultural grounds. al-Shābushtī vividly describes the connection between the physical environment and festivities of St John's Monastery, stating:

> Dayr Mar Ḥannā [Yūḥannā] lies on the banks of Lake Ḥabash, near the river, and there are gardens beside it . . . near the monastery is a fountain, called the Fountain of Najjātī, and near this stands a great sycamore tree, under which people gather and drink. This area is a place of constant revelry, dancing, and enjoyment. It is a pleasant area in the days of the rising Nile, when the lake is full, and during the time when the fields are filled with crops and all is green and flourishing. The people flock to this place, and they amuse themselves there. Poets have sung of the beauty and charm of this location.[75]

At other times the allure appears to be further elevated by the presence of religious artefacts or relics reputed to be in a monastery's possession, maintaining the capacity to draw pilgrims of varying confessional affiliations. The drawing power of icons is clearly demonstrated in the case of Dayr al-Quṣayr in Egypt, which apparently held an appeal for Muslims well into the late-ninth century. According to al-Shābushtī, the monastery was even visited on occasion by the Muslim elite, citing the case of the Ṭūlūnid ruler of Egypt, Abū al-Jaysh Khumarāwayh (r. 884–96), as an example:

> This monastery sits atop a mountain, on the terrace of its highest point. It is a monastery of beautiful construction, masterfully done in its workmanship, and it is a pleasing spot. There are many monks residing in it. And there is a spring there, boring out through the rock, which supplies them with water. In its temple (*haykal*) there is an image (*ṣūra*) of Mary, with Jesus (*al-masīḥ, ʿalayhi al-salām*) sitting in her lap. People visit this place to look upon the image. There is, in its upper portion, a large hall constructed by Abū al-Jaysh Khumarāwayh ibn Aḥmad ibn Ṭūlūn, with four windows facing the four directions. He was a frequent visitor to this monastery, to admire this image within it (*muʿjabān bil-ṣūra allatī fīhi*), taking drink as he looked at it.[76]

Near the conclusion of the *Kitāb al-diyārāt* there is an entire section dedicated to monasteries that possess other wondrous objects and where miraculous occurrences take place. For Dayr al-Khanāfis, near Mosul, al-Shābushtī reports that people gather to it on a certain day of the year to witness the appearance of a swarm of dung beetles, for which the monastery is named.[77] These scarabs appear and envelope the walls and roofs of the monastery, as well as the surrounding land, covering everything in blackness. The following day, the day of the monastic festival, the people congregate in the temple church (*haykal*) to worship and make offerings. Thereupon the dung beetles vanish and are not seen again until the next year.[78] The author also tells of a hot spring at the Jacobite Monastery of al-Qiyāra, outside of Mosul, that people visit for its curative powers.[79] The Monastery of Bār Qūmā is reported to have held the remains of a saint, believed to be one of the original disciples, in a wooden case. The doors of it are flung open on the feast days, revealing the body, and people come to view the saint.[80] A similar ritual takes place at Dayr Yuḥnas, where the saint is brought out for the festival in his sarcophagus. Adding to the miraculous sense here, however, the saint then briefly returns to life and walks about the grounds.[81]

Yāqūt likewise relates a story from Dayr Mīmās, a monastery revered for the healing power of the saint interred there, demonstrating an acceptance for the mystical nature of certain tombs. Though the report clearly displays a legendary quality, the details might suggest that Muslims of the region also subscribed to the same view of this tomb:

> The monastery lies between Damascus and Ḥomṣ, along the river . . . in a pleasant spot. Inside it, there is a martyr whom they consider as one of the original apostles (*ḥawārī*) of Jesus, peace be upon Him, and these monks believe that he is able to heal the infirm. The poet, al-Butayn, took ill and went there to be healed. It was said that the people there were neglectful of him, so he urinated in front of the grave of the saint. It then happened that he died right after doing that. Word spread amongst the people of Ḥomṣ that the saint had killed the poet and they went straight for the monastery to demolish it, saying: 'A Christian killed a Muslim, we cannot accept it! Give up the bones of the saint, so that we might burn them.' The Christians however bribed the amīr of Ḥomṣ so that he might relieve their common people.[82]

As in the case of Muslim participation at the Christian festivities of al-Ḥīra, a similar phenomenon has been suggested in connection to the Shrine of St Sergius at Ruṣāfa, where the Umayyad caliph Hishām (r. 723–43) intentionally constructed a palace and mosque adjoining the basilica dedicated to the early fourth-century Christian martyr. Yāqūt claims to have actually seen the monastery at Ruṣāfa, calling it a 'marvel of the world for its beauty and buildings . . . with monks and houses of worship within'.[83] He likewise acknowledges that Hishām constructed his city there alongside the monastery.[84] Muslims were clearly engaging in worship at this site during the Umayyad period, and there is some evidence that this *ziyāra* too involved participation in the cult of St Sergius.[85] As explained by Josef Meri, 'the *ziyāra*, the Arabic word for pilgrimage and visiting holy places, was a multi-dimensional phenomenon influenced by geography and local custom as well as by religious tradition'.[86] Adding to this potential for flexible religious affiliation, it should be remembered that many of those who converted to Islam within this early period of Muslim rule over the Levant, Iraq and North Africa had originally come from Christian backgrounds.[87]

As such, it seems likely that some of these burgeoning Muslim communities would have only been a few generations removed from active participation in monastic pilgrimage and celebrations on feast days, indeed as part of the Christian laity. This would make a continuing reverence for the ascetic and monk across confessional divides all the more plausible. In present-day Syria, Muslims still visit the Convent of Our Lady of Ṣaydnāyā, an activity which traces its origins to the early medieval period.[88] The shrine of Ṣaydnāyā, near Damascus, has been revered for centuries as a place of healing for both Christian and Muslim communities, due to its possession of a purportedly miraculous icon of the Virgin.[89]

Another striking contemporary example of this phenomenon regarding the blending between confessional groups comes from Palestine. In an ethnographic study on religious practices in the village of al-Khaḍr, near Bethlehem, Lance Laird discusses Muslim and Christian pilgrimage to the local shrine.[90] The Greek Orthodox church and monastery dedicated to Mār Jirjis (Saint George) has drawn people in need of healing, protection and blessings for centuries. As in the case of Ṣaydnāyā, this veneration is apparently carried out without regard to confessional distinction. The identity of the Christian saint, Mār Jirjis, has however become intertwined with a seemingly unrelated Muslim religious figure known as al-Khiḍr,[91] for whom the village is named.[92] On feast days, both Christian and Muslim communities converge on the shrine and venerate Mār Jirjis and al-Khiḍr as a single saint.[93] According to Ignaz Goldziher, the evolution of saint veneration within Islam, including visitation to sacred shrines, was a direct product of the survival of local religious customs, being ultimately re-interpreted to fit into a Muslim context.[94] In this case it relied upon the influence of newly converted Muslims, coming from Christian heritages, and neighbouring Christian communities. Those that had recently converted would have brought with them, into their new religious affiliation, a great many traditions and practices of the generations before them.[95] The observance of Christian festivals and interest in monasteries, as a component to this 'popular religion', would therefore indicate considerable latitudes for confessional interaction on the local level.

Such a situation clearly allows for considerable fluctuations in confessional self-identity throughout the period in question, to the extent that one might then contend that the very notion of definable religious barriers, as a method of verifying conversion or designating the other in early Islam, would become somewhat dubious. We must take into account the potential knowledge of doctrinally specific beliefs on the local level, the difference in vernacular languages of various religious groups in the initial contact period, and the continued intimate social interaction between religious groups.

This kind of flexibility would then seem to be a continuation of fluid religious parameters, particularly concerning the veneration of the holy man and his abode that had characterised the late antique world. Peter Brown has stated that these ascetic personalities 'functioned as "monasteries without walls" for a wide network of religiously-minded clients'[96] within this malleable confessional milieu of the late antique Near East. This kind of pietistic orientation would perhaps help to contextualise the visit of ʿUmar ibn ʿAbd al-Azīz to Dayr Simʿān. Would it not seem possible that the caliph, who literally 'walked like the monks' (*yamshī mishya al-ruhbān*),[97] could have held some kind of spiritual connection to the monks of his region? On the caliph's own familiarity with monasticism, or at least the recognition of monastic wisdom, Abū Nuʿaym al-Iṣfahānī reports of an encounter between ʿUmar ibn ʿAbd al-Azīz and a monk:

> A monk once came to visit ʿUmar ibn ʿAbd al-Azīz, and ʿUmar said to him: 'Is it not reported that you are constantly weeping? Why do you go on this way?' and the monk responded: 'Verily, by God, O Command of the Faithful, I have closely looked after the people, and there was nothing more important to them than their faith, but today there is nothing more important to them than this material world, and I know that death today is better for the righteous man (*al-barr*) than the impudent (*al-fājir*)', and as the monk departed, ʿUmar said: 'This is indeed a truth, O Abū Ayyūb, the monk.'[98]

Notes

1. Al-Ṭabarī, *Taʾrīkh al-rusūl waʾl mulūk* (5 vols) (Beirut: Dār al-Kutub al-ʿIlmiyya, 1987), vol. 4, 67; Leiden edition 1362–3 (Leiden: Brill, 1879–1901). Alternatively, however, Ibn ʿAbd al-Ḥakam's *Sīrat ʿUmar ibn ʿAbd al-Azīz* (Damascus: al-Maktab al-ʿArabiyya, 1966), 158–60, and al-Dhahabī's *Tadhkirat al-Ḥuffāẓ* (5 vols) (Beirut: Dār al-Kutub al-ʿIlmiyya, 1998), vol. 1, 130–1, report that the caliph was poisoned by a servant. In one report, Ṭabarī suggests that the poisoning of ʿUmar was carried out by the Banū Marwān.

2. Al-Ṭabarī, *Taʾrīkh* 1, 67–8 (Leiden edition 1362–3). There is likewise a brief report of the caliph staying at Dayr Simʿān in the report by Ibn ʿAbd al-Ḥakam, *Sīrat*, 156–7. This account of his stay at the monastery is however altogether unrelated to the report in al-Ṭabarī. There is some confusion as to whether or not this is the more famous Monastery of St Simeon, near Aleppo, or another monastery by the same name. Eutychius, for example, places this monastery near Ḥimṣ. See *Annales, Corpus Scriptorum Christianorum Orientalium, Scriptores Arabici*, ed. L. Cheikho (Paris, 1905), part 3, tome 6, 276. According to Yāqūt as well, there is some discrepancy about the location of this particular monastery: the *Muʿjam al-buldān* placing the Monastery of St Simʿān outside Damascus and being dedicated to Simon Peter and not the stylite ascetic. See Yāqūt, *Muʿjam al-buldān* (5 vols) (Beirut: Dār al-Sādir, 1955–7), vol. 2, 517.
3. Al-Dhahabī, *Tadhkirat al-ḥuffāẓ* 1, 90. According to the teachings of al-Shāfiʿī, he was considered *al-khulafā al-rāshidūn khamsa*. See also W. W. Barthold, 'The Caliph ʿUmar II and Conflicting Reports on His Personality', trans. from Russian by Jan W. Weryho, *The Islamic Quarterly: A Review of Islamic Culture* 15:2/3 (April–September 1971), 69; Ignaz Goldziher, *Muslim Studies*, vol. 2, ed. S. M. Stern, trans. from German by S. M. Stern and C. R. Barber (Albany, NY: State University of New York Press, 1967–71) 43.
4. Al-Ṭabarī, *Taʾrīkh* 4, 68 (Leiden edition 1362–3).
5. Sidney Griffith, *Arabic Christianity in the Monasteries of Ninth-Century Palestine* (Aldershot: Ashgate Variorum, 1992), *The Beginnings of Christian Theology in Arabic: Muslim-Christian Encounters in the Early Islamic Period* (Aldershot: Ashgate Variorum, 2002), 'Michael, the Martyr and Monk of Mar Sabas Monastery, at the Court of the Caliph ʿAbd al-Malik: Christian Apologetics and Martyrology in the Early Islamic Period', *ARAM* 6:1 (1994), 115–48; G. Troupeau, 'Les Couvents Chrétiens dans la Littérature Arabe', *Études sur le christianisme arabe au Moyen Âge*, Variorum Collected Series 515 (London: Variorum, 1995), 265–79; Hilary Kilpatrick, 'Monasteries Through Muslim Eyes: The Diyārāt Books', in *Christian-Muslim Relations: A Bibliographical History*, vol. II, eds D. Thomas and A. Mallett (Leiden: Brill, 2003), 19–37; Elizabeth and Garth Fowden, 'Monks, Monasteries and Early Islam', in *Studies on Hellenism, Christianity and the Umayyads*, eds G. Fowden and E. K. Fowden, *Meletemata* 37 (Athens: Diffusion de Boccard, 2004), 19–37; Suleiman Mourad, 'Christian Monks in Islamic Literature: A Preliminary Report on Some Arabic Apophthegmata Pratum', *Bulletin for the Royal Institute on Inter-Faith Studies* 6 (2004), 81–98; Elizabeth Fowden, 'The Lamp and the Olive Flask: Early

Muslim Interest in Christian Monks', in *Islamic Cross Pollinations: Interactions in the Medieval Middle East*, eds Anna Akasoy, James Montgomery and Peter Pormann (Exeter: Gibb Memorial Trust, 2007), 1–28; Ofer Livne-Kafri, 'Early Muslim Asceticism and the World of Christian Monasticism', *Jerusalem Studies in Arabic and Islam* 20 (1996), 105–29; Christian Sahner, 'Islamic Legends about the Birth of Monasticism: A Case Study on the Late Antique Milieu of the Qur'ān and Tafsīr', in *The Late Antique World of Early Islam: Muslims Among Christians and Jews in the Eastern Mediterranean*, ed. R. Hoyland (Princeton, NJ: Darwin Press, 2015), 393–435.

6. Fred Donner has refined this concept on the basis of a 'believers' movement, which allowed for inclusion into a nascent Islamic community on the basis of righteous belief as well as pious action, surpassing the boundaries of traditional confessional allegiances. See Fred Donner, 'From Believers to Muslims: Confessional Self-Identity in the Early Islamic Community', *al-Abhath* 50–1 (2002–3), 9–53 at 17–21, and also *Muhammad and the Believers: At the Origins of Islam* (Cambridge, MA: Belknap Press of Harvard University Press, 2010), which presents an expansion on the original article.
7. Donner, *Muhammad and the Believers*, 69.
8. Ibn Sa'd, *Ṭabaqāt al-kabīr* (11 vols) (Cairo: Maktabat al-Khanjī, 2001), vol. 7, 326. He literally 'walked like the monks'.
9. Al-Dhahabī, *Tadhkirat al-ḥuffāẓ* 1, 130. The depiction of 'Umar as intensely 'fearful of his Lord', used here in the Arabic as *fariqān*.
10. Ibid. 130.
11. Suliman Bashear, 'Qibla Musharriqa and Early Muslim Prayer in Churches', *The Muslim World* 81:3–4 (1991), 268–82 at 278.
12. Ibn Sa'd, *Ṭabaqāt* 7, 374. Bashear makes the observation that this tradition does not seem to have been in wide circulation after the middle of the ninth century. See 'Qibla Musharriqa', 278.
13. See Donner, 'From Believers to Muslims', 19–21.
14. Donner further suggests that the core of Muḥammad's message was composed of moral and pietistic themes, based on unremitting mandates for such observance in the Qur'ān. Fred Donner, *Narratives of Islamic Origins: The Beginnings of Islamic Historical Writing*, Studies in Late Antiquity and Early Islam 14 (Princeton, NJ: Darwin Press, 1998), 67.
15. Yazīd himself, it should be noted, had a prominent Christian mother, Maysūn, from the Banū Kalb. She was not only the wife of Mu'āwiya, but sister to the Kalbī leader, Ibn Baḥdal. Henri Lammens suggested that Yazīd's affinity for

Christianity may have been the result of spending much of his childhood with his mother's tribe in Syria. On the caliph's background, see Lammens, *Le Califat de Yazid Ier*, Extrait des Mélanges de la Faculté Orientale de Beyrouth (Beirut: Imprimerie Catholique, 1921).

16. Irfan Shahîd, *Byzantium and the Arabs in the Sixth Century* (2 vols) (Washington, DC: Dumbarton Oaks Research Library, 2002), vol. 2, 387.
17. Boaz Shoshan, 'High Culture and Popular Culture in Medieval Islam', *Studia Islamica* 73 (1991), 67–107 at 69.
18. See Elizabeth Fowden, 'Christian Monasteries and Umayyad Residences in Late Antique Syria', *Studies on Hellenism, Christianity, and the Umayyads*, eds Garth and Elizabeth Fowden, *Meletemata* 37 (Athens, 2004), 175–92.
19. Paulus Peeters, 'La Passion de St. Pierre de Capitolias', *Analecta Bollandiana* 57 (1939), 299–333 at 309–12.
20. See Lawrence Conrad, 'Historical Evidence and the Archaeology of Early Islam', in *Quest for Understanding: Arabic and Islamic Studies in Memory of Malcolm H. Kerr*, eds S. Seikaly, R. Baalbaki and P. Dodd (Beirut: American University of Beirut Press, 1991), 263–82 at 271. In the case of Hishām, the retreat to this unnamed monastery was in an effort to avoid an outbreak of plague.
21. See Andrew T. Crislip, *From Monastery to Hospital: Christian Monasticism and the Transformation of Health Care in Late Antiquity* (Ann Arbor, MI: University of Michigan Press, 2005), 100–2.
22. Mourad, 'Christian Monks in Islamic Literature', 82–3.
23. See chapter IV 'Asceticism and Sufism' in I. Goldziher, *Introduction to Islamic Theology and Law*, trans. A. and R. Hamori (Princeton, NJ: Princeton University Press, 1981), and T. Andrae, 'Zuhd and Mönchtum', *Le Monde Oriental* 25 (1931), 296–327.
24. Mourad, 'Christian Monks in Islamic Literature', 85.
25. Among several examples of this phenomenon within the *Ḥilyat al-awlīyāʾ* is the passage concerning Mālik ibn Dīnār of Baṣra (d. 749) and his visit to a Christian hermit. See Abū Nuʿaym al-Iṣfahānī, *Ḥilyat al-awlīyāʾ wa-ṭabaqāt al-aṣfiyāʾ* (10 vols) (Beirut: Dār al-Kitāb al-ʿArabī, 1967–8), vol. 2, 365.
26. Louis Massignon, *Essay on the Origins of the Technical Language of Islamic Mysticism*, trans. and intro. Benjamin Clark (Notre Dame, IN: The University of Notre Dame Press, 1997).
27. Tor Andrae, *In the Garden of Myrtles*, trans. Birgitta Sharpe (Albany, NY: State University of New York Press, 1987).
28. Gedaliahu Stroumsa, 'From Master of Wisdom to Spiritual Master in Late

Antiquity', in *Religion and the Self in Antiquity*, eds David Brakke, Michael L. Satlow and Steven Weitzman (Bloomington, IN: Indiana University Press, 2005), 183–96.

29. Stroumsa provides the examples of Lucilius and Seneca to make this point. See Stroumsa, 'From Master of Wisdom', 189.
30. Andrae, *In the Garden of Myrtles*, 12. Annemarie Schimmel also commented on this contact between Christian hermits and the early Islamic mystical traditions but tended to downplay the possibility of any direct Christian influence. See Schimmel, *The Mystical Dimensions of Islam* (Chapel Hill, NC: The University of North Carolina Press, 1975). 34–5.
31. The tenth-century bibliographer Ibn al-Nadīm references several books dedicated to monasteries in his *Kitāb al-fihrist*; unfortunately, none of these works has survived. See Ibn al-Nadīm, *Kitāb al-fihrist*, ed. M. Riḍā Tajaddud, 3rd edn (Beirut: Dār al-Masīrah, 1988), 105–28. The only extant example of this literary genre is the *Kitāb al-diyārāt* of al-Shābushtī, which likely contains some of the information found in the earlier volumes. Working with Ibn al-Nadīm's index, there are several other works within the category of *diyārāt* books listed in the editor's introduction, including ones by prominent medieval Muslim authors, such as Abū al-Faraj al-Iṣfahānī. It is suggested that al-Shābushtī likely incorporated much of this material into his own compilation, *Kitāb al-diyārāt.* See introduction in *Kitāb al-diyārāt*, ed. Kūrkīs ʿAwwād (Beirut: Dār al-Rāʾid al-ʿArabī, 1986), 36–48.
32. See Kilpatrick, 'Monasteries Through Muslim Eyes', 21–3.
33. Ibid. 23. Perhaps particularly involving young, unveiled women.
34. Habīb Zayyāt, *al-Diyārāt al-naṣrāniyya fī al-Islām* (Beirut: Dār al-Mashriq, 1999), 69.
35. Intoxicants had of course been categorically prohibited in the Qurʾān, at least in terms of their consumption by Muslims. See Qurʾān 5:90 and 2:219.
36. Lukas Schachner, '"I Greet You My Brethren. Here are 15 shentasse of Wine": Wine-Production in the Early Monasteries of Egypt and the Levant', *ARAM* 17 (2005), 157–84 at 174. There are some indications in existing papyri that seventh-century monasteries even met their tax obligations with deliveries of wine to local authorities.
37. Philip Mayerson, 'The Wine and Vineyards of Gaza in the Byzantine Period', *Bulletin of the American Schools of Oriental Research* 257 (Winter 1985), 75–80. Mayerson ties the popularity of the Gaza wine (*vinum Gazetina*) with the rise

of monasticism in the area and an increasing number of western pilgrims to the region from the fourth to sixth century.

38. *Vita Sancti Hilarionis*, ed. J. P. Migne, Patrologia Latina 23 (1864), 42–4. It seems that at times Hilarion would intentionally time his visits to other monastic centres in accordance with the harvesting of the grapes from their vineyards. One report claims that a miracle resulted from Hilarion's blessing of the grapes that belonged to a certain monk known as Sabas, increasing the yield to 300 jars of wine from the estimated 100 jars prior to his arrival.
39. Troupeau, 'Les Couvents', 270–5. The wine-production capacity of monasteries would not have been the only facilitating component to any would-be disreputable intentions on the part of Muslim visitors, for these monastic settlements of the Levant were often located well away from the major towns and population centres. They would have been detached therefore from the prying eyes of the general population as well as from the judgemental gaze of the urban *ʿulamāʾ*. See Ira M. Lapidus, *A History of Islamic Societies* (Cambridge: Cambridge University Press, 2002), 100–1. Lapidus asserts here that 'Urban Islam embodied fundamentalist, conservative, puritanical, accomodationist, realist, and millenarian religious attitudes.' As well he states, 'the urban ʿulamāʾ affirmed religious equality, political accountability, and personal values based on the Qurʾanic revelation'.
40. The caveat to using a book like the *Kitāb al-diyārāt* for historical research has been noted. It is, in reality, not strictly designed as a work of history. In addition to a collection of anecdotes concerning monasteries, al-Shābushtī includes historical information, topographical and architectural data, the works of Arab poets on monasteries, and information concerning Christian festivals. While this compilation of material has been previously characterised as 'guide to the night-life in Iraq and Egypt', rather than a book of history, much of the material contained in the *Kitāb al-diyārāt* still contains valuable information concerning the status of monasteries into the Islamic period, as well as the manner in which these entities were interpreted by contemporary Muslims. See Ewald Wagner, *Grundzüge der klassischen arabischen Dichtung*, vol. 2, *Die arabische Dichtung in islamischer Zeit* (Darmstadt: Wissenschaftliche Buchgesellschaft, 1988), 43, and Hilary Kilpatrick, 'Representations of Social Intercourse between Muslims and non-Muslims in Some Medieval Adab Works', in *Muslim Perceptions of Other Religions: A Historical Survey*, ed. J. Waardenburg (Oxford: Oxford University Press, 1999), 213–24 at 217.
41. Al-Shābushtī, *Kitāb al-diyārāt*, 54. The monasteries mentioned here are all

situated on the banks of the Tigris near Baghdād. For the Arabic *khimār*, I have translated as 'taverns/wine-sellers'.

42. Ibid. 69.
43. Ibid. 62.
44. Ibid. 46.
45. David Rice, 'Deacon or Drink: Some Paintings from Samarra Re-Examined', *Arabic* 5:1 (January 1958), 15–33 at 32.
46. See Elizabeth Fowden, 'Christian Monasteries and Umayyad Residences in Late Antique Syria', 175–92.
47. Barthold, 'The Caliph ʿUmar II and Conflicting Reports on His Personality', 80–1.
48. The production of wine was lauded as a dignified pursuit in some circumstances and condemned as a potentially morally damaging endeavour at other times. See Schachner, 'I Greet You My Brethren', 158–9. The consumption of wine amongst the brethren was commonly the subject of strict legislation for monastic communities. For several examples of such guidelines, see *Rules of Mar Rabbūlā*, in *Syriac and Arabic Documents Regarding Legislation Relative to Syrian Asceticism*, ed. Arthur Vööbus, Papers of the Estonian Theological Society in Exile no. 40 (Stockholm: ETSE, 1960), 27.
49. Al-Shābushtī, *Kitāb al-diyārāt*, 241.
50. Adam Mez, *The Renaissance of Islam: History, Culture and Society in the 10th Century Muslim World* (New York, NY: AMS Press, 1975), English trans. Salahuddin Khuda Bukhsh and D. S. Margoliouth, at 40–1 and 418–26.
51. Muhammad Umar Memon, *Ibn Taymiyyah's Struggle Against Popular Religion: with an annotated translation of his 'Kitāb iqtiḍāʾ al-ṣirāṭ al-mustaqīm mukhālafat aṣḥāb al-jaḥīm'* (The Hague: Mouton, 1976), 1–4; cf. Boaz Shoshan, 'High Culture and Popular Culture in Medieval Islam', *Studia Islamica* 73 (1991), 67–107 at 86.
52. It should perhaps be recalled too that, according to the *Sīra* of Ibn Isḥāq, it was the beauty of Christian liturgical chant (*fa-samiʿatu aṣwātahum fīhā wa hum yuṣallūna*) that first prompted Salmān al-Fārisī to abandon his ancestral Zoroastrianism and embrace Christianity, prior to his conversion to Islam. See Ibn Hishām, *al-Sīra al-Nabawiyya*, ed. Mustafa al-Saqqa *et al.* (4 vols) (Beirut: Dār al-Khayr, 1997), vol. 1, 186.
53. Shahîd has mentioned a similar possibility in relation to the Arab ethnic identity of the Ghassānids and the early Islamic interest in monastic sites. See *Byzantium and the Arabs in the Sixth Century* (Washington, DC: Dumbarton Oaks, 1995–),

vol. 2, 92. This is not however to suggest that these types of interactions were observed exclusively on the most rural or outlying level. The tenth-century historian Eutychius, for instance, mentions Muslims gathering at the Church of Bethlehem and at the Church of Constantine in Jerusalem for prayer. See *Annales, Corpus Scriptorum Christianorum Orientalium. Scriptores Arabici*, ser. 3, tome 6, 17.

54. For a discussion as to when and why the more rigidly defined confessional structures may have emerged, see Donner, *Muhammad and the Believers*, chapter 5.
55. The monastic rules initiated by Basil of Caesarea, in the fourth century, demanded this philanthropic directive under the auspices of the μιμητὴς Χριστοῦ, stating: 'Whosoever is engaged in the imitation of Christ . . . you must engage in charitable giving, and do not withhold kindness for humanity, and do not disregard humanity . . . each day you must endeavor to help those in need, and be of assistance to those before yourselves.' See *Sanctus Basilius Magnus, Sermo Asceticus*, Patrologia Cursus Completus, Series Graeca 31, ed. J. P. Migne, col. 648B. Also see Demetrios J. Constantelos, *Byzantine Philanthropy and Social Welfare* (New Brunswick, NJ: Rutgers University Press, 1968), 88–9.
56. Constantelos, *Byzantine Philanthropy*, 90.
57. John Binns, *Ascetics and Ambassadors of Christ: The Monasteries of Palestine 314–631* (Oxford: Clarendon Press, 1994), 54–5.
58. The monastic colonies at Sketis and Kellia developed these *xenodocheion* by the late fourth century. See Marilyn Dunn, *The Emergence of Monasticism: From the Desert Fathers to the Early Middle Ages* (Oxford: Blackwell Publishers, 2000), 14. Andrew Crislip ultimately traces this concept to the rise of the medieval hospital. By the fifth century the term *nosokomeion*, or 'place for the care of the sick', had become virtually interchangeable with the monastic-associated designations of the *xenodocheion/xenon*, 'hostel for strangers' and *ptôchotropheion*, 'place for the nourishment of the poor'. See Crislip, *From Monastery to Hospital*, 102.
59. *Life of George of Choziba*, 'Sancti Georgii Chozebitae: Confessoris et Monachi Vita Auctore Antonio ejus discipulo', ed. and Latin trans. C. Houze, *Analecta Bollandiana* 7 (1888), 115.
60. Al-Shābushtī, *Kitāb al-diyārāt*, 171.
61. See ibid. editor's footnote no. 1 at 163.
62. The narrator's full name is al-Faḍl ibn al-ʿAbbās ibn Māʾmūn, meaning that he was, by birth, a ranking prince within the ʿAbbāsid administration.
63. Al-Shābushtī, *Kitāb al-diyārāt*, 163–5. It is also worth noting here that at one

point in this encounter the monk pulls aside al-Faḍl to inquire as to who exactly the two men with him were. He simply answers that they were 'young men involved in military service'. In other words, the superior apparently had no idea that his monastery was granting hospitality to people as important as the caliph himself and his entourage. The fourteenth-century historian al-ʿUmarī also refers to the concept of monastic hospitality in a number of passages within the *Masālik al-abṣār*. In one example, a group of Muslims visit Dayr Bārīshā at Mosul and actually object to the lavish reception they encounter, feeling it unnecessary. The monk in charge responds, 'By God, this is our custom which we do for all those who enter into this abode.' Although this particular episode refers to a later, tenth-century encounter, it clearly illustrates the continued image of monastic hospitality, even as it applied to Muslims, well into the Islamic period. See al-ʿUmarī, *Masālik al-abṣār fī mamālik al-amṣār*, ed. A. Zakī Pasha (5 vols) (Cairo: Dār al-Kutub al-Miṣriyya, 1924), vol. 1, 205.

64. Al-Shābushtī, *Kitāb al-diyārāt*, 177.
65. Yāqūt, *Muʿjam al-buldān* 2, 512.
66. Steven Judd, 'Reinterpreting al-Walīd ibn Yazīd', *Journal of the American Oriental Society* 128 (2008), 439–58 at 451. The author makes the point that al-Walīd's habitual immoral behaviour, at least as perceived by the more religious factions within the caliphate, would ultimately cost him the throne and his life.
67. Yāqūt, *Muʿjam al-Buldān* 2, 512.
68. Judd, 'Reinterpreting al-Walīd ibn Yazīd', 439–40.
69. Robert Hamilton, *Walid and His Friends: An Umayyad Tragedy* (Oxford: Oxford University Press, 1988), 86. Hamilton discusses this appreciation in an Umayyad context, citing several instances of al-Walīd ibn Yazīd visiting monasteries.
70. See the Muslim appreciation for Christian art in Gerard Troupeau, 'Les Églises d'Antioche chez les Auteurs Arabes', in *L'Orient au coeur*, eds F. Sanagustin *et al.* (Paris: Maisonneuve et Larose, 2001), 319–27.
71. Yāqūt, *Muʿjam al-buldān* 2, 533. Could this perhaps be a reference to a religious icon? The word employed here (*ṣura*) is ambiguous in this context.
72. Troupeau, 'Les Églises d'Antioche', 319–27.
73. The book is traditionally attributed to Abū al-Faraj al-Iṣfahānī (d. 967), though this is perhaps inaccurate. See the introduction to *The Book of Strangers: Mediaeval Arabic Graffiti on the Theme of Nostalgia*, trans. Patricia Crone and Shmuel Moreh (Princeton, NJ: Markus Wiener Publishing, 2000).

74. Al-Iṣbahānī, *Kitab adab al-ghurabā'* (Beirut: Dār al-Kitāb al-Jadīd, 1993), 24–5.
75. Al-Shābushtī, *Kitāb al-diyārāt*, 289–90.
76. Ibid. 284.
77. Ibid. 300. The meaning of *khanāfis* is 'dung beetles/scarabs'.
78. Ibid. 300.
79. Ibid. 302.
80. Ibid. 304.
81. Ibid. 312.
82. Yāqūt, *Mu'jam al-buldān* 2, 538. Similar stories form a relatively common topoi of legends circulating between Christian groups of the Near East as well. Christian Sahner references an example, from the writings of Anastasius of Sinai, of Muslims striking an image of Saint Theodore with an arrow while visiting a church near Damascus. As recounted, because of this sacrilege, the Muslims were struck dead by God's wrath. See Christian Sahner, *Christian Martyrs Under Islam: Religious Violence and the Making of the Muslim World* (Princteon, NJ: Princeton University Press, 2018), 91.
83. Yāqūt, *Mu'jam al-buldān* 2, 510.
84. Ibid. 510.
85. Elizabeth Key Fowden, *The Barbarian Plain: Saint Sergius between Rome and Iran* (Berkeley, CA: University of California Press, 1999), 189. See also Dorothée Sack, 'St Sergios in Resafa: Worshipped by Christians and Muslims Alike', in *Religious Identities in the Levant from Alexander to Muhammad: Continuity and Change*, eds M. Blömer, A. Lichtenbeger and R. Raja (Turnhout: Brepols, 2015), 271–82. In pre-Islamic times the shrine at Ruṣāfa served to solidify the social bonds between the local nomadic and sedentary communities. The mutual acceptance of the importance of the saint, particularly concerning religious festivals and fairs associated with the shrine, would have been instrumental in establishing economic partnerships between the sedentary and nomadic elements. In this way the popular devotion to St Sergius in Syria may be comparable to the ties between the Quraysh and Tamīm, a nomadic tribe that assisted in the Meccan caravan trade. The bond between them was ultimately consolidated through patronage of the pagan sanctuary at Mecca in the pre-Islamic era, by granting these nomads certain functions during urban cultic rituals. See Fred Donner, *The Early Islamic Conquests* (Princeton, NJ: Princeton University Press, 1981), 28.
86. Josef M. Meri, *The Cult of Saints among Muslims and Jews in Medieval Syria* (Oxford: Oxford University Press, 2002), 5. For a similar situation of mutual

saint veneration for Muslims and Jews in North Africa as well as communal veneration of sacred sites between Christians and Muslims in Palestine, see Mahmoud Ayoub, 'Cult and Culture: Common Saints and Shrines in Middle Eastern Popular Piety', in *Religion and Culture in Medieval Islam*, eds Richard G. Hovannisian and Georges Sabagh (Cambridge: Cambridge University Press, 1999), 103–15.

87. Troupeau, 'Les Couvents', 276–7.
88. Meri, *The Cult of Saints*, 4.
89. Ibid. 210.
90. Lance Laird, 'Boundaries and Baraka: Christians, Muslims and a Palestinian Saint', in *Muslims and Others in Sacred Space*, ed. Margaret Cormack (Oxford: Oxford University Press, 2013), 40–73.
91. Khiḍr, or al-Khaḍir, has been associated through exegesis, *ḥadīth* and the *qiṣaṣ al-anbiyā'* with the unnamed companion to Moses in the Qur'ān, 18:60–2. See A. J. Wensinck, 'al-Khadir', in the *Encyclopedia of Islam, 2nd edition* (Leiden: Brill, 1990), 902–5, and also Ethel Sara Wopler, 'Khiḍr and the Politics of Place: Creating Landscapes of Continuity', in *Muslims and Others in Sacred Space*, ed. Margaret Cormack (Oxford: Oxford University Press, 2013), 147–63.
92. Laird, 'Boundaries and Baraka', 46–7.
93. Ibid. 47.
94. Ignaz Goldziher, 'Veneration of Saints in Islam', *Muslim Studies* 2 (1971), 290–305.
95. Boaz Shoshan, 'High Culture and Popular Culture in Medieval Islam', *Studia Islamica* 73 (1991), 86.
96. Peter Brown, 'Holy Men', in *The Cambridge Ancient History*, vol. 14, eds A. Cameron, B. Ward-Perkins and M. Whitby (Cambridge: Cambridge University Press, 2001), 781–810 at 796. The concept of pilgrimage as a highly developed ritual system flourished among the Arabs of Late Antiquity, even prior to their encounter with Christianity. As Shahîd has pointed out, the extensive vocabulary associated with pilgrimage rites in the Arabic language is a testament to the importance of the institution. Shahîd indeed suggests that the breadth of the Arabic vocabulary associated with pilgrimage is 'almost unique': in addition to the most basic verb of *ḥajja*, meaning 'to perform pilgrimage', there are the derivatives such as *ḥajj*, 'pilgrimage'; *ḥājj*, 'a pilgrim'; *maḥajja*, 'pilgrimage route' and/or 'pilgrimage centre'; as well as the month known as *Dhū al-Ḥijja*, originally denoting the time of the annual pilgrimage. See 'Arab Christian Pilgrimages in the Proto-Byzantine Period (V–VII Centuries)', in *Pilgrimage*

and Holy Space in Late Antique Egypt, ed. D. Frankfurter (Leiden: Brill, 1998), 373–89, see footnote on 374. This is contrasted with the scarcity of pilgrimage terms in Greek. One of the Greek terms used in Ottoman times, that being χατζής for 'pilgrim', was itself a derivation from the Arabic root of *ḥajj*.

97. Ibn Saʿd, *Ṭabaqāt al-kabīr* 7, 326.
98. Abū Nuʿaym al-Iṣfahānī, *Ḥilyat al-awliyāʾ* 4, 91.

5

Refuge in the Bosoms of the Mountains: Medieval Muslim Appreciation for Christian Monasticism and Intersecting Boundaries of Confessional Identity

Towards the Possibilities for Ecumenism

The previous chapters have been devoted to demonstrating the flexible parameters for monastic existence as well as substantiating an elevated religious and social distinction for monastic communities throughout the early Islamic period. The question remains, however, as to precisely why these institutions and their guardians would have been accorded such a privileged position within Islam during its formative era. In other words, what was the origin of this reverence for Christian ascetic communities that appears to have been transferred into a Muslim context? In turn, what can this tell us about the nature of Islam and confessional distinctions in the early period?

In an attempt to answer such a query, this section of research will posit that the ultimate source of early Muslim interest in monasteries is articulated through an inclusive, piety-centred religious orientation that extends from the late antique period. As demonstrated in the previous sections, flexible parameters for confessional identity would appear to have been a defining characteristic of devotion throughout this period. This inclination, at least in its nascency, may then be considered a component in an early 'believers' movement.[1] In turn, membership within such a group would have been based upon a shared core of spiritual doctrines, without regard to exclusive sectarian identities.

Fred Donner has suggested, based on a certain limited criteria of beliefs and actions (for example: the absolute conviction in the one God, an impending Day of Judgement, and personal righteousness),[2] that it is not unreasonable to conclude that in the earliest stages of Islam, people from amongst the *ahl al-kitāb* would have been included in the 'community of believers'. Christians and Jews could therefore have fallen under the rubric of 'believers', or *mu'minūn*, provided they individually fit into these set categories. In other words, 'the community of Believers was originally conceptualized independent of confessional identities'.[3] In such a case, this attention to personal righteousness would appear to have been the driving force behind the cross-confessional appreciation for monastic life.

This theory revolves around distinct terminology employed within the Qur'ān concerning the identification of communities of 'Believers', or *mu'minūn*, and communities of 'Muslims', or *muslimūn* – the latter having the literal meaning of 'those who submit'. According to Donner's thesis, these two terms are neither interchangeable nor synonymous, though later Muslim tradition has tended to emphasise the equivalency of the two designations.[4] Due to the frequency of occurrences in the text of *mu'minūn* as opposed to the term *muslim/muslimūn* – a comparison of nearly a thousand occurrences to fewer than seventy-five – the claim could be put forth that a 'community of Believers' may have been the way the early community actually conceived of itself above any other categorisation.[5]

It is important to also mention here that the term *muslim*, possessing a rather general meaning of 'those who submit' in the context of the origins period as well as its employment in the Qur'ān, became increasingly more defined by classical exegetes and historians in the Islamic tradition. The term itself has since come to have a more technical meaning.[6] The core concept behind the term, in its original sense, was potentially more inclusive in the early period, as would have necessarily been the case for the term *mu'minūn*. In the terminology of the sacred text, therefore, a *muslim* would have essentially been defined as a 'committed monotheist'[7] and *islām* as 'committed monotheism in the sense of committing oneself to God's will'.[8] Such a conclusion is supported in *Sūrat Āl 'Imrān*:

> O People of the Book, why do you argue about Abraham when both the Torah and the Gospel were not revealed until after him? Have you no sense? Indeed, you have argued about things of which you have some knowledge.

> Must you now argue about that which you know nothing? God knows, but you know not. Abraham was neither Jew nor Christian. He was a *ḥanīfan musliman* and not an idolater. (*Sūrat Āl ʿImrān* 3:65–7)

Though the exact translation of the term *ḥanīf* has been subject to debate, it is clear within the passage that the term *muslim* is the adjective of *ḥanīf*. G. R. Hawting has taken this problematic term as an identification of pure monotheism; a non-denominational form of the original *dīn Ibrāhīm*.[9] Wellhausen similarly concluded that the religion of the *ḥanīfiyya* represents those that had shunned paganism, but alternatively had not fully embraced either Judaism or Christianity.[10] If such an explanation is accepted, then the phrase would be referring to the religion practised by Abraham, the *ḥanīfan musliman*, as a kind of primitive and non-distinct monotheism – with the adjectival phrase referring to Abraham perhaps being translated as 'he was a submitting monotheist'.

As the passage in *Sūrat Āl ʿImrān* suggests, the religion of Abraham was viewed by early Muslims as the original, untainted form of monotheism. It is precisely this fundamental type of monotheistic belief that the Qurʾān was seeking to confirm. Other scriptures as well, such as the Torah and the Gospel, had been delivered in a continuum of this divine message since the time of Abraham; but either through ignorance or wilful distortion, the message had become confused over the ages.[11] The Qurʾān counsels that if Jews and Christians truly understood their own sacred texts, they would realise that the Muslim scripture validates what had been previously revealed. *Sūrat al-anʿām* claims as much in the following verse:

> This is the Book which we have sent down, blessed and confirming what has come before it, that you might warn the mother city and those that dwell around it. Those who believe in the Hereafter believe in it, and they are maintaining their prayers. (*Sūrat al-anʿām* 6:92)

Donner further proposes that this proper Belief, in terms of the Qurʾānic usage, is actually tantamount to pious behaviour.[12] It is enjoined to the believers in this way by virtue of *Sūrat al-baqara*, for example, which states:

> Righteousness (*al-birr*) does not consist in whether you turn your face toward the East or the West. Rather the righteous man is he who believes

in God and the Last Day, in the angels and the Book of the prophets; who, though he cherishes it, gives his own wealth to kinsfolk, to orphans, the indigent, to the traveler in need, and beggars, and for the redemption of slaves; who attends his prayers and renders the alms levy; who is true to his promises and steadfast in trial and adversity and in times of war. Such are the true believers; such are those who fear God (*hum al-muttaqūna*). (*Sūrat al-baqara* 2:177)

Christian ascetics of Late Antiquity would have easily identified with such a set of precepts, as fundamental importance was traditionally placed on the holy man's personal conduct.[13] For the fourth-century monk Paphnutius of Scetis, this meant that virtuous thought must necessarily be translated into righteous action:

For the faithful and good man must think the thoughts sent by God; he must speak what he thinks and act according to what he says. For if the way a person lives is not in accord with the truth of his words, then such a person is like bread without salt.[14]

The uncompromising demand for righteousness in personal conduct is also exhibited in various ways throughout the cycles for monastic regulations in the Syriac tradition. To this effect, the fourth-century *Admonitions* (*ṭōb zawhrē*) *of Mār Ephrēm* begin:

My brother: be vigilant in your true teaching which you receive from your teachers. Nothing should be before your sight except a constant obedience (*mushtam'unutē amīnutē*).[15] When you walk on the street, dignify your steps and discipline your look; and control your countenance; and do not eat anything on the street so that the discipleship should be despised. Select for yourself foremost diligence in learning; give great honor to your fathers, to your masters, and to those who see you; your brothers will profit by you, and your companions will imitate the manner of your steadfastness.[16]

In addition to devout belief, the good deeds that were so much a part of the monastic vocation would have been particularly concerned with the care of the poor and the sick. The conviction of charity in this sense was institutionalised by monastics in the form of the *διακονίαι*, or hospices for the needy.[17] The late sixth-century ecclesiastical historian John of Ephesus not only sees these acts in terms of their practical value but views them as an integral spiritual exercise within asceticism; ultimately undertaken as an expression of 'humility before God'.[18] As will be further discussed, the association between humility and piety was emphasised in the early Islamic tradition as well.[19]

The emphasis placed on rigorous piety for inclusion into the community of 'believers' could certainly seem to have applied to the concept of monasticism in its late antique context, perhaps above any other categories of religious identity. While the possibility for the inclusion of such piety-minded Jews and Christians into the 'believers' community applies more specifically to the first few decades of the early Islamic period, after which such boundaries would have become increasingly more defined, this research proposes that the relics of this ecumenical perspective, or non-confessional stance toward acceptance of non-Muslims into the 'community of believers', was an important determinant in the initial interactions between monastic communities and Muslims. This would also have played a significant role in the shaping of later policies governing monks and monasteries under state control.

'The Monks whom Salmān Served' and a Fluid Confessional Matrix

We should now return to the conversion narrative of Salmān al-Fārisī, as discussed in the opening chapter of this book, as a key to understanding the perception of monasticism on the part of medieval Muslim commentators. It is worth remembering that the 'guides' along this spiritual sojourn of Salmān are explicitly identified as Christian ascetics. The years spent serving and studying under these various religious masters is ultimately the way in which the path to Islam is slowly revealed. The relationship between Salmān and his teachers is analogous to that of an initiate, or acolyte, and his monastic mentor. The narrative elements of travel between spiritual advisers, each in turn pointing the way to another source of further illumination, clearly parallels themes found in late antique monastic literature and hagiographies.[20] The *topos* of the itinerant ascetic, it has been suggested, may actually constitute an early form of monastic pilgrimage. The wanderer here is not necessarily a *peregrinus* to a particular shrine or sacred place,[21] but rather a seeker of knowledge via the peripatetic life. The deliberate quest to make contact with holy people, or at least the prospect of meeting other pious figures along the road, sharing their life stories, and gaining wisdom from collective experience are themes that resonate throughout the literature of this period.[22] Moreover, these figures are acknowledged within the narrative as supreme fonts of religious virtue and knowledge. Such a motif occurs as well throughout sources from Late Antiquity[23] and even into the Islamic period in the form of Muslim hagiographical texts.[24] The defining characteristics of the holy men in this account do indeed correspond to a severity in ascetic practice and wisdom in spiritual affairs. It is likely not a coincidence that a location such as Naṣībīn, or Nisibis, for instance, had been recognised as a premier centre of monastic scholarship since antiquity.[25]

As this portion of the narrative comes to a close, an alternate ending is supplied in the form of an *isnād* traced to ʿUmar ibn ʿAbd al-Azīz. The variant account claims that Salmān's teacher in ʿAmmurīya does not send him directly to the prophet among the Arabs, but instead to a particular place in Syria where he will find a man of exceeding virtue and miraculous powers. Salmān follows his instructions and finds this man living between two thickets,[26] periodically healing the masses of sick and infirm that appear before him. In phrasing, that is perhaps reminiscent of the travels by the unnamed Arabian prophet,[27] this holy man 'passes between each thicket (*yakhruj fī kull sana min hādhihī al-ghayḍa ilā hādhihī al-ghayḍa mustajayzā*), where people gather for his curative attention'. When Salmān eventually makes his way through the throngs of witnesses, he inquires of this mystic concerning the *dīn Ibrāhīm*, the *ḥanīfiyya*; and the narrative takes an unexpected turn. The last lines of the passage state:

> The man replied, 'you have questioned me about something that people today do not ask about! The time has arrived that a prophet will be sent forth with this religion [the *dīn Ibrāhīm*] from among the people of the *ḥaram*. Go to him, and he will deliver it to you.'. Then he again entered [into the thicket]. The Messenger of God then said, 'if what you have told me is true, ʿO Salmān, then you met Jesus the son of Mary.'[28]

So, in this latter, alternate account at the narrative's conclusion the figure of Jesus[29] is invoked to provide the seeker, Salmān, with a final set of instructions for his religious quest. The end of the passage then depicts the Persian sitting before the Prophet Muḥammad and relating this story of his encounter with the mystic 'between the thickets'. What is in effect being described here is a continuum of revelation on the basis of this *ḥanīfiyya*, from the Prophet Abraham, through Jesus, and culminating in the message of Muḥammad. Quite literally, in the case of this last passage, Jesus is depicted as pointing the way to Islam. The wise teachers of Salmān as well are represented as junctures along this spiritual path, apparently without regard to denominational constraints. It is only by virtue of his long spiritual journey as a monastic acolyte amongst these pious Christians that his position as a *ṣaḥābī*, or Companion, comes to be realised. The quest for the *ḥanīfiyya*, or the purest expression of ancient monotheism, is at the heart of this sojourn. In its Qurʾānic context the *ḥanīfiyya* is itself entirely devoid of confessional affiliations, as demonstrated by the aforementioned verses 65–7 of *Sūrat Āl ʿImrān*.

In post-Qurʾānic Arabic terminology, the *ḥanīfiyya* tends to become synonymous with true belief or being a Muslim, the community itself sometimes being referred to as *al-ḥanīfa*.[30] The concept of a continuum of revelation applies here in that all of the prophets from antiquity to Muḥammad have revealed this same message – though it had become distorted over the ages by both the Jews and Christians.[31] If Christian monks, or at least factions within the monastic fold, were being understood by the early Muslim community to represent some of the few remaining repositories of this ancient tradition, it stands to reason that they should have also been seen as occupying an 'intermediate phase' along the continuum. Such would seem to indicate a fluid religious environment in which confessional distinction was of less concern than the level of personal piety demonstrated by a particular individual or institution. This *in-between stage* regarding the perception of monasticism appropriately parallels the presentation of ascetic teachers in the narrative of Salmān. They appear for the acolyte as a middle ground or transitional level of spiritual awareness, serving as necessary points of guidance down the path to Islam.

Aside from the traditional reverence for the 'holy man' that permeated across late antique confessional divides, the principal motif of piety that is so fervently stressed within the Qurʾān,[32] by virtue of terms like *birr* and *taqwā*,[33] may then provide an additional basis for a laudatory appraisal of Christian monasticism amongst early Muslims. This is surely the case with the exposition of al-Ṭabarī concerning monasticism. Though the terms *ruhbān*[34] and *rahbāniyya*[35] occur in a few passages within the Qurʾān itself, there is again the caveat of determining a harmonised scriptural assessment of the monastic institution.[36] Thus, we find in these Qurʾānic allusions what appear to be both positive and negative evaluations on the monastic station. As Christian Sahner has expressed in sharp terms: 'We see the Qurʾānic monk as both hero and villain: a loyal follower of Jesus and Muḥammad, but also a perverter of the true Christianity.'[37] The *Sīra*, in its capacity as scriptural exegesis, provides a model for this contrasting view. Still, there does seem to exist a particular connection between the Muslim *umma* and their monastic counterparts from the earliest stages of the Prophet's movement. These communities subscribed to remarkably similar ideas of religious devotion, chief among them being an uncompromising and demanding sense of personal piety.

Adding to the complexity of the early Muslim perception of monasticism are cases in which the institution may appear to be condemned, or at least specifically prohibited, within Islam.[38] A particular *ḥadīth*[39] is commonly cited as proof for the condemnation of monasticism by the Prophet Muḥammad, which states, 'There is no monasticism in Islam (*lā rahbāniyya fi-l-Islām*), the monasticism of this community is *jihād*.'[40] This reproach, as has been argued by Massignon,[41] may however not necessarily be directed against the religious merits of monasticism itself, but rather represents a criticism of the social values attached to the monastic lifestyle; the primary affront in this case being the institution of celibacy within ascetic circles. Ibn Saʿd (d. 845) therefore rejects monasticism as an innovation within Islam (*al-rahbāniyya al-mubtadaʿ*), likewise expressly due to the connection to an 'un-married life' as it existed in its Christian parameters.[42]

Early variations of this *ḥadīth* are also reported by ʿAbdallāh ibn al-Mubarāk (d. 797) in the *Kitāb al-jihād* in the following two formats:

> Every community has its monasticism (*li-kull umma rahbāniyya*), and the monasticism of this community is *jihād* in the path of God (*fi sabīl Allāh*).[43]

> A person mentioned itinerant asceticism (*al-sīyāḥa*) in front of the Prophet, to which the Prophet replied: 'God has given to us instead jihād in the path of God, and the extolment of God (*takbīr*) throughout every lofty place.'[44]

Reuven Firestone provides the basic meaning of the root j-h-d as

> exerting one's utmost efforts and abilities in relation to an 'other', and that other is usually defined as 'an object of disapprobation' that could range from a concrete human enemy, to Satan, or to the evil inclinations in one's own self (based on Lane 1863). *Jihād* can thus take on a range of meanings and can be applied to a number of different kinds of action. It easily becomes a religiously laden term because it represents the most basic ethical message of religion, that one must strive to do the good by overcoming the bad.[45]

The term *jihād* is frequently used as part of this aforementioned idiomatic expression 'in the path of God' to convey a sense of deep religious commitment to certain defined acts of devotion. Though in particular usage this term can be applied to the concept of war in defence of Islam and the community, it can also be employed in a more general sense referring to 'religious piety'.[46]

Massignon has moreover argued against the authenticity of this *ḥadīth*, claiming that it appears to have come into use no earlier than the middle to late second century of the Islamic era.[47] The reasoning behind Massignon's rejection of the *ḥadīth*, in its varied incarnations, is that the statement apparently comes into common acceptance at a time when Muslim polemics concerning Christianity were on the rise. Given the historical context suggested by Massignon, the statement could then be understood as forming part of a larger theological reproof against rival confessions. As well, he suggests that the *lā rahbāniyya* statement may have a connection to criticisms against the emerging Sufi traditions, stemming from the more conservative elements, as having arisen from foreign imports. Given the similarities between Christian and early Muslim ascetic practices, a statement such as this against monasticism could have concurrently served as a denunciation of Sufism and other mystical/ascetic developments within Islam.[48]

Even if Massignon's theory of dubious authenticity is accepted, the problematic interpretation of monasticism within the Qur'ān itself remains. The allegation that monasticism is an unwarranted innovation in religious practice, even in terms of its development within Christianity, may appear to be presented as such in *Sūrat al-ḥadīd*, which states:

> Then We sent Our messengers, following in their footsteps, and followed them with Jesus the son of Mary, and gave him the Gospel. And We placed in the hearts of those who followed him compassion (*ra'fa*), and mercy (*raḥma*). As for monasticism (*rahbāniyya*), they instituted themselves (*ibtad'ūhā*), We did not prescribe it for them except that they were seeking to please God; but they did not observe it faithfully (*fa-mā ra'awhā ḥaqq ri'āyatihā*). So, We rewarded those among them who are true believers; but many of them are disobedient (*wa-kathīr minhum fāsiqūn*).[49] (*Sūrat al-ḥadīd* 57:27)

According to Massignon, however, this passage is not to be understood in a pejorative sense. In clarification of this proposal, he claims that during the first three centuries of exegesis the passage was unanimously interpreted in terms of praise for the monastic life; but rather has been tendentiously interpreted by later exegetes, as well as contemporary orientalists, as a confirmation of the *lā rahbāniyya* thesis.[50] This would, according to his argument, essentially then be an illustration of an anachronistic projection of a spurious *ḥadīth* in an attempt to explain a problematic passage within the Qur'ān. Massignon further insists that a key phrase within the passage has been consistently misinterpreted. He then offers his own translation[51] of verse 27 of *Sūrat al-ḥadīd*, differing in certain critical elements from traditional interpretation, which reads:

> Then . . . Jesus, the son of Mary, and We gave him the gospel, and in the hearts of those who followed him We placed the seeds of readiness to forgive, compassion, and the monastic life (*rahbāniyya*). It was they who instituted it. We only prescribed it for them in order to make them desire to conform to what pleases God, but they have not followed the obligatory method of this rule for living; to those among them who have remained faithful We have given their recompense, but many among them have been sinners.

When juxtaposing the two interpretations of the passage, it is clear that the central issue concerns precisely where the term *rahbāniyya* should fit within the grammatical confines of the verse. Ultimately this is a question of whether or not the term belongs as a component to the phrase 'We placed in the hearts of those who followed him compassion, and mercy and monasticism' or rather begins a new clause such as 'As for monasticism, they invented it'. The essence of the verse, of course, changes considerably depending upon the resolution of this issue.

In an essay entitled *Das christliche Mönchtum im Koran*, Edmund Beck favours the view that *rahbānīya* is here syntactically joined to *ra'fa* (compassion) and *raḥma* (mercy) as attributes placed in the hearts of the pious.[52] Beck further interprets the passage to reflect that Muḥammad, particularly during the early Medinan period, revered the ascetic ideal and monasticism due to the extreme versions of piety exhibited by their devotees. The meaning of the passage is, however, that such radical devotion was ultimately incompatible with human frailty and was therefore not explicitly enjoined to the pious by divine decree.[53] Beck is essentially arguing that while the merits of monasticism were lauded, practical concerns compelled the Prophet to advocate for a more moderate set of parameters for worship.

Though not directly cited by Massignon or Beck, these interpretations for a reverent view of monasticism in *Sūrat al-ḥadīd* reflect the position reached by the twelfth-century exegete al-Zamakharī. In the *Kitāb al-kashshāf* he discusses, in positive terms, the impetus behind the development of monasticism. The explanation is two-fold: first, being a withdrawal into the spiritual in an attempt to distance oneself from external temptations (*fitan*), and secondly, as a necessary device to avoid persecution in the early years of the church.[54] Within this historical context, some members of the community had to seek refuge in the mountains and outlying areas. It was in this tradition of flight or retreat that the concept of monasticism first originated, according to al-Zamakharī's understanding. While not mandated by God, those who initiated this lifestyle were simply trying to please God as the verse implies.[55] He then goes on to explain that on a grammatical level, the phrase in question should be read as 'We placed in their hearts compassion and mercy and monasticism . . . We did not prescribe it for them except that they should seek, through it, the approval of God.'[56]

Of particular interest is that al-Zamakharī uses the term 'believers' (*mu'minūn*) when referring to the pious followers of the teachings of Jesus, those that were forced into virtual self-exile as a means of escaping oppression.[57] In other words, the exegete acknowledges that many of these 'true believers' resorted to the monastic lifestyle in an effort to preserve their religion. In contrast, the 'sinners' referred to later in the verse, the *fāsiqūn*, are those who had failed to uphold their contract with God. The idea of monasticism therefore holds considerable merit and is seen as a binding agreement between man and the divine: worthy of reward when practised faithfully but reprimanded when the terms of the monastic station were not carefully observed.[58]

The Qur᾽ānic exegete Muqātil ibn Sulaymān (d. 767), in an explanation of a seemingly unrelated verse (verse 87 within *Sūrat al-mā᾽ida*), provides an example from the life of Muḥammad that would appear to specifically prohibit severe versions of asceticism as a part of his community.[59] The Qur᾽ānic verse in question states: 'O you who have believed, do not prohibit the good things which God has made lawful for you (*mā ʿāḥalla Allāh lakum*), and do not transgress. Verily, God does not like transgressors.'[60] Muqātil then cites a *ḥadīth* in which several of the Prophet's leading Companions, among them ʿAlī ibn Abī Ṭālib and ʿUmar ibn al-Khaṭṭāb, had attempted to express rigorous piety by refusing food, maintaining an abstinence from women (their wives), and the wearing of course garments. Going even further, the group intended to set up monastic cells (*yabnū ṣawāmiʿa*) and take upon themselves the monastic life (*fa-yatarahhabū fihā*). The Prophet discovered their plans and promptly issued the following injunction: 'He who does not follow my example (*sunna*) is not one of my people . . . Our *sunna* concerns clothing, eating, and [the taking of] wives. Whoever averts this *sunna*, he does not belong to me.'[61]

The citation above clearly serves as another example from the *ḥadīth* corpus that seeks to restrict the influence of extreme asceticism within the Muslim community. In an article entitled 'Wa-Rahbāniyatan Ibtadʿūhā', Sarah Sviri uses this type of material to conclude that there was indeed a trend within early Islam to denounce monasticism.[62] For Sviri the strong stance against monasticism reflects the highly aggressive mentality of the early *umma*, as the traditionally monastic preference for being non-combatants and engaging in spiritual withdraw from the material world would have been seen as anathema to a militaristic society.[63] Her thesis represents a reaction against the scholarship of both Massignon and Beck.[64] However, there are reasons to believe, as suggested by Massignon, that this negative view of monasticism appears rather late in the Islamic tradition and may have held ulterior purposes than just admonishing Christian asceticism. In a consonant analysis of this *ḥadīth*, Sahner has juxtaposed the eighth- and ninth-century Muslim views of monasticism as both 'an emblem of pure, undiluted monotheism, but on the other hand, as a symbol of a corrupt and decadent church'. A powerful denunciation of the practice therefore, canonised by virtue of the words of the Prophet himself, was perhaps intended to help Muslim ascetics differentiate themselves from their Christian parallels, at a time of 'heightened conversion and social mixing'.[65]

It may also be suggested that a key component within the *ḥadīth* provided by Muqātil has gone undervalued. While the centrepiece of the tradition is, of course, the Prophet's mandate concerning the *sunna*, there can also be found a subtle indication of the early view of monasticism as demonstrated by some of the Companions. It would appear that within their understanding, the truly pious existence could perhaps be achieved by emulating the example of monastic life (*fa-yatarahhabū fīhā*).[66] Though spurned by the Prophet in this instance, the episode may reveal an early Muslim inclination toward a connection between the monastic station and radical piety. Due to the grammatical ambiguity of the passage in *Sūrat al-ḥadīd*, the ninth-century theologian Muḥāsibī attempted to provide an exposition of verse 27 with the following statement:

> There is disagreement concerning this verse. Mujāhid interprets it to mean, 'We had only prescribed it for them in order to make them desire to conform to what pleases God, but it was they who instituted it. God placed in them the monastic life, for their own sake, and He reprimanded them later because they had abandoned it,' But Abū Imāma and others have made this interpretation: 'We did not prescribe it for them, rather they have instituted it only in order to please God, yet God has chastised them for abandoning it.' This second opinion is the most likely and it is the one that the majority of the learned within the community agree upon.
>
> Therefore, God said, 'They have not followed the method required for this rule of life.' If God criticized them because they did not follow a rule that He had not even prescribed as an obligation or part of the sacred law, what then will He do to those who do disavow obligatory rites, which if neglected will bring His wrath and separation from Him? So, He has made

piety the core element in the performance of these duties and all happiness in this world and the next.[67]

In both of the opinions cited by Muḥāsibī, the general view of monasticism appears to be laudatory, though ultimately dependent upon the degree of dedication held by the initiate. The monastic institution itself is therefore valid, even though it was not mandated by the divine. The taking of the monastic vow however, implies a serious commitment, and one that must be followed through to completion. It is the forsaking of the practice, once the sacred oaths had been sworn, or the inability to fulfil the requirements of the oath that comes under censure.

There are likewise two passages within *Sūrat al-tawba* that seemingly reveal a negative attitude toward monks and/or the perception of their status:

> The Jews say Ezra is the son of God, while the Christians say the Messiah is the son of God. Such are their assertions, by which they imitate the infidels of ancient times. God confound them! How perverse they are! They take their rabbis and monks as lords, in addition to God, as well as the Messiah, the son of Mary. (*Sūrat al-tawba* 9:30–1)

> O Believers, many are the rabbis and monks who devour the wealth of the people in falsehood and hinder them from the path of God. To those that gather up gold and silver and do not spend it in the cause of God, announce for them a woeful punishment. (*Sūrat al-tawba* 9:34)

It should be noted, however, concerning the two verses above, that there is no indication here that monasticism itself is being denounced a priori. In the case of *Sūrat al-tawba* verses 30–1, it would appear that the perception of monks and other clerical figures as deities themselves, as the people have 'taken them to be lords in addition to God' (*ittakhadhū ʿārbābān min dūni llāhi*), is the objectionable offence. Essentially then the passage has greater concerns over the popular view of such figures than with the lifestyle of its practitioners. In addition to the obvious reprimand against some members within the Christian and Jewish community who were guilty of 'associating' men with God, Wansbrough has interpreted these verses as part of a larger polemic against paganism and idolatry that fits into a specific historical context within the life of the Prophet.[68] It is, however, the existence of fraudulent monks that cheat people out of their possessions that prompts the criticism in verse 34. In both of these examples therefore, it is not the practice of monasticism that is under scrutiny, but rather the misconduct of some of its adherents or those associated with the institution that serve as the targets of reproach.[69]

Monastic Piety through an Ecumenical Lens

> Until the disciple of God seeks refuge in the bosoms of the mountains and the wombs of the wadīs and caverns, taking shelter with the wild beasts, settling at their watering holes and eating from the gardens of trees in its shade, he will not see that a blessing, complete as this one, is laid before him.

> . . . ḥattā yāwā murīd Allāh ilā aknāf al-jibāl wa-baṭūn al-awdiya wa-l-ghīrān yaẓallu maʿa al-waḥsh yaridu muwāridahā, yākul min ajinna al-shajar fī aẓillahā, lā yarā fī dhalika anna al-niʿma atamma ʿalā aḥadin minhā ʿalayhi.

The above passage, which opened the first chapter of this book, is contained within the *Kitāb al-ruhbān* (*The Book of Monks*) of the ninth-century Muslim moralist Ibn Abī al-Dunyā (d. 894 CE).[70] That a religious scholar such as Ibn Abī al-Dunyā would dedicate this degree of attention to the compilation of a text highlighting the merits of Christian monasticism is quite telling. The topical range of his own literary corpus was extensive, of which there were recorded to have been more than a hundred treatises,[71] yet the concern for ascetic practices forms a consistent thread throughout his work. The *Kitāb al-ruhbān* therefore certainly fits within his general pattern of illuminating the virtues of humility, fasting, fear of the divine, ritual weeping, silence in contemplation, and chiefly, the denunciation of the physical world.[72] The text likewise parallels certain elements of the *Apophthegmata Patrum*[73] that appear in medieval Muslim hagiographical accounts, often depicting Muslim ascetics, or *zuhhād*, in dialogue with Christian monks.[74] The collection of edifying sayings in this way is typical of the *akhbār* (singular *khabar*) genre for the period, which generally appear as recorded anecdotes involving the Companions of the Prophet (*ṣaḥāba*) as well as knowledgeable men from later generations.[75] The distinction here in the *Kitāb al-ruhbān* is that these *akhbār* relate to Christian ascetics and holy men, the separate accounts therein taking the form of short stories or dictums demonstrating monastic wisdom.

Though regarded as an ascetic himself, Ibn Abī al-Dunyā was also a highly public figure and was engaged in extensive teaching activities in and around his native Baghdād throughout the mid- to late ninth century. Such was his renown as a man of learning that he was granted an appointment as tutor for two future ʿAbbāsid caliphs, al-Muʿtaḍid (r. 279–89/892–902) and al-Mukhtafī (r. 289–95/902–8). That being said, however, Ibn Abī al-Dunyā is not easily confined within the conventional rubrics of *muḥaddith*, *mutakallim* or *faqīh*, in the classical sense of those terms.[76] Rather, his approach to scholarship rested more on the promotion of piety and advocating for a moral life than a demand for strict observance of dogmatic principles. Despite his legacy of erudition, in addition to his voluminous literary output, Ibn Abī al-Dunyā has remained a relatively minor figure in contemporary western scholarship, particularly when contrasted with other literary titans of the age such as al-Jāḥiẓ (d. 869) and Ibn Qutaybah (d. 889).[77]

It is here that the broader literary and cultural background of the author should merit mention, for the historical context of ninth-century Baghdād situates Ibn Abī al-Dunyā at the very epicentre of a vibrant intellectual landscape within the *formative period* of Islam.[78] It was, after all, in this period that a distinctly Muslim confessional identity was being formally articulated. The blossoming of Arabic literature and the advancement of the religious sciences facilitated the expression of this identity, with the great legal traditions, *ḥadīth* sciences, Qurʾānic exegesis, and the theological discipline of *kalām* all coming to maturity by the late ninth century. Michael Cook has described Muslim society in this period as a 'debate culture', a civilisation marked by religious diversity and pluralism but also one of polarisation between the more populist religion of traditionalists and those of elitist theologians.[79] As a component to this formative period framework there also appears to have been a fairly well-established mystical orientation within Islam,[80] and it is within this cross-section of religious society that Ibn Abī al-Dunyā would have yielded the greatest influence. Refining the concept of *zuhd*, which might be broadly interpreted here as 'asceticism',[81] was a concern for Muslim mystics and fits well within the theological 'debate-culture' of this period. This evolving ṣūfī tradition was, as judged by Montgomery Watt, a reaction against contemporary conditions; the piety and austerity-minded constituents of that movement voicing grievances against the materialism of their wider community and the misguided fervour of those in the more traditional religious sciences, judges and jurists. As Watt stated, 'Perhaps the ṣūfīs were seeking to escape from the frustration of living in a society that claimed to be religious, yet was controlled by men who only paid lip-service to the established religion.'[82] The *Kitāb al-ruhbān* champions such a disposition, held by Muslim *zuhhād* throughout this period, but interestingly, utilises the figure of the Christian monk as its exemplar.

Yet, the first ʿAbbāsid century is also characterised by the development of religious polemic between Christian and Muslim,[83] and it is within this aspect of the debate-culture that a treatise praising the monastic station might seem somewhat antithetical to the currents of that time. The *Risāla fi-l-radd ʿalā al-naṣārā* (*Response to the Christians*) of al-Jāḥiẓ was composed at the express commission of the caliph al-Mutawakkil (r. 232–47/847–61) and stands as a fine example of the emerging anti-Christian theological discourse. The promotion of this material by the Muslim court demonstrates not only awareness of a growing rivalry towards the *dhimma* of the realm, but also the conscious distillation of a categorically Islamic ideology into the imperial apparatus. The interest and intrusion of the state on religious matters, most importantly being the crystallisation of orthodoxy, reaches its zenith at approximately this moment, the period between the caliphates of al-Maʾmūn and al-Mutawakkil.[84] Other comparable polemical treatises were written in this same era – for example, the anti-Christian discourses of al-Qāsim ibn Ibrāhīm al-Rassī, Ibn Isḥāq al-Kindī and Muḥammad ibn Hārūn al-Warrāq – but these were carried out by experienced theologians and specialists.[85] The fact that al-Jāḥiẓ, known for the breadth of his literary interests, also endeavoured to refute Christian dogma illustrates the spread of such a movement into wider areas of scholarship and literature.[86] On the other side, Christian apologists were likewise active in defending their own traditions and critiquing Islam, adding to the tense nature of sectarian dialogue throughout the period.[87]

There are a multitude of reproaches laid upon Christians here in the *Risāla fi-l-radd ʿalā al-naṣārā* of al-Jāḥiẓ, including their proselytising zeal, their skill at convoluted philosophical arguments, their haughtiness, and their often-elevated positions within Muslim society. Doctrinally, however, the refutation against the concept of the Trinity takes centre stage, with al-Jāḥiẓ infamously attempting to demonstrate its absurdity by suggesting that even two Christian brothers, raised by the same father and mother, would necessarily have contradictory understandings of the tenet.[88] Disputations of this type against the Trinity, as well as their counterpoints in Christian apologetic justifications, had by this time become part of the standard practice of early ʿAbbāsid intellectual culture.[89]

The considerable range of medieval Muslim texts involving Christian monks[90] does however attest to the unremitting vitality of Near Eastern monasticism into the early Islamic centuries, and demonstrates a continued appreciation for their spiritual authority, even within a political milieu that was increasingly dominated by Islamic principles. As far as texts illustrating inter-confessional discourse, the *Ḥilyat al-awliyā*ʾ (*The Ornaments of the Saints*) of Abū Nuʿaym al-Iṣfahānī (d. 1038) should be listed here as an example of precisely this type of purported interaction between Christian monks and Muslim ascetics. Such encounters within the *Ḥilyat al-awliyā*ʾ commonly take the structure of *akhbār*, or anecdotes, that feature monks as the instruments of spiritual advice to Muslims. An account of the celebrated early Muslim mystic of Baṣra, Mālik ibn Dīnār (d. 749), seeking the counsel of an unnamed Christian ascetic serves this point well:

> Mālik ibn Dīnār stated: 'I journeyed up to a mountain, and upon it there lived a monk, so I went aloft to meet him,' saying: 'O monk, teach me about these things, which of the world, you have abandoned.' [the monk] then said: 'Are you not a follower of the Qurʾān and the *furqān*?' and then I replied: 'Yes! Yet I still need your advice concerning the renunciation of the world,', and he said: 'Verily then, I implore you, if you are able to construct a wall of iron between yourself and the desire for the things of this world, then that is what you must do!'[91]

A close approximation to this report by Mālik ibn Dīnār also appears in the *Kitāb al-ruhbān*, which states:

> A certain monk said: 'O Mālik ibn Dīnār. If you are able to construct a wall of iron between yourself and people, then you must do it!'

> qāla rāhib min al-ruhbān: yā Mālik ibn Dīnār, in istaṭaʿta an tajʿala baynak wa-bayna al-nās sūrān min al-ḥadīd, fa-ifʿil![92]

For both Massignon and Andrae, the formulation of later Muslim ascetic practices was indeed an inheritance of, or at least greatly influenced by, monasticism. Early Muslim communities, particularly those of the post-conquest era, would have lived amongst a great variety of Christian communities. As monasticism was a widespread phenomenon throughout North Africa, Arabia and the Levant, a degree of cultural exchange between Christian ascetics within those communities and their Muslim counterparts would seem implicit.[93] Additionally, many of those Christians from the regions of Ḥīra, Kūfa and Najrān were Arabs, perhaps furthering the potential for dialogue.[94] These areas too were prominently recognised from pre-Islamic antiquity for their monastic practices.[95]

As previously mentioned, the archetypal Christian holy man was that of a misanthropic outsider to society, clearly acknowledged as such within the late antique Christian tradition itself,[96] yet there was still much spiritual knowledge to be gained from personal interaction with these figures. This model for the transmission of esoteric wisdom transcended any rigid boundaries between religious orientations. Accounts of Muslim mystics visiting Christian ascetics therefore actually harmonise with even more ancient Mediterranean patterns for the diffusion of knowledge.[97] The paradigm proposes that one recognised as a sage himself/herself, regardless of a particular philosophical alignment, could greatly enhance their own insight from dialogue with other enlightened personalities.[98] While adherents of Islam were able to consult their own sacred scripture for purely theological concerns, those particular individuals that were seeking an experiential knowledge regarding ascetic piety and its methods of praxis would appear to have been naturally drawn to such practitioners from other religious backgrounds. The above-mentioned accounts relating to Mālik ibn Dīnār demonstrate precisely this kind of interaction. As well, this kind of contact reinforces Tor Andrae's insistence upon shared spiritual values between confessional groups in the early period of Islam.[99]

Throughout the late antique Christian tradition this model for the transmission of mystical knowledge is exemplified in the itinerant ascetic, traversing great distances to interact with 'living saints' as a kind of pilgrimage rite. The peripatetic life in this context presented an opportunity for spiritual growth by means of contact with other holy people.[100] Just as a traditional pilgrim in the Near East might expect to receive *baraka*, or 'blessings', in visitation to a certain shrine,[101] the wandering faithful could have achieved similar measures of sanctification by learning and studying with living holy men; the *baraka* in this case being embodied in the saints themselves and the wisdom they might impart.[102] In the early Christian imagination, these holy men served as reminders of the divine presence in the world, providing testimony of God's proximity to mankind through the charisma of the ascetic, the potency of his intercessory prayers, and/or the miracles conducted through his agency.[103] The Christian monk was thus perceived as endowed with this degree of spiritual insight based upon a rigorous austerity of lifestyle. Given the paramount mandate for personal piety found within Qur'ānic scripture,[104] it would appear reasonable for devout Muslims to seek out other like-minded, but not necessarily sectarian-aligned, wellsprings of religious knowledge.

The virtues of Christian asceticism as illustrated by the *Kitāb al-ruhbān* suggests that the image of the monk had changed little during the transition into the Islamic period. All the more important to this proposition is the palpable absence of a rigid confessional stance within the material. The *Kitāb al-ruhbān* is therefore devoid of any strictly theological or Christological controversies, its content simply conforming to issues of morality, piety and the inner life. With the lack of an explicitly Christian dogma here, many of these sayings, in other words, could just as easily have been interpreted as moral maxims from learned Muslim sages. This would seem to be in stark contrast to the aforementioned rise of polemical literature that dates from precisely the same period.

Our author, Ibn Abī al-Dunyā, also composed a short book entitled the *Kitāb al-wajal wa-tawaththuq bi-l-ʿamal* (*On Fear and Confidence in Activity*), in which there appears a section concerning an ancient Christian ascetic. This portion of the text, known as the *Ḥikāyat Anṭūnis al-sāʾiḥ* (*The Tale of Anthony the Anchorite*), is comprised of a series of parables demonstrating the wisdom of the hermit and his exhortation to the spiritual life.[105] While there have been a number of holy men bearing this name in the Christian tradition and the historical context of the treatise is ambiguous, Franz Rosenthal, in his study of this text, suggested a 'faint echo' of the life of Saint Anthony the Great (d. 356), the Father of Christian monasticism.[106] In particular, the content of this work involves advice for avoiding the temptations of the physical world. As claimed by Ibn Abī al-Dunyā at the beginning:

> Now, among the works of the ancients dealing with wise sayings and parables, we have found a book of wise sayings and parables that will make a sensible person want to abandon the fleeting life of this world and inspire him to working with confidence for the other world. This is a book ascribed to Antony, the saintly ascetic.[107]

The precise source of the sayings and parables in *The Tale of Anthony* are obscure. It may well be that Ibn Abī al-Dunyā was, in fact, the original architect of the piece – though he could have reproduced the story from familiar elements, freely making additions or withdrawing material according to his purpose.[108] Whatever the provenance of the *The Tale of Anthony* and despite its differing form and content from *The Book of Monks*, there remains a remarkable thematic consistency within both texts for their positive assessment of Christian asceticism. The main parallel, as indicated by the passage above, concerns the abandonment of the world and its materialistic trappings. In the *Kitāb al-ruhbān*, Ibn Abī al-Dunyā employs Muslim transmitters, some of whom were well-known mystics in their own right, to recall the sage advice of Christian monks for how this elevated state of spirituality can be attained.

The contrast, struggle and asymmetry between physical reality and the transcendent life are clearly demonstrated by several passages within the *Kitāb al-ruhbān*. As reported by Ibn Abī al-Dunyā:

> On the authority of Sufyān ibn ʿUyayna:
> They saw a monk going about on a mountain and they said to him: 'Where are you going?' He replied: 'I am searching for the good life.' They said back: 'but you have left that life behind you in the city.' He then said: 'What do you consider life to be?' They answered: 'food, clothing, and desires.' The monk then said: 'It is not like this with us. Verily, a good life for us is when you summon your senses to the obedience of God and they answer you.'

> ʿan Sufyān ibn ʿUyayna, qāla: nadharū ilā rāhibin wa-huwa yakhruju min naḥw al-jabal, fa-qālū lahu: ayna turīdu? qāla: āṭlubu al-ʿaysh. qālū: khallafta al-ʿaysh warāʾika fī-l-madīna. qāla: wa-mā taʿudūn al-ʿaysh fīkum? qālū: al-ṭaʿām wa-l-libās wa-shahawāt. qāla: laysa huwa ʿindanā hākadhā. innamā al-ʿaysh ʿindanā an tadʿū ṭawārak ilā ṭāʿa Allāh fa-yujibinuka.[109]

Here we find the classic precept for a rejection of human institutions, a universal theme in the oldest stratum of monastic literature from the Near East.[110] John of Lycopolis, the fourth-century Egyptian anchorite, for instance, viewed proximity to a village as a threat to the ascetic way of life, instructing his followers to 'flee to the furthest parts of the desert . . . for living in villages has often harmed even the perfect'.[111] This same spirit of withdrawal can be witnessed throughout late antique Syriac regulations for monastic life. The sixth-century *Canons of Jōḥannan Bar Qūrsos*, the West Syrian bishop of Tellā de-Mauzelat in northern Syria, for instance begins his 'rules' with a comparable precept:

> Those who have taken it upon themselves to live monastic life, it is evident that they have made a promise for the way of life of the angels, to live for the Messiah. For this like of another world, they have moved from towns and villages to the ancoritic monasteries (*l-ʿōmrē iḥidāyē*). They crucify themselves to the world, and to its lusts in order that the Messiah may dwell and live in them.[112]

The desert, the traditional locus of this self-exile, in this case is really to be understood as the antithesis of urban life, or the world of humanity, which was commonly deemed as corruptive to the soul. The rejection of village-life therefore necessarily removed any obstacles between the pious seeker and the divine, the wilderness offering harmony, purity and silence.[113] Only the emptiness of the wilderness could facilitate the quintessential *ἡσυχία* (hesychia), the quiet and inner stillness of Christian contemplation.[114] For the Syriac-speaking monastic communities of the Levant and Mesopotamia, this directive was exemplified in the middle fourth-century *Demonstrations of Aphrahāṭ*. The views concerning a strict isolation from humanity are confirmed in the passages stating, 'We should be aliens from this world, as Christ was alien from this world' and 'Whoever would resemble the angels, must alienate himself from men.'[115] While the desert offered a tangible destination for this movement away from mankind, it also presented a pathway into a realm where the pious seeker could most authentically encounter the divine; both Jesus and Paul had, after all, sought withdrawal into the desert for such reasons.[116] Saint Jerome, in his *Letter to Eustochium* (c. 384), professed this familiar view for the sanctity of the desert, in contrast to the civilised world:

> How often, when I was living in the desert, in that lonely wasteland (*in illa uasta solitudine*), scorched by the burning sun, which affords to hermits a savage dwelling place, did I fancy myself surrounded by the pleasures of Rome . . . Now, in my fear of Hell I had confined myself to this prison, where I had no companions but scorpions and wild beasts . . . I used to dread my very cell as though it knew my thoughts and filled with anger directed at myself, I made my way alone into the desert (*rigidus solus deserta penetrabam*). Whenever I saw hollow valleys (*concaua uallium*), craggy mountains (*aspera montium*), steep cliffs (*rupium praerupta*), there I made my oratory, there at that place of torture for my unhappy flesh. There – the Lord Himself as my witness – after many a tear and straining my eyes toward heaven, I felt myself in the presence of angelic hosts.[117]

The *Kitāb al-ruhbān* echoes this early Christian sentiment that an ascetic withdrawal into the holy should require a specific topographical dimension, as is suggested with the quote from the beginning of this book. A number of these sayings likewise connect monasticism with caves, ravines and mountains. The concept of aligning the pietistic pursuits with a particular landscape appears to have been later adopted into the Islamic mystical tradition as well. As an example of this, when asked to describe those who 'worried for their souls' (*mahmūmūn*), the Muslim ascetic Dhū al-Nūn of Egypt (d. 862) poetically instructed that:

> Sadness is firmly affixed to their inmost hearts, their ambitions dedicated to seeking God, their hearts filled with longing fly towards him. Fear lays them down in beds of distress and hope has slaughtered them with a wrathful sword. Intense weeping has ruptured the blood of their hearts, their souls at the brink of destruction from the incessant sorrow. It is the promise of their bodies, to flee from their places of origin and their homes . . . they scatter into the caverns and desolate wastes (*fi-l-kuhūf wa- fi-l-qafr*) . . . Their only food is the grass and their drink is pure water. They rejoice in the words of al-Raḥmān and their spirits wail out before Him like the crying of doves.[118]

Here in the *Kitāb al-ruhbān*, a solitary life in 'the bosoms of the mountains and the wombs of the wadīs' is indeed idealised as the conduit for salvation. Not only is there a sense of denial for human society in this passage, but also an appreciation for the tranquility of living in concert with the natural world. Without question, the vocabulary used in this section, such as the phrase '*aknāf al-jibāl wa-baṭūn al-awdiya*', is explicitly feminine and maternal. The extreme isolation for the ascetic, while fraught with hardships, was nonetheless being interpreted as a virtual return to the womb. This same metaphor is later utilised within another report to describe ascetics as:

> Lions by day, monks at night, they do not enter into homes except by permission and they only eat an eighth of a portion of food . . . the land has been emptied of them, they have become enveloped within the wombs of the wadīs and ravines.

> luyūth bi-al-nahār wa ruhbān bi-l-layl, lā tadkhulūna al-buyūt illā bi-idhn wa-lā ya'kalūna al-ṭa'ām illā bi-thumn . . . akhlū lahum al-arḍ wa-ulḥiqū bi-buṭūn al-awdiya wa-shi'āb.[119]

The maternal imagery is worth noting however, for while the place of refuge in Near Eastern and Egyptian asceticism, traditionally cast in the desert landscape typology, could offer the peace of *ἡσυχία*, it was often portrayed as a place of suffering, danger and temptation.[120] Such locales offered considerable risk and were only appropriate to the truly worthy practitioners.[121] Of these kinds of hazards, two are specifically mentioned by Ibn Abī al-Dunyā in this collection. The first involves a situation in which Iblīs comes to a hermitage to tempt a monk away from his prayers:

> On the authority of Wahb ibn Munnabih:
> He approached a monk who was sitting alone in his cell at the time of the Messiah. Iblīs intended to inflict hardship [on the monk] but he held no sway over him. He then came to him in the image of the Messiah and called out: 'O monk! Come near that I might have a word with you.' He answered: 'Take your leave as you please, but I am not able to do so for some time because of my age.' He said: 'come to me, I am the Messiah.' The monk replied: 'if you are the Messiah, what need of me do you have? Is it not that you commanded us to worship and promised us resurrection? On your way as you please, I have no need of you.' So, the Accursed One took leave of him and departed.

atā rāhiban takhulā fī ṣawmaʿatihi fī zaman al-masīḥ. fa-arādahu Iblīs [bi-kāraba] fa-lam yaqdur ʿalayhi. fa-atāhu mutashabihan bi-l-masīḥ fa-nādāhu: ayyuhā al-rāhib! ashrif ḥattā ukallimuka. qāla: inṭaliq li-sha'nika, fa-lastu aqdir ʿalā radd mā maḍā min ʿumrī. qāla: fa-ashrif ʿalayya fa-anā al-masīḥ. qāla: in kunta al-masīḥ fa-mā bī illayka min ḥājatin[?] a-laysa qad amartanā bi-al-ʿibāda wa waʿadtanā al-qiyāma[?] inṭaliq li-sha'nika fa-lā ḥāja lī bi-ka. fa-anṭalaqa ʿanhu al-laʿīn wa-taraktahu.[122]

Here 'the Accursed One' (*al-laʿīn*), as he is referred to at the conclusion of the passage, disguises himself as the Messiah, bidding the monk to stop his devotions and come out of the cell to speak with him. This kind of temptation, visited upon the Christian recluse by demons, is a relatively common feature in the hagiographical literature from Late Antiquity, projecting evil spirits as part of the desert 'trials' that a monk must necessarily undergo.[123] John Climacus, a seventh-century *hegoumenos* of St Catherine's Monastery in Sinai,[124] for instance, specifically warned his fellow ascetics on the dangers of demons interfering with contemplation and prayer. In his *Ladder to Paradise*, John urges them to 'Without display, concentrate, withdraw into your own heart. For demons fear this concentration just as thieves fear dogs' (Γίνου σύννους ἀφιλένδεικτος, πρὸς τὴν ἑαυτοῦ καρδίαν ἐξεστηκώς. Δεδοίκασι γὰρ σύννοιαν οἱ δαίμονες, ὡς οἱ κλέπται τοὺς κύνας).[125]

The specific designation of this supernatural tempter in the text as *Iblīs*[126] does however potentially suggest a definitively Muslim view. This figure is mentioned by name in nine *sūras* of the Qurʾān, seven of these containing the story of the *Fall of Iblīs*[127] (Qurʾān 2:34, 7:11, 15:31, 17:61, 18:50, 20:116 and 38:74). Iblīs is in some facets synonymous with al-Shayṭān, though the role that each personification plays within scripture is quite distinct.[128] Iblīs, in the Qurʾān, is the name given when the context concerns opposition or disobedience to God,[129] hence the *Fall of Iblīs* when refusing God's command to bow to Adam. Alternatively, al-Shayṭān is invoked when passages concern the primary role of this evil to be the 'deception or temptation' of mankind.[130] Why the role of Iblīs has shifted within this passage of the *Kitāb al-ruhbān* is elusive, here being the embodiment of 'temptation', yet it would still seem to demonstrate a noticeably Muslim terminology. This would obviously make sense given Ibn Abī al-Dunyā's audience, yet it should be said that the core frame of this story does bear remarkable resemblance to one told by Palladius of Galatia (d. c. 430) involving a monk being tempted away from his spiritual duties by Satan. In this account too the 'Evil One', designated in the Syriac with *bīšē*, appears in disguise and claims to be Christ.[131] One might assume that such a story would have been adapted to fit a specific need of the author, particularly in the substitution of titles or designations that would be clearly familiar to a Muslim constituency.

The second example features a rather more physical form of danger in which a monk saves his attendant (*ghulām*) from the appetites of a lion that appeared within their cell. Fearing what was about to transpire, the lion looking hungrily upon the men, the attendant calls out to his master to 'Call upon your God, the one you became a monk for, so that he might turn away from me the cunning of this beast!' The monk soothes the animal and preserves the spirit of the attendant by offering a prayer to God in 'either Hebrew or Aramaic'. The story concludes with the lion leaping into the servant's lap and wagging his tail (*fa-wathaba al-sabuʿ ʿanhu yanfuḍu dhanabahu*).[132] Such an account also recalls motifs found across ancient Christian Greek, Coptic and Syriac literature, attempting to demonstrate the power of the saint over the natural world. Examples of the more ferocious animals, such as crocodiles, serpents, hyenas, leopards and panthers being tamed by Christian mystics were often employed as proofs of sainthood.[133] Of these varied and miraculous interactions with wild animals, encounters with lions are the most repeated across the hagiographical material.[134]

Even though these creatures are savage beasts and would be extremely dangerous to the average person, they possess the ability to intuitively recognise the innocence and sanctity of holy people.[135] One of the most popular of these types of stories, the tale of 'Saint Jerome and the Lion', was widely circulated in Western Europe during the late Middle Ages.[136] From the writings of Jerome (d. 420) himself also comes the narrative concerning the death of Paul of Thebes and the discovery of his corpse in a desert cave by his former acolyte, Antony the Great. According to the *Vita S. Pauli Primi Eremitae*, Antony begins to weep because he did not possess the tools necessary to bury his monastic mentor, but just then two lions appear out of the wilderness and dig a hole with their paws so that the venerable old man can be laid to rest. Moreover, the lions actually lament the death of the monk, fawning at his feet and roaring loudly in distress ('*Ecce duo leones ex interioris eremi parte currentes . . . et illi quidem directo cursu ad cadaver beati senis substiterunt, adulantibusque caudis circa ejus pedes accubere: fremitu ingenti rugientes, prorsus ut intelligeres eos plangere*').[137] Far from posing a threat to Antony, the lions were docile, helpful, appearing to him as though they were doves ('*quasi columbas videret*').[138] The final line in this section of the *Kitāb al-ruhbān* similarly closes by stating that the lion 'went away and did not harm him [the servant] at all' (*thuma walliya wa-lam yaḍurrahu shai'ān*).[139]

Such stories were also used to conceptualise the deep connection between the holy man and the natural world, the saint being a restorative agent for a primordial paradise,[140] a utopia in which lions and mystics could live side by side in harmony. As Catherine Osborne has suggested:

> the true holy man, unlike the city-dweller, will be in a position to recognize that the beasts are not vicious . . . the desert, unlike the human city, is a society in which justice is respected and nature's proper order is restored, as before the Fall. Thus, the desert becomes a model of heaven.[141]

Forsaking the world in such a way should be interpreted, in its early Christian context, as a profound fracture with the traditions of the late-classical world, in contrast to its emphasis on civic virtues and collective values. Communing with nature, as well as with beasts within that environment, is a demonstrative feature for that rejection of human institutions. As put by Charles Segal,

> For the desert saints . . . man's real goal is the heavenly kingdom, and civic life constitutes a state of alienation from his true condition. Hence to negate civilized life, to replace culture by nature, is to bypass the fallen condition of humankind. To draw closer to the beasts is, paradoxically, to regain a lost proximity to the divine.[142]

Given the incorporation of such fairly common literary tropes from Late Antiquity, it seems reasonable to suggest that much of the material in the *Kitāb al-ruhbān* was actually compiled from the *Apophthegmata Patrum* and other Christian sources. Though not all of the reports within *Kitāb al-ruhbān* take the form of dialogues between confessional groups, they invariably situate a Muslim sage recounting the knowledge of a Christian ascetic. Again, it should be emphasised that there is a total disregard for theological arguments here, the paramount concern conforming strictly to issues of a moral or pious nature. The only reference that seems, in any way, to compare Islam and Christianity comes in the form of a conversation between a monk and Caliph ʿUmar ibn ʿAbd al-Azīz (d. 101/720) at Dayr Simʿān.[143] At the end of their exchange, the caliph, having been impressed during his dialogue with the monk, reportedly exclaims, 'if only you had embraced Islam!' (*lau dakhalta fī al-Islām*).[144] The monk, for his part, then attempts to reveal the parallel issues that both faiths have in common, that being that each one's followers tend to become less and less faithful over time. The contrast between the two traditions here, offered by the monk, is that Christianity is an old, well-established faith and Islam is new and pristine. Yet according to the monk's lament they will eventually suffer the same fate, not through any defect of the religions themselves, but through the frailties of their adherents. This attitude is made clear in the monk's avowal, 'But my faith is old, and its people have been changed. Would that you live so long that your religion becomes old and you will see its people changed, such that it becomes distorted and you no longer recognize it' (*wa-dīnī qad khalaq wa-taghayara ahluhu. Wa-in taʿish yā amīr al-muʾminīn ḥattā yakhlaq dīnuka fa-satarā min taghayara tunkaruhu lā mā taʿarifuhu*).[145] There is surely a remarkable sense of ecumenism or solidarity in such a statement; a mutual lament for the shortcomings of the human condition, far from the contempt seen across the polemical standard fare of that time.

In concert, the only semblance of reproach against monasticism comes in the final report of the book, by virtue of ʿAlī ibn Abī Ṭālib's exposition on a verse from *Sūrat al-kahf*. The Qurʾānic passage reads:

> Say: Shall We inform you of those who are the greatest failures with respect to their deeds? (*Sūrat al-kahf* 18:103)

According to ʿAlī, the *al-akhsarīn* or 'greatest failures' here applies to a particular group of Christian monks. The reprimand is being directed at 'those monks who have jailed themselves in their places of worship' (*hum al-ruhbān alladhīna ḥabasū anfusahum fi-l-sawārī*). Careful attention should however be given to the specificity of the charge. This clearly does not apply to all monks, or even the institution of monasticism itself. It would merely appear to be an admonishment to those monks who have become overzealous in their duties. This could be Ibn Abī al-Dunyā's way of praising the piety of those who rejected the world, while managing the expectations of similarly minded mystics from his own confessional community. That pious mode of life could most profoundly be expressed in its Christian context by virtue of a spiritual abandonment of the world; the ἀναχώρησις, being the ascetic's physical removal from humanity, would have been, as such, implicit within the monastic mandate for righteousness.

Notes

1. See Fred Donner, 'From Believers to Muslims: Confessional Self-Identity in the Early Islamic Community', *al-Abhath* 50–1 (2002–3), 19–21.
2. The core beliefs are mentioned as well in Fred Donner's *Muhammad and the Believers: At the Origins of Islam* (Boston, MA: Belknap Press of Harvard University Press, 2010), which is an expansion of the original article. See pages 57–61.
3. Donner, 'From Believers to Muslims', 19–21.
4. Donner, *Muhammad and the Believers*, 57. As well, D. Z. H. Baneth has discussed the use of the related term *aslama*, originally meaning 'the act of submitting oneself to God', being gradually interpreted by the Muslim community as 'to become a follower of Muhammad'. See Baneth, 'What Did Muhammad Mean When He Called His Religion "Islam"? The Original Meaning of Aslama and Its Derivatives', in *The Qur'an: Style and Contents*, ed. A. Rippin (Farnham: Ashgate, 2001), 90.
5. Ibid. 58.
6. James Robson, 'Islām as a Term', *The Muslim World* 44: 2 (1954), 103. Robson does however conclude that depending on the chronology of the revelation, whether they be dated to the Meccan or Medinan period, the meaning of the term islām vacillates between the vague notion of 'submission' to a decidedly more precise designation. In the later passages the term appears to have taken on a more defined sense of a particular religious creed. See pages 104–5.
7. Donner, *Muhammad and the Believers*, 71.
8. Ibid. 71. Montgomery Watt has suggested that the original name for the movement founded by Muḥammad was not *Islam*, but rather *tazakkī*, or 'righteousness'. It is after the *Hijra* that the most numerous references to a community of *mu'minūn* begin to occur. It appears that in the early terminology of 'believers', Jews would have been included under this general rubric. During the period

of the Prophet's break with the Jews of Medina, he claimed to have been following the religion of Abraham, the *ḥanīfiyya* – and the Prophet's religion may have been called exactly that for some time afterward. See Watt, *Muhammad at Medina* (Oxford: Clarendon Press, 1977), 301–2.

9. G. R. Hawting, *The Idea of Idolatry and the Emergence of Islam: From Polemic to History* (Cambridge: Cambridge University Press, 1999), 21. Also, Hawting suggests on the basis of this verse that Islam was seeking to bind itself to an Abrahamic lineage in much the same way as the apostle Paul had attempted to bind Christianity with Judaism. The example provided comes from Galatians 3:7 in which Paul states, 'they whom are of faith, the same are the children of Abraham'. For Hawting this is a question of Islam striving for legitimacy and using the figure of Abraham for support (see pages 36–7). Waardenburg gives a similar assessment in the use of the term *ḥanīfiyya* as one of the original names for the movement, which was not only a reaction against the paganism of Mecca, but also a 'reform movement' with regard to the local Christian and Jewish communities. See Jacques Waardenburg, 'Towards a Periodization of Earliest Islam According to Its Relations with Other Religions', in *Proceedings of the Ninth Congress of the Union Européene des Arabisants et Islamisants, Amsterdam 1978*, ed. Rudolph Peters (Leiden: Brill, 1981), 305–26.
10. Julius Wellhausen, *Reste arabischen Heidentums* (Berlin: Walter de Gruyter & Co, 1961), 234. Cf. Hawting, *The Idea of Idolatry*, 27.
11. Khalid Blankenship, 'The Early Creed', in *The Cambridge Companion to Classical Islamic Theology*, ed. T. Winter (Cambridge: Cambridge University Press, 2008), 33–54.
12. Donner, 'From Believers to Muslims', 19–21.
13. Robert Kirschner, 'The Vocation of Holiness in Late Antiquity', *Vigiliae Christianae* 38 (1984), 112.
14. *Historia Lausiaca* 47, 13–14, trans. R. T. Meyer, *The Lausiac History*, Ancient Christian Writers 34 (London: Newman Press, 1965), 129.
15. *Admonitions of Mār Ephrēm*, in *Syriac and Arabic Documents Regarding Legislation Relative to Syrian Asceticism*, ed. Arthur Vööbus, 19, no. 1–3. It should be noted that the word here for 'obedience' (*mushtam'unutē*) comes from the root *sham'a*, which has a core meaning of 'listening'.
16. Ibid.
17. Daniel Caner, 'Charitable Ministrations (*Diakoniai*), Monasticism, and the Social Aesthetic of Sixth-Century Byzantium', in *Charity and Giving in*

Monotheistic Religions, eds Miriam Frenkel and Yaacov Lev (Berlin: de Gruyter, 2009), 45–74.

18. John of Ephesus, *Vitae Sanctorum Orientalium*, ed. and trans. E. W. Brooks, *Patrologia Orientalis*, vol. 18 (Paris: Firmin-Didot, 1923–5), 671–2.
19. For the possible influence of Christian institutions on the later development of the Islamic *waqf*, see Peter Charles Hennigan, *The Birth of a Legal Institution. The Formation of the Waqf in Third-Century* A.H. *Hanafi Legal Discourse*, Studies in Islamic Law and Society 18 (Leiden: Brill, 2004), 50–70.
20. See discussion of 'Desert Ascetics and Distant Marvels' in Georgia Frank, *The Memory of the Eyes. Pilgrims to Living Saints in Christian Late Antiquity* (Berkeley, CA: University of California Press, 2000), 35–78. This journey also recalls the conversion story of Kaʿb al-Aḥbār, which involves travelling and studying under various Jewish scholars to finally reach Islam. See Ibn Saʿd, *Ṭabaqāt al-kabīr*, vol. 8 (Cairo: Maktabat al-Khanjī, 2001), 2, 156 in biographical form. For an analysis of Kaʿb's conversion, see both Moshe Perlmann's 'The Legendary Story of Kʿab al-Aḥbār's Conversion to Islam', in *The Joshua Starr Memorial Volume* (New York: The Conference on Jewish Relations, 1953), 85–99, and 'Another Kʿab al-Aḥbār Story', *The Jewish Quarterly Review* 45:1 (1954), 48–58.
21. Maribel Dietz, 'Itinerant Spirituality and the Late Antique Origins of Christian Pilgrimage', in *Travel, Communication and Geography in Late Antiquity: Sacred and Profane*, eds Linda Ellis and Frank Kidner (London: Routledge, 2016), 125–34 at 126. Dietz suggests that the *instabilitas* aspect of pilgrimage was the ritual in and of itself, without regard to an explicit destination. This is 'monastic' in the sense of retreat from the familiar and dedication to the hardships of a wandering life.
22. Ibid. 127–9. Munʾim Sirry has discussed a rather analogous phenomenon in medieval Muslim hagiography, in which the pious seeker reaches a pinnacle of asceticism through direct contact with an imminent teacher. See Munʾim Sirry, 'Pious Muslims in the Making: A Closer Look at the Narratives of Ascetic Conversion', *Arabica* 57:4 (2010), 437–54. The 'conversion' here is not however between confessional traditions, but rather from within traditional Islam and moving to a more ascetic or 'Sufi' lifestyle.
23. See Thomas Sizgorich, 'Narrative and Community in Islamic Late Antiquity', *Past and Present* 185 (2004), 9–42 at 11. The quote from Sizgorich is specifically referencing Muḥammad's encounter with the monk Baḥīrā, but it applies here as well: 'these narratives employ a figure – the monk – which had been

recognized and acknowledged for more than four centuries in communities of variant confessional alignments as a discerner of truth and godliness to support truth claims crucial to early Muslim programmes of communal self-fashioning'.

24. See Suleiman Mourad, 'Christian Monks in Islamic Literature: A Preliminary Report on Some Arabic Apophthegmata Pratum', *Bulletin for the Royal Institute on Inter-Faith Studies* 6 (2004), 81–98.
25. See Arthur Vööbus, *History of the School of Nisibis, Corpus Scriptorum Christianorum Orientalium*, Subsidia 26 (Louvain: Secrétariat du CSCO, 1965), as well as Adam Becker, *Fear of God and the Beginning of Wisdom: the School of Nisibis and Christian Scholastic Culture in Late Antique Mesopotamia* (Philadelphia, PA: University of Pennsylvania Press, 2006). The story of the temporary conversion to Christianity of the Jewish philosopher David b. Merwān al-Mukkammaṣ (d. 937) takes place in Nisibis under a prominent Christian teacher. See Jacob Mann, 'An Early Theologico-Polemical Work', *Hebrew Union College Annual* 12–13 (1968), 417–18.
26. The word in the *Sīra* here is *ghaiḍatayn*, with the dual ending. Identical terminology is preserved in the *Ṭabaqāt al-kabīr* 4, 74.
27. The dual is utilised in both cases, with the terms *ḥarratayn*/'two lava fields' and *ghaiḍatayn*/'two thickets', respectively, accompanied by terms indicating motion between these areas. Ibn Isḥāq, *Sīra*, vol. I, 178.
28. Ibid. 179.
29. For the differing views on the life, and death, of Jesus in the Islamic tradition, see Gabriel Said Reynolds, 'The Muslim Jesus: Alive or Dead', *Bulletin of the School of Oriental and African Studies* 72:2 (2009), 237–58.
30. François De Blois, 'Naṣrānī (Ναζωραῖnos) and ḥanīf (ἐθνικόσ): Studies on the Religious Vocabulary of Christianity and Islam', *Bulletin of the School of Oriental and African Studies* 65:1 (2002), 1–30 at 18.
31. Blankenship, 'The Early Creed', 33–54. On *taḥrīf*, or 'alteration of scripture', see also Gabriel Said Reynolds, 'On the Qur'anic Assessment of Scriptural Falsification (taḥrīf) and Anti-Jewish Polemic', *Journal of the American Oriental Society* 130:2 (April–June 2010), 189–202.
32. Fred Donner, *Narratives of Islamic Origins: The Beginnings of Islamic Historical Writing*, Studies in Late Antiquity and Early Islam 14 (Princeton, NJ: Darwin Press, 1998), 67.
33. For a discussion on the nuance of these terms, see Fazlur Rahman, *Major Themes of the Qur'an* (Chicago, IL: The University of Chicago Press, 1980/2009), at 29, 61, 110 and 137.

34. Qur'ān, *Sūrat al-mā'idah*, verse 82 (5:82); *Sūrat al-tawbah*, verses 31 and 34 (9:31, 9:34).
35. Qur'ān, *Sūrat al-ḥadīd*, verse 27 (57:27).
36. Edmund Beck, 'Das Christliche Mönchtum Im Koran', *Studia Orientalia* 13:3 (Helsinki, 1946), 3–29; Daniel Sahas, 'Monastic Ethos and Spirituality and the Origins of Islam', in *Acts of the XVIIIth International Congress of Byzantine Studies*, eds I. Ševčenko and G. Litavrin (Shepherdstown, WV: Byzantine Studies Press, 1996), issue 2, 27–39; Sara Sviri, 'Wa-Rahbāniyatan Ibtad'ūhā: An Analysis of the Traditions Concerning the Origins and Evaluation of Christian Monasticism', *Jerusalem Studies in Arabic and Islam* 13 (1990), 195–208; see also section on the 'Vocation of Monasticism' in Louis Massignon, *Essay on the Origins of the Technical Language of Islamic Mysticism*, trans. and intro. Benjamin Clark (Notre Dame, IN: The University of Notre Dame Press, 1997), 98–104.
37. Christian Sahner, 'Islamic Legends about the Birth of Monasticism: A Case Study on the Late Antique Milieu of the Qur'ān and Tafsīr', in *The Late Antique World of Early Islam: Muslims Among Christians and Jews in the Eastern Mediterranean*, ed. R. Hoyland (Princeton: Darwin Press, 2015), 294–395.
38. See Sviri, 'Wa-Rahbāniyatan Ibtad'ūhā', 195–201, as well as Emran El-Badawi, 'From "Clergy" to "Celibacy": The Development of *Rahbānīyyah* Between the Qur'ān, Ḥadīth and Church Canon', *Al-Bayān* 11:1 (June 2013), 1–14.
39. One of the earliest incarnations of this statement comes from the *Kitāb al-ṭabaqāt al-kabīr* of Ibn Sa'd (d. 845).
40. See Ibn Sa'd, *Kitāb al-ṭabaqāt al-kabīr* (Cairo: Maktabat al-Khānjī, 2001), vol. 5, 70. For a comprehensive explanation of this nuanced term *jihād*, see Reuven Firestone, 'Jihād', in *The Blackwell Companion to the Qur'ān*, ed. A. Rippin (Oxford: Blackwell Publishing, 2006), 308–20.
41. See section on the 'Vocation of Monasticism' in Massignon, *Essay on the Origins of the Technical Language of Islamic Mysticism*, 98–104.
42. Ibid. 98–104. Cf. Ignaz Goldziher, *Introduction to Islamic Theology and Law*, trans. A. and R. Hamori (Princeton, NJ: Princeton University Press, 1981), 134–6.
43. 'Abdallāh ibn al-Mubarāk, *Kitāb al-jihād*, ed. Nazīh Ḥammād (Mecca, 1978), 37. For a comprehensive analysis of this statement, see Christian Sahner, '"The Monasticism of My Communtiy is Jihad": A Debate on Asceticism, Sex, and Warfare in Early Islam', *Arabica* 64 (2017), 149–83.
44. Ibid. 38.

45. Firestone, 'Jihād', *The Blackwell Companion to the Qur'ān*, 308–9.
46. Ibid. 311.
47. Massignon, *Essay on the Origins of the Technical Language of Islamic Mysticism*, 99.
48. Ibid. 99–100.
49. Qur'ān, *Sūrat al-ḥadīd*, verse 27. The translation provided above represents a traditional rendering of this verse, as to be found in the Qur'ānic translations of A. J. Arberry, for example.
50. Massignon, *Essay on the Origins*, 100.
51. Ibid. 100–1.
52. Beck, 'Das christliche Mönchtum im Koran', 18.
53. Ibid. 17.
54. Al-Zamaksharī, *Kitāb al-kashshāf 'an ḥaqā'iq ghawāmiḍ al-tanzīl wa-'uyūn al-aqāwīl fī wujūh al-ta'wīl* (Riyadh, 1998), vol. 6, 52–3.
55. Ibid. 53.
56. Ibid. 53.
57. Ibid. 53.
58. Ibid. 53.
59. Muqātil ibn Sulaymān, *Tafsīr Muqātil ibn Sulīmān*, vol. 1, ed. Shiḥātah (Egypt, 1979), 498–99.
60. Qur'ān, *Sūrat al-mā'idah*, verse 87.
61. Muqātil ibn Sulaymān, *Tafsīr*, 499.
62. Sviri, 'Wa-Rahbāniyatan Ibtad'ūhā', 195–201.
63. Ibid. 201.
64. Ibid. 196–8.
65. Sahner, 'The Monasticism of My Community is Jihad', 152
66. Muqātil ibn Sulaymān, *Tafsīr*, 499.
67. Al-Ḥārith ibn Asad Muḥāsibī, *Kitāb al-ri'āya liḥuqūq Allāh*, ed. Margaret Smith, E. J. W. Gibb Memorial Series XV (London, 1940), folio 4–5.
68. John Wansbrough, *Quranic Studies: Sources and Methods of Scriptural Interpretation* (Oxford: Oxford University Press, 1977), 123.
69. It should also be noted that certain types of monks even received reprimand within the late antique Christian monastic tradition. The loftiest ideal for monastic life, as it was generally considered, was the anchoritic existence that had been established by Anthony in the fourth century. The 'highest rung' on the ladder of monastic perfection was however diluted with less admirable forms of monastic life: those, for instance, who sought fame or power

through the rigours of asceticism. See section on 'Monastic Typologies' in Maribel Dietz, *Wandering Monks, Virgins, and Pilgrims: Ascetic Travel in the Mediterranean World A.D. 300–800* (University Park, PA: Pennsylvania State University Press, 2005), 73–4.

70. His full name is ʿAbd Allāh ibn Muḥammad ibn ʿUbayd ibn Sufyān ibn Qays Abū Bakr al-Qurashī. See Carl Brockelmann, 'Ibn Abī al-Dunyā', *The Encyclopedia of Islam 1913–1936* (Leiden: E. J. Brill, 1987), vol. 3, 335; A. Dietrich, 'Ibn Abī al-Dunyā', *The Encyclopedia of Islam: New Edition*, eds H. A. R. Gibb *et al.* (Leiden: E. J. Brill, 1960–2002) vol. 3, 684.
71. For a listing of some of the major works by Ibn Abī al-Dunyā, see Ibn al-Nadīm, *Kitāb al-fihrist*, ed. Gustav Flügel (2 vols) (Leipzig: F. C. W. Vogel, 1871–2), vol. 1, 185. Nearly sixty of his works have survived from antiquity. See Carl Brockelmann, *Geshichte der Arabischen Litteratur* I 153, Suppl. I (Leiden: Brill, 1937–42), 247–8, and Reinhard Weipert, 'Die erhaltenen Werke des Ibn Abī al-Dunyā. Fortsetzung und Schluss', *Arabica* 56:4/5 (July 2009), 450–65.
72. Among the relevant titles listed here in the *Fihrist* are the *Kitāb fiqh al-Nabī* (The Knowledge of the Prophet), *Kitāb dhamm al-malāhī* (The Reproach against Music), *Kitāb dhamm al-fuḥsh* (The Reproach against Indecency), *Kitāb ʿafw* (Compassion), *Kitāb al-hamm wa al-ḥuzn* (Solicitude and Grief) and the *Kitāb dhamm al-dunyā* (Condemnation of the World).
73. On this collection, see William Harmless, *Desert Christians: An Introduction to the Literature of Early Monasticism* (Oxford: Oxford University Press, 2004), 169–90; Benedicta Ward (trans.), *The Sayings of the Desert Fathers: The Alphabetical Collection*, Cistercian Studies 59 (Kalamazoo, MI: Cistercian Publications, 1984).
74. See Mourad, 'Christian Monks in Islamic Literature', 81–98.
75. James A. Bellamy, 'Pro-Umayyad Propaganda in Ninth-Century Baghdad in the Works of Ibn Abī al-Dunyā', *Prédiction et propogrande au Moyen Âge: Islam, Byzance, Occident* (Paris: Presses universitaires de France, 1983), 71–86.
76. Leonard Librande, 'Ibn Abī al-Dunyā: Certainty and Morality', *Studia Islamica* 100/101 (2005), 5–42 at 6–7.
77. This is perhaps a result of the increasing importance attributed to legalistic and juridical tracts within the Islamic tradition, a trend that can be traced back to his own era, from which Ibn Abī al-Dunyā's writings stand apart. See James A. Bellamy, 'The Makārim al-Akhlāq by Ibn Abī al-Dunyā: A Preliminary Study', *The Muslim World* (2 April 1963), 106–19; Brockelmann, 'Ibn Abī al-Dunyā', *EI*, 335; Dietrich, 'Ibn Abī al-Dunyā', *EI: New Edition* III, 684.

78. The phrase 'formative period' is borrowed from Montgomery Watt, *The Formative Period of Islamic Thought* (Edinburgh: Edinburgh University Press, 1973). See specifically Chapter 9, 'The Polarity of Sunnism, and Shīʿism', 253–78, and subsection 'The End of the Formative Period' in chapter 10, 316–18. Watt argues here that both Sunnī and Shīʿī doctrines had assumed their 'more or less' definitive form, as had the legal traditions, by the middle of the tenth century. Thus the 'formation' of such development has a terminus around the year 950 CE, just before the Būyid interlude in Baghdād.
79. Michael Cook, 'Ibn Qutayba and the Monkeys', *Studia Islamica* 89 (1999), 43–74. Cf. Librande, 'Ibn Abī al-Dunyā: Certainty and Morality', 7.
80. Montgomery Watt, 'Some Mystics of the Later Third/Ninth Century', *Islamic Studies* 7: 4 (December 1968), 309–16.
81. Leah Kinberg has discussed the varying and nuanced definitions of this term. While the implication of *zuhd* may be slightly altered depending on which particular medieval Muslim scholar is utilising the term, it can ultimately be understood as 'a web of instructions on how to behave in day-to-day life'. Principally, this has roots in the concept of moderation and the manner in which a pious Muslim should deal with the material world. See Kinberg, 'What is Meant by Zuhd?', *Studia Islamica* 61 (1985), 27–44.
82. Watt, 'Some Mystics of the Later Third/Ninth Century', 309.
83. For this polemical tradition, see Sidney H. Griffith, 'Jews and Muslims in Christian Syriac and Arabic Texts of the Ninth Century', *Jewish History* 3:1 (Spring 1988), 65–94; David Thomas, 'Dialogue with Other Faiths as an Aspect of Islamic Theology', in *Religious Polemics in Context: Papers Presented to the Second International Conference of the Leiden Institute for the Study of Religions*, eds T. L. Hettema and A. Van Der Kooij (Assen: Koninklijke Van Gorcum, 2004), 93–109. On the theological content of the polemical arguments, see Reynolds, 'On the Qur'anic Accusation of the Scriptural Falsification', 189–202; Hava Lazarus-Yafeh, 'Some Neglected Aspects of Medieval Muslim Polemics against Christianity', *The Harvard Theological Review* 89:1 (January 1996), 61–84.
84. Jacques Waardenburg, 'The Medieval Period: 650–1500', in *Muslim Perceptions of Other Religions: A Historical Survey*, ed. Jacques Waardenburg (Oxford: Oxford University Press, 1999), 18–69 at 42. See also Christopher Melchert, 'Religious Policies of the Caliphs from al-Mutawakkil to al-Muqtadir, AH 232–295/AD 847–908', *Islamic Law and Society* 3:3 (1996), 316–42.
85. David Thomas, 'The Doctrine of the Trinity in the Early Abbasid Era', in

Islamic Interpretations of Christianity, ed. Lloyd Ridgeon (New York: St Martin's Press, 2001), 78–98; Gabriel Said Reynolds, *A Muslim Theologian in the Sectarian Milieu: 'Abd al-Jabbār and the Critique of Christian Origins* (Leiden: Brill, 2004), 32–5.

86. Reynolds, *A Muslim Theologian in the Sectarian Milieu*, 33.
87. Of these Christians apologists that might be mentioned are John of Damascus (d. c. 748), Theodore Abū Qurra (d. c. 826) and the Nestorian Patriarch Timothy I of Baghdad (d. 823). See Mark Beaumont, 'Speaking of the Triune God: Christian Defense of the Trinity in the Early Islamic Period', *Transformation* 29:2 (April 2012), 111–27; Thomas, 'The Doctrine of the Trinity in the Early Abbasid Era', 78–98; Sidney H. Griffith, 'Jews and Muslims in Syriac and Arabic Texts of the Ninth Century', *Jewish History* 3:1 (Spring 1988), 65–94.
88. Al-Jāḥiẓ, *Thalāth Risā'il*, ed. Joshua Finkel (Cairo: al-Matba'at al-Salafiyya, 1926), 14–20. Finkel translated this section in 'A Risāla of al- Jāḥiẓ', *Journal of the American Oriental Society* 47 (1921), 311–34.
89. Thomas, 'The Doctrine of the Trinity', 80. This treatise by al-Jāḥiẓ, however, bears conspicuous juxtaposition to the laudatory appraisal of monasticism within the *Kitāb al-ruhbān*, which specifically lays a scathing attack upon Christian ecclesiastical and ascetic practices on the basis of their institutional resolve for celibacy. See al-Jāḥiẓ, *Thalāth Risā'il*, 18–20. For more information on the theological development of anti-Trinitarian polemic, see *Early Muslim Polemic against Christianity: Abū 'Īsā al-Warrāq's 'Against the Incarnation'*, ed. David Thomas (Cambridge: Cambridge University Press, 2002).
90. Mourad, 'Christian Monks in Islamic Literature', 82.
91. Abū Nu'aym al-Iṣfahānī, *Ḥilyat al-awliyā' wa-ṭabaqāt al-aṣfiyā'* (10 vols) (Beirut: Dār al-Kitāb al-'Arabī, 1967–8), vol. 2, 365. On the problematic word *furqān* here, see Fred Donner, 'Quranic furqān', *Journal of Semitic Studies* 52:2 (Autumn 2007), 279–300.
92. MS Rampur 565 *al-Muntaqā min Kitāb al-ruhbān*, fol. 191a, section 11, lines 22–3.
93. Tor Andrae, *In the Garden of Myrtles*, trans. Birgitta Sharpe (Albany, NY: State University of New York Press, 1987), 8–9.
94. Massignon, *Essay on the Origins of the Technical Language of Islamic Mysticism*, 50–1.
95. For information on the history of Christianity in the region, see Irfan Shahîd, *Byzantium and the Arabs in the Fifth Century* (Washington, DC: Dumbarton Oaks Research Library, 1989), 405–19; on church and monastery construction

in these areas, Shahîd, 'Byzantium in South Arabia', *Dumbarton Oaks Papers* 33 (1979), 23–94.

96. Kirschner, 'The Vocation of Holiness in Late Antiquity', *Vigiliae Christianiae* 38 (1984), 105–24; Peter Brown, 'Holy Men', in *The Cambridge Ancient History*, vol. 14, ed. A. Cameron, B. Ward-Perkins and M. Whitby (Cambridge: Cambridge University Press, 2001), 781–810.
97. Guy G. Stroumsa, 'From Master of Wisdom to Spiritual Master in Late Antiquity', *Religion and the Self in Antiquity*, eds David Brakke, Michael L. Satlow and Steven Weitzman (Bloomington, IN: Indiana University Press, 2005), 183–96.
98. Stroumsa provides the examples of Lucilius and Seneca to make this point. See Stroumsa, 'From Master of Wisdom', 189.
99. Andrae, *In the Garden of Myrtles*, 12.
100. Georgia Frank, 'Desert Ascetics and Distant Marvels', *The Memory of the Eyes: Pilgrims to Living Saints in Christian Late Antiquity* (Berkeley, CA: University of California Press, 2000), 35–78; Maribel Dietz, 'Itinerant Spirituality and the Late Antique Origins of Christian Pilgrimage', in *Travel, Communication and Geography in Late Antiquity: Sacred and Profane*, eds Linda Ellis and Frank Kidner (Burlington, VT: Ashgate, 2004), 125–34.
101. Josef Meri, *The Cult of Saints among Muslims and Jews in Medieval Syria* (Oxford: Oxford University Press, 2002), 17–18.
102. Ibid. 102–7.
103. Claudia Rapp has written on the power of the holy man as intercessor between human society and the sacred. See '"For Next to God, you are my salvation": Reflections on the Rise of the Holy Man in Late Antiquity', in *The Cult of Saints in Late Antiquity and the Middle Ages: Essays on the Contribution of Peter Brown*, eds James Howard-Johnston and Paul Antony Hayward (Oxford: Oxford University Press, 1999), 63–83.
104. Donner, 'From Believers to Muslims', 9–53; Donner, *Muhammad and the Believers.*
105. Franz Rosenthal, 'The Tale of Anthony', *Oriens* 15 (31 December 1962), 35–60.
106. Ibid. 36–7.
107. Ibid. 44. Cf. Leah Kinberg, *Morality in the Guise of Dreams: A Critical Edition of the Kitāb al-Manām of Ibn Abī al-Dunyā*, Islamic Philosophy, Theology and Science: Texts and Studies volume 18, eds H. Daiber and D. Pingree (Leiden: Brill, 1994), 31.

108. Ibid. 38. Rosenthal does not see any evidence that this work is a translation from another language, such as would potentially indicate a Greek or Syriac hagiographical origin for the parables. Rather, the figure of Anthony in this text quotes from the Qur'ān and exhibits a distinctively Muslim tone when addressing Jewish and Christian scripture. This would perhaps reflect the natural inclination of a religious Muslim author, who may have adapted an existing set of stories for their own objective.
109. MS Rampur 565 *al-Muntaqā min kitāb al-ruhbān*, fol. 190b, section 1, lines 9–13.
110. Arthur Vööbus, *A History of Asceticism in the Syrian Orient: A Contribution to the History of Culture in the Near East* (2 vols) (Louvain: Corpus Scriptorum Christianorum Orientalium Secrétariat du Corpus, 1958–60) vol. 2, 19–28.
111. Translation by Norman Russell, *The Lives of the Desert Fathers: Historia Monachorum in Aegypto* [Cistercian Studies 34] (Kalamazoo, MI: Mowbray, 1981), 56. David Brakke has also discussed the early monastic principle that temptation, and specifically demonic temptation, was connected to living near villages. See David Brakke, *Demons and the Making of the Monk: Spiritual Combat in Early Christianity* (Cambridge, MA: Harvard University Press, 2006), 132–4.
112. Canons of Jōḥannan Bar Qūrsos, in *Syriac and Arabic Documents Regarding Legislation Relative to Syrian Asceticism*, ed. Arthur Vööbus (Stockholm: Etse, 1960), 57, no. 1–2.
113. Shafiq AbouZayd, *Iḥidayutha: A Study of the Life of Singleness in the Syrian Orient: From Ignatius of Antioch to Chalcedon 451 A.D.* (Oxford: ARAM Society for Mesopotamian Studies, 1993), 198.
114. Harmless, *Desert Christians*, 228–9.
115. See Aphraatis Demonstrations, Demonstratio De Monachis, *Patrologia Syriaca complectens opera Omnia SS. Patrum, doctorum scriptorumque Catholicorum* (Paris: F. Didot, 1894–) 1, col. 241 and 248, respectively. The typical designations of μοναχός, from the Byzantine and Coptic tradition, and *iḥidayē*, most commonly utilised in Syriac – both having the core meaning of 'single' or 'solitary' – serve as a testament to this fundamental emphasis on the individuality of the eremetic existence. In both of these cases the central element, from which the designations arise, concerns a retreat from the material world into spiritual seclusion. See Claire Fauchon, 'Les forms de vie ascétique et monastique en milieu syriaque, Ve–VIIe siècles', in *Le Monachisme Syriaque*, Études Syriaques 7, ed. F. Jullien (Paris, 2010), 37–63. The Syriac term also carries the

sense of celibacy, as the *iḥidayē* is isolated from both worldly affairs and from the bonds of married life.

116. John Chryssavgis, *Ascent to Heaven: The Theology of the Human Person According to Saint John of the Ladder* (Brookline, MA: Holy Cross Orthodox Press, 1989), 56–7. See Gospel of Mark 4:1, Gospel of Luke 4:1–2 and Galatians 1:17.
117. Jerome/Sancti Hieronymi, *Epistula* XXII:7, ed. Hilberg, Corpus Scriptorum Ecclesiasticorum Latinorum 54, Epistularum Pars I (Vindobonae: F. Tempsky, 1910–18). For a full translation of the 'Epistle of Jerome to Eustochium', see *Select Letters of St Jerome*, ed. and trans. F. A. Wright (London, 1933), 67–9.
118. Al-Iṣfahānī, *Ḥilyat* 9, 385–6.
119. *Kitāb al-ruhbān*, fol. 191b, section 14, lines 5–7.
120. Claudia Rapp, 'Desert, City, and Countryside in the Early Christian Imagination', *Church History and Religious Culture* 86:1/4 (2006), 93–112.
121. AbouZayd, *Iḥidayutha: A Study of the Life of Singleness in the Syrian Orient*, 199.
122. *Kitāb al-ruhbān*, fol. 191a, section 5, lines 1–5. A similar story appears in the *Ḥilyat al-awlīyā* 4, 44.
123. See David Brakke, 'The Making of Monastic Demonology: Three Ascetic Teachers on Withdrawal and Resistance', *Church History* 70:1 (March 2001), 19–48; on the intimate connection between prayers and contending with demons, see Brouria Bitton-Ashkelony, 'Demons and Prayers: Spiritual Exercises in the Monastic Community of Gaza in the Fifth and Sixth Centuries', *Vigiliae Christianae* 57:2 (May 2003), 200–21.
124. Little is definitively known about the author, aside from his composition of *The Ladder of Divine Ascent*. See John Duffy, 'Embellishing the Steps: Elements of Presentation and Style in the *Heavenly Ladder* of John Climacus', *Dumbarton Oaks Papers* 53 (1999), 1–17.
125. John Climacus, *Scala Paradisi*, Gradus VII, ed. Migne, *Patrologia Cursus Completus*, Series Graeca, 88.805 A in the Greek text.
126. The name 'Iblīs' comes from the Arabic verbal root of b-l-s, according to Ibn Manẓūr. The meaning of the root is comparable to the terms *quṭiʿa* ('to be cut-off from'), *sakata* ('to be silenced'), *yaʾisa* ('to have lost hope') and *nadima* ('to regret'). The entry also claims that the original name of this figure was ʿAzāzīl, but having been cursed by God for his disobedience, the name was changed to Iblīs. Reflecting the verbal root, the figure was therefore effectively severed or 'cut-off' from God. See Ibn Manẓūr, *Lisān al-ʿarab* (Beirut: Dār Iḥyāʾ al-Turāth al-ʿArabī, 1418/1997), vol. 1, 482. However, western

scholars have claimed that the name/term is of foreign import, *a'jamī*, to the Qur'ān. Its rendering may have been derived through the New Testament and Greek patristic term διάβολοσ, to which iblīs bears phonological similarity. See Gabriel Said Reynolds, 'A Reflection on Two Qur'ānic Words (Iblīs and Jūdī) with Attention to the Theories of A. Mingana', *Journal of the American Oriental Society* 124:4 (October–December 2004), 675–89.

127. For more on this narrative, see Jean Butler, 'Reading Satan, Remembering the Other', *Numen* 58:2/3 (2011), 157–87.
128. Reynolds, 'A Reflection on Two Qur'ānic Words', 681.
129. Butler, 'Reading Satan', 162–3.
130. Reynolds, 'A Reflection on Two Qur'ānic Words', 680–1.
131. For the story of the monk Nathaniel being unsuccessfully tempted by Satan in disguise, see 'Anān-Īshō, *The Book of Paradise*, ed. and trans. Ernest A. Wallis Budge (2 vols) (London: Chatto and Windus, 1907), vol. 1, 163 English translation; vol. 2, 136–7 Syriac text. A bit later in the text a similar example is given, where the monk Eucarpus is visited by Satan. When the tempter proclaims to the monk that 'I am Christ', Eucarpus actually believes in the falsehood and is mislead into giving up his life of humility and solitude. See *Book of Paradise* 1, 404–5.
132. *Kitāb al-ruhbān*, fol. 191b, section 16, lines 13–19.
133. See Dominic Alexander, *Saints and Animals in the Middle Ages* (Woodbridge: Boydell Press, 2008), 38–56.
134. Alison Goddard Elliott, *Roads to Paradise: Reading the Lives of the Early Saints* (Hanover, NH: The University Press of New England, 1987), 144–60. This fact may be owed to the numerous stories of Christian martyrdom involving lions.
135. David Salter, *Holy and Noble Beasts: Encounters with Animals in Medieval Literature* (Cambridge: D. S. Brewer, 2001), 11–24.
136. Ibid. 11–24.
137. Jerome/Sancti Hieronymi, *Vita S. Pauli Primi Eremitae*, ed. Migne, Patrologia Latina 23, col. 17–28. This passage appears in section 16.A, 'Christiana traditio', lines 7–15.
138. Ibid.
139. *Kitāb al-ruhbān*, fol. 191b, section 16, line 19. Alison Goddard Elliott cites biblical precedent for man's dominion over lions in the story of Daniel (The Book of Daniel, chapters 6 and 14), in connection to the prophet's 'innocence and purity'. See Elliott, *Roads to Paradise*, 152.

140. Patricia Cox Miller, *In the Eye of the Animal: Zoological Imagination in Ancient Christianity* (Philadelphia, PA: University of Pennsylvania Press, 2018), 119–54.
141. Catherine Osborne, *Dumb Beasts and Dead Philosophers: Humanity and the Humane in Ancient Philosophy and Literature* (Oxford: Clarendon Press, 2007), 160. Cf. Miller, *In the Eye of the Animal*, 120.
142. Charles Segal, 'Foreword' on page x, to Elliott, *Roads to Paradise*. Cf. Salter, *Holy and Noble Beasts*, 20–1.
143. ʿUmar ibn ʿAbd al-Azīz reportedly died and was buried at Dayr Simʿān. See al-Ṭabarī, *Taʾrīkh al-rusūl waʾl mulūk* (5 vols) (Beirut: Dār al-Kutub al-ʿIlmīyya, 1987), vol. 4, 67; Leiden edition 1362–3 (Leiden: Brill, 1879–1901).
144. *Kitāb al-ruhbān*, fol. 191a, section 8, lines 8–12.
145. Ibid. lines 8–12.

6

The God-fearers: A Righteous Tie that Binds

The *Ktābā d-Rīsh Mellē* of John bar Penkāyē again makes explicit reference to an accord for the safeguarding of monastic communities under Muslim rule. This particular section of the *Rīsh Mellē* states that 'God had prepared them [ie. the Muslim occupiers of the region] to hold Christians in honor, also possessing a special ordinance (*pūqdānā maram*) from God concerning our monastic station, that they should hold it in honor.'[1] This reference to a 'special ordinance' may have some relationship to conquest reports and early legal statutes concerning the protection of monasteries and the treatment of their residents. As discussed in the third chapter of this research, it would appear that these institutions were therefore understood as distinct communities, somewhat partitioned from the larger Christian fold.

The terminology employed by John bar Penkāyē as it applies to the 'monastic station' – referring to the socio-political position of monasticism – is likewise significant and seems to find analogous formulations in related texts. The Pact of Najrān, for example, as preserved by al-Balādhurī, uses a similar phrasing in 'nor will a monk [be removed] from his monastic position (*rahbāniyya*)'.[2] This particular attitude toward monasticism is revealed in similar fashion by a recension of the Najrān treaty found in the *Chronicle of Seert*, stating:

> This establishes the protection of their persons, their churches, their chapels, their oratories, the abodes of their monks and the places of their anchorites,

> wherever they are found – in mountains, valleys, in caves, in settled places, in plains or deserts . . .[3]

Comparable to such sentiments that appear to indicate a certain endorsement for monastic privilege is a passage from an early eighth-century Christian account, known as the *Disputation against the Arabs*.[4] This account alleges to possess some independent knowledge of statements attributed to Muḥammad that render a similar tone, suggesting at one point through the words of a Muslim figure in the text that 'even Muhammad our Prophet said about the inhabitants of monasteries and the mountain dwellers that they will enjoy the kingdom'.[5] There is unfortunately no further clarification in the text regarding this statement.

It may well be argued that since the *Disputation against the Arabs* as well as the aforementioned passage from the *Ktābā d-Rīsh Mellē* were composed by monks there would have been a natural inclination to promote the security of monasteries, singled out above any other religious or civil body in the most explicit of terms. Thus, the direct references to monasteries along with their political pacts or assurances for asylum can perhaps be interpreted as merely instruments of self-preservation.[6] Given the apparent interreligious concern specifically applied to monastic sanctuary, expressed through the passages above, it seems likely however that there was something more to this issue. In such a case the general reverence for ascetics, across confessional boundaries, would have served as a central motivating factor.

Though there are instances in which the institution of monasticism may appear to be condemned, or at least prohibited within Islam,[7] there also exist a range of more moderate statements that perhaps reflect a reverential perspective on asceticism.[8] The Qurʾānic usage of the terms *ruhbān* and *rahbāniyya*, as mentioned above, referring to monks and monasticism respectively, serves as an illustration of this range of viewpoints. A few of these statements merit discussion here, as it seems plausible that such regard for holy men and hermits, or at minimum an ambivalence to their existence, may have had considerable impact on the later formulation of Christian monasteries as subjects for both administrative procedure and popular interest. Among the most important of these is the statement found in *Sūrat al-māʾida*, which is as follows:

> You will find the people most intensely hostile to the believers are the Jews and pagans, and that the nearest in affection to them are those that say: 'we are Christians'. That is because there are priests (*qissīsīn*) and monks (*ruhbān*) among them who are free from arrogance (*lā yastakbirūna*). (*Sūrat al-mā'ida* 5:82)

The isolation of these two categories of Christian ecclesiastical positions, particularly the monks in this context, is most instructive in supporting a reverential connection. According to the exegesis of al-Ṭabarī, the verse directly refers to monks on the basis that their approach to religion is so near to that of Muslim belief (*bi-qurb mūdatihim li-ahl al-īmān bi-llāhi wa-rasūlihi*).[9] The parallels concern three main characteristics: their absolute dedication to religious observance, in this case by withdrawing to monasteries and hermitages apart from the secular world; the presence of a learned class among them who focus on holy scripture; and their resolute humility.[10] In essence, idealised monastic figures would have been considered amongst the foremost paragons of righteousness, regardless of sectarian affiliation.

The absence of haughtiness or pride among this group, here referred to by the phrase *annahum lā yastakbirūna*, serves as a key element within the verse. The usage here clearly presents a contrast to the impious monks mentioned in *Sūrat al-tawbah*, verse 34.[11] It likewise appropriately describes one of the central facets of the pious monastic existence: an unyielding sense of humbleness before the divine, a dissolution of tendencies for self-exaltation. The issue of humility, *ταπείνωσις* in the Greek monastic tradition of the Near East, was recognised as one of the key components for spiritual self-transformation as evidenced by teachings of late antique monastic leaders to their brethren.[12] It was through this cultivation of self-surrender and a total willingness to obey their masters, in matters of discipline, that spiritual perfection could be achieved.[13]

In an anthropological study of self-imposed submissiveness in this type of medieval religious context, Talal Asad states that

> a remarkable feature of monastic discipline is that it explicitly aims to create, through a program of communal living, the will to obey . . . the obedient monk is a person for whom obedience is his virtue – in the sense of

> being his ability, potentiality, power – a Christian virtue developed through discipline.[14]

The sense of humility in supplication and human inadequacy before the divine is a palpable theme in the Syriac hymnal cycles (*memrē*) of the monk Jacob of Serūgh (d. 521). In many cases this awareness of human limitations is accompanied by appeals for mercy from God and self-reproach.[15] Hymns from his third cycle, for instance, state: 'Accept with compassion the imperfection of my hymn *(la'mḥilōteh d-memrō qabell ḥabīboīt)*, and let my coin fall upon your table with favor'[16] and 'In exchange for what I have sung here feebly (*nashīshoīt*), may your mercies (*raḥmaīk*) endure so that I may live through them to eternity'.[17] Later cycles from Jacob also display a deep sense of humility and recognition of the necessity for divine mercy – clemencies which are undeserved, yet sought in earnest supplication: 'May your compassion be the defender of my weakness (*ḥnonok nehwē snēgrō l'shaplōtī*) when You rise for Judgment and may it approach You on my behalf'[18] and 'Let it speak loudly about my misery so that with Your grace You might bring life to this weakling without merit' (*l'honō bad lō showē*).[19] The admonition of the self is likewise present, including a call to action in *memrō* thirty-five: 'O, you who is idle, while you live, awaken and praise *('ett'īr shabaḥ)*, for there is time for all things and now [is the time] to profess Him.'[20]

The paramount distinction between humility and arrogance, in terms of proper devotion, can also be seen in *Sūrat al-sajda*:

> None believe in Our verses except those who, when reminded of them, prostrate themselves in adoration and give glory to their Lord; they are not arrogant (*wa-hum lā yastakbirūna*). They rise from their beds to pray to the Lord in fear and hope; who spend what has been provided for them. No mortal knows what bliss will be in store for these as a reward for their labors. (*Sūrat al-sajda* 32:15–16)

This characteristic of submission or obedience to the divine is clearly reflected in the Arabic term traditionally employed for 'monk', *rāhib*, carrying an intrinsic root meaning of 'veneration', 'reverence', 'awe' and perhaps most significantly 'fear'.[21] The verbal extension of this root, *rahiba*, appears as an example of this usage in the Qur'ān 7:154, stating: 'And when the anger in

Moses subsided, he took up the tablets; and in their inscription was guidance and mercy for those who are fearful of their Lord' (*hum li-rabbihim yarhibūna*). It may even be suggested that this connotation of 'fear of the divine' is more heavily pronounced in the Arabic terminology than in other languages from the region, in which the monk can literally be understood as 'one who fears God'. In the typical designations of both μοναχός and the practice of ἀναχωρειν,[22] from the Byzantine tradition, and *iḥidayē*,[23] most commonly utilised in Syriac, the emphasis falls on the solitary nature of the monastic existence. In either of these cases the central element, from which the designations arise, concerns a retreat from the material world into spiritual seclusion.[24]

It would appear, however, that the fear of the divine, ultimately being understood as a significant component to pietistic observance, serves as the defining characteristic of monasticism in general Arabic terminology as well as its designation in the Qur'ān. The connection between these two ideas of piety and fear is further illuminated in the Qur'ānic usage of the term *taqwā*, generally being translated as 'righteousness' or 'piety'. Yet once again the root itself, w-q-a, carries a specific meaning of the 'fear of God'.[25] The truly pious individual, a *muttaqin*, therefore necessarily possesses fear as a core attribute. It is the reverence for the divine that presupposes an obedient and righteous life. The early Muslim mystic Ḥasan al-Baṣrī (d. 728) even stated of Muḥammad that 'Fear (*khawf*) guided the Prophet in his conduct with respect to God and kept him restrained from neglecting His charge.'[26] In the *Iḥyā' 'ulūm al-dīn*, al-Ghazālī (d. 1111) includes an entire section dealing with the importance of fear yielding to piety.[27] For al-Ghazālī, fear can initially be classified in terms of knowledge or an awareness of God; and secondly, in appropriate actions taken concerning this knowledge. In this way, when one's knowledge of God has reached perfection, only then will one also be filled with a total awe of the divine, leading to absolute submission.[28] A *ḥadīth* of the Prophet is then provided as testimony for this position:

> The person most filled with fear in respect of His Lord is the man who has the most knowledge of himself and his Lord. For that reason, Muḥammad said: 'I am the one who fears God most among you.' And likewise, God said: 'Only the knowledgeable among his creatures fear God.'[29]

The gravity of this type of submission, born from awe, and its reward is referred to in *Sūrat al-anfāl*, stating:

> O you who have believed, if you fear God (*tattaqū Allāh*), he will grant you salvation and cleanse you of your sins and forgive you. Great is the bounty of God. (*Sūrat al-anfāl* 8:29)

It seems as no coincidence that certain features within the cycles of Syriac rules for monastic conduct also provide a virtually analogous assessment of the bond between fear, humility and the pious existence. The regulations imposed on monastic communities by the fourth-century Mār Ephrēm of Edessa, for example, contain the following passage:

> It is good for you that you are being educated in the fear (*deḥltē*) of your masters; and becoming humble (*makīk*), and chaste (*nekhef*), and disciplined (*maṭkus*). Do not become undisciplined.[30]

The sixth-century *Rules of Jōḥannan bar Qūrsos* likewise provide guidelines for the initiates that highlight a particular concern over the 'fear of God':

> They shall be sent into monasteries to read books and to learn the conduct of the fear of God (*deḥlṯ ʿElohē*). For if many send their children to far off countries because of the instruction of this world, how much more fitting it is for those who have set apart and offered their children to God, that they must send them into the holy mountains for spiritual wisdom.[31]

The significantly later *Canons of Tīmāteʿos II*, composed in the fourteenth century, confirm the long tradition of this connection within eastern monasticism. The opening line to the *Regulations for Leaders of Monasteries* (*Qanūnē ʿal rīsh ʿūmrē*) as formulated by Tīmāteʿos II, the metropolitan of Mosul, reads: 'It is in all fear of God (*d-bikolḥe deḥlṯ ʿElohē*) that they shall rule.'[32]

The religious status of monks, based on the aforementioned principles submitted by al-Ṭabarī (chief among them being their consummate humility), is therefore interpreted by the commentator to be rather close to that of the true believers, that is Muslims (*fa-hum lā yabʿdūna min al-mūʾminīn*).[33] It also bears noting that the same phrasing (*lā yastakbirūna*) appears in both *Sūrat al-sajda*, in the characterisation of 'those who believe in Our verses', and in *Sūrat al-māʾida*, with the explicit determination of monks 'who are not arrogant'. Muqātil ibn Sulaymān provides one of the earliest hermeneutical expositions of this passage from *Sūrat al-mā'ida*. In the explanation he suggests that when the word *ruhbān* appears in scripture it is to be understood as 'those pious men of the cells' (*muta'abbid aṣḥāb al-ṣawāmi'a*),[34] 'those who do not act pridefully in matters of faith' (*lā yatakābirūna 'an al-īmān*).[35] This is, in fact, his definition of *monasticism*.

In general, it could then be suggested that it is indeed this rigorous solemnity and personal piety in the ascetic existence that most defines monasticism in its Qur'ānic usage. Sebastian Brock has compared the development of late antique asceticism to a kind of martyrdom, with the Christian ascetic replacing the martyr as the fulcrum of truly pious existence.[36] With the last waves of persecutions against Christians coming to an end just prior to the advent of monasticism, the life of the martyr as the standard of righteousness in the early Church was no longer attainable. The rise of monasticism and asceticism, however, could be seen as a 'successor' to the ideal of martyrdom.[37] The pious death in this instance was not a physical one brought about through persecution by temporal authorities; rather it concerned the complete rejection of the material world and a withdrawal into the spiritual. The monastic and ascetic figures of Late Antiquity would then have become generally associated with this type of spiritual perfection; therefore, ultimately being recognised as the premier representatives of religious piety. As such was the case throughout the late antique period, it seems reasonable to suggest that the principle would have been maintained to some extent within the early Islamic era as well. In its original conception of a movement with righteousness at its core, would these figures not have sustained a certain validation within the 'Believers' movement regardless of confessional affiliation?

The rigour of personal piety associated with monasticism, and particularly as it concerned the strict observance of daily prayer rituals, is clearly the reason why some Muslim ascetics were on occasion reverently referred to by the term *rāhib*.[38] This would of course not suggest that these figures were actually monks, but that they had embraced a pietistic way of life that was reminiscent of a monastic ideal. It was, by way of an example, excessive praying that led to Abū Bakr ibn 'Abd al-Raḥmān being called the *rāhib* of Quraysh.[39] The ritualised act of prayer (*ṣalāt*) is of course one of the central tenets for a pious life as mandated in the Qur'ān. One of the fundamental physical acts of the ritual is the *sujūd*, or prostration before the divine. A. J. Wensinck has postulated that the development of this Muslim practice may be traced to eastern Christian ritualistic influences.[40]

The references to prayer occur frequently within the Qur'ān, including the directions for its dutiful observance: concerning manner of ritual and when they are supposed to be performed.[41] In the latter regard, the Qur'ān dictates that prayer must be performed before dawn, before sunset, during the night, and during the day. Verses from *Surāt hūd* and *Surāt al-isrā'* provide the following examples:

> Attend to your prayers, morning and evening, as well as in the night. Good deeds shall make amends for sins. That is the admonition for thoughtful men. Therefore, have patience; God will not deny the reward for those who do good. (*Surāt hūd* 11:114–15)

> Recite your prayers at sunset, at nightfall, and at dawn; the dawn prayer has ever witnessed. Pray during the night also; an additional duty (*nāfila*) upon you for the fulfillment of which your Lord may exalt you to a station of honor. (*Surāt al-isrā'* 17:78–9)

Early mystical traditions within Islam often regarded *ṣalāt* as a kind of ascension. Just as the Prophet's *mi'rāj* (the ascension into heaven as part of the Prophet Muḥammad's Night Journey) had conveyed him closer to God, so the mystics were inclined to believe that prayer could transport them into the immediate presence of the divine.[42] Such was the absolute necessity for ritual prayer in the world of early Islamic mysticism. A similar demand for the uncompromising observance of prayer existed in the world of Christian monastics. Even in the formative stages of monasticism, under the guidance of Pachomius (d. 348), the monks were ordered to pray in community at fixed times during the day and night, as well as performing solitary prayers throughout the hours of their labour.[43] This cycle of prayer typically developed into seven or eight offices during the day, in addition to the nocturnal vigil.[44]

John Cassian (d. 435) likewise insisted, based on the teachings of Abba Isaac of Scetis, that 'The end of every monk and the perfection of his heart incline him to constant and uninterrupted perseverance in prayer; and, as much as human frailty allows, it strives after an unchanging and continual tranquility of mind and perpetual purity.'[45] This type of unceasing prayer, referred to as ἀδιάλειπτος προσευχή in the Greek Palestinian tradition, as well as the remembrance of God, μνήμη Θεοῦ, were considered pivotal aspects of monastic devotion and were believed to ensure the chances of a genuine encounter with the sacred.[46] As well, the concept of prayer was one of the foundational principles of progress, προσκοπή, in the monastic understanding of the search for spiritual perfection.[47]

The sayings attributed to the fifth-century monastic leader Agathōn of Scetis remark that his brethren once questioned him: 'among all good works, which is the virtue that requires the greatest effort?' His reply was: 'Forgive me, but I think that there is no greater labor than that of prayer to God. For every time a person wants to pray, his enemies, the demons, want to prevent him from praying, for they know that only by turning him away from prayer can they hinder his journey.'[48] It is also claimed that Anthony practised a 'watchfulness', spending entire nights in prayer vigil.[49] The peace that such prayer granted a monk was known as ἡσυχία, representing an inner calm. Abba Rufus of Scetis is reported to have stated of this ἡσυχία, 'interior stillness means to remain sitting in one's cell with fear and knowledge of God, holding far off the remembrance of wrongs suffered and pride of spirit'.[50]

The prayer during the night hours is generally accorded a more lofty significance in the early monastic sources, in part signifying the adherent's rejection of sleep in preference for worship.[51] The special force behind this office of prayer, known as *nocturns*, was maintained within the western monastic tradition as well, typically being recognised as the longest and most important of the daily liturgical cycles.[52] These prayers were not seen as simply performing an anticipatory function of heralding the dawn but held a distinct theological and cosmological spirit of their own. For the monks of early medieval Europe, the office of *nocturns* represented a deeply symbolic connection between their own communities and the primordial darkness into which creation was brought forth. It was in these moments, through chant and meditation amidst the darkness, that monks perceived themselves to be closest to the divine.[53] As stated by Mary Helms, 'within the context of a nocturns-centered existence that consumed so much of their time and attention, monks can appropriately be thought of as men of the night'.[54]

The Arabs of the late antique and pre-Islamic Near East seem to have particularly associated monasticism with the night vigil as well. The lamps used in the observance of the night prayers by the monk and hermit would have served as a welcome guide to nomads or travellers along the fringes of society. These physical signs of humanity within the desert environment, along with the ardent conviction of hospitality connected to the monastic ethos, made an impression within pre-Islamic poetry. The light from these lamps is one of the defining features of the hermit or anchorite, as the poet Imrū' al-Qays recalls in these verses:

> She illuminates the darkness at evening, like a lamp set by a praying monk (*tuḍi'a al-ẓalām bi-l-'ishā', manāra mumsa rāhib mutabattil*).[55]
>
> . . . and the stars were as the lamps of monks that they light for travelers (*wa al-nujūm ka-ānnahā, maṣābīḥ ruhbān tushabb li-quffāl*).[56]

In particular, this image of the lamp burning throughout the night, as the monk engages in ritual prayer, is the potent element within the verses. It has been suggested that the famous 'light verse' of the Qur'ān, *Sūrat al-nūr* verse 35, as well as its surrounding verses, may provide an allusion to precisely this type of monastic tradition. The Qur'ānic verses here read:

> And We have sent down to you, distinct verses and examples of those who passed on before you and an admonition to those who fear God.
>
> God is the light of the heavens and the earth. The likeness of His light is as a niche (*mishkāt*) wherein is a lamp (*miṣbāḥ*), the lamp in a glass (*zujājā*), the glass as it were a glittering star, kindled from a blessed tree, an olive that is neither of the East or West, whose oil would shine even if no fire had touched it; light upon light (*nūrun 'alā nūrin*). God guides to His light whom He will. And God strikes similes for men, and God has knowledge of all things.
>
> In houses (*fī buyūt*) which God has allowed to be raised up, and within which His name has been commemorated; therein glorifying Him, in the mornings and the evenings, are men whom neither trade nor commerce

> diverts from the remembrance of God and the performance of the prayer, and paying the alms (*zakāt*), fearing a day when hearts and eyes will be turned about. (*Sūrat al-nūr* 24:34–37)

In an examination of the 'light verse', Gerhard Böwering maintains that this reference to the *buyūt*, those places where the name of God is recalled in morning and evening prayers, is a reference to ritual observance within eastern monasteries.[57] It is true enough though that the traditional word *ādyār*, for 'monasteries', is not explicitly provided within the text. The usage of the term *buyūt* could then be argued to have a more general meaning, as simply 'houses of prayer'. As well, as noted by Bell in his commentary, the payment of *zakāt* would typically not have been applied to priests or monastics.[58] Still, Böwering insists on a peculiar use of terminology[59] and imagery[60] within the verses that point to a non-Arab, or more specifically eastern Christian origin. In the words of Böwering, '

> Christian readers of the Qur'ān may picture this verse against the solemn atmosphere of altars lit for worship in eastern Christian churches and monasteries, and detect in the Qur'ānic wording phrases that recall 'the Light of the World' in John's Gospel and the 'Light from Light' from the Nicene Creed.[61]

This concept likewise finds resonance within a particular passage from the *Kitāb al-ruhbān* of Ibn Abī al-Dunyā, drawing the parallel between monastic prayer and candlelight. The dictum here, based upon the authority of al-Faḍīl ibn Shaʿba, is as follows:

> 'Behold! Do not let the lamp in your house go out, lest thieves come in and make off with you.' He continued: 'let your house be illuminated by the remembrance of God' (*nawwara baytak bi-dhikr Allāh*).[62]

Daniel J. Sahas has likewise drawn the conclusion that the verses from *Sūrat al-nūr* directly reference the observance of prayer in a monastic context, drawing the subtle parallels between the duties of the Muslim faithful and pious monks.[63] It is also worth observing that here, within these verses, one could make the argument that the emphasis on prayer, prostration before the divine, the anticipation of a Final Judgement – 'a day when hearts and eyes will be turned about' – and social responsibility toward others are precisely the themes that Donner addresses relating to a non-confessional orientation of the early *umma*.[64]

Though the reference to these *buyūt* in which the performance of prayer is characterised as a virtually perpetual act of devotion is rather obscure, it is tantalising to consider the possibility that the 'light verse' could be understood within the context of monastic life. The devotion of the chanting remembrance of God, μνήμη Θεοῦ, could conceivably have a favourable comparison here as well. The instructions for monastic prayer according to John Cassian include precisely this type of unending devotion, so that through constant integration the 'monk and prayer become ever one'.[65] This section of the *Conferences* of John Cassian states:

> Therefore, before we pray we should make an effort to cast out from the innermost parts of our heart whatever we do not wish to steal upon us as we pray, so that in this way we can fulfill the apostolic words: 'Pray without ceasing' . . . for we shall be unable to accomplish this command unless our mind, purified of every contagion of vice and given over to virtue alone as a natural good, is fed upon the constant contemplation of almighty God.[66]

While the suggestion that the 'light verse' within *Sūrat al-nūr* specifically references monasteries may be inconclusive, the emphasis placed upon ritual prayer, rigorous personal piety, and fear of the divine in both the early Islamic and eastern monastic traditions maintains certain parallels. If these sentiments for the attainment of a truly righteous life between the traditions are as analogous as they appear, then the case can be made for inter-confessional overlapping of religious identities: that is, a 'Believer's movement'.

Above all other factors, it would seem, the relentless pursuit of piety within one's own life appears to have been the dominant factor. Regardless of confessional stance, the behaviour, humility and attention to prayer would seem in accordance with the basic Qur'ānic tenets for leading a righteous life. The claim that the lives of monks represent a close approximation to pious Muslim behaviour (*fa-hum lā yab'dūna min al-mū'minīn*),[67] as presented earlier by al-Ṭabarī, adds further weight to the existence of a kind of amorphous religious milieu of the early Islamic period; one in which monks and their abodes may have represented a certain lofty spiritual ideal. The boundaries of confessional distinction in such a case would have been flexible and could be traversed depending upon certain shared concepts of righteous behaviour.

Based on this association with piety and spiritual awareness, it stands to reason that according to the *Sīra* of Ibn Isḥāq (d. 767), the first person to recognise the future prophetic significance of Muḥammad was a Christian monk[68] from Buṣrā, in southern Syria. According to the text, the monk, known as Baḥīrā,[69] possessed a great knowledge of religion by virtue of a book he kept in his dwelling. The young[70] Muḥammad passed by the hermitage (here called a *ṣawmiʿa* or 'cell') as part of a trading mission in the company of his uncle Abū Ṭālib to al-Shām. The monk took special notice of him and subsequently, upon consulting his sacred works, predicted the boy's forthcoming greatness. The text explains that the monk then examined a particular physical mark on the young boy, which is referred to as the *khatam al-nabuwwa*[71] or 'the seal of prophecy', a telling sign of this future eminence, as a way of confirming his forecast.[72]

There is likewise another encounter between a monk and Muḥammad preserved in the *Sīra*, framed within the account of the Prophet's marriage to Khadīja. Once again, in this instance, set at a later period in which the Prophet was already twenty-five years old, the encounter takes place as Muḥammad is on a trading mission to Syria. When Muḥammad and his travelling companion Maysara stop to rest in the vicinity of a monastic cell, an unnamed monk approaches Maysara to inquire about the identity of the man resting under the nearby shade tree. Maysara then informs the monk that his companion, Muḥammad, was 'from the tribe of Quraysh, the people of the Ḥaram in Mecca'. The monk then exclaims, 'no one has ever sat beneath this tree except a prophet' (*mā najala taḥta hādhihi al-shajara qaṭṭu illā nabī*).[73] Though this account does not contain the depth of detail seen in the encounter with Baḥīrā, it is still a prophetic device that, once again, establishes the figure of the monk as an early harbinger for the future significance of Muḥammad.

While the development of monasticism could be considered an unwarranted innovation in religious practice, as earlier presented by the classical Muslim exegetes, the institution as a whole would appear to have maintained a certain degree of honour even within an Islamic context. The continuation of this elevated status for monasticism would at least potentially account for the appearance of both Baḥīrā and the unnamed monk in the *Sīra* narratives. For Muqātil, the entire development of both Christianity and Judaism were, in fact, also innovations.[74] The separation of these two confessional traditions was thereby not in conjunction with the original teachings of Jesus. The authentic doctrine is referred to as the *dīn ʿIsā*,[75] and would clearly be bound to the non-confessionally specific *dīn Ibrāhīm* in the exegete's understanding.

There were, however, groups of devout men who remained loyal to the original message up until the time of Muḥammad. A total of forty such devotees existed at the emergence of Islam as explained by Muqātil. These believers among the people of the Gospel (*min muʾminī ahl al-Injīl*), referring to the uncorrupted teachings of Jesus, were dispersed throughout Abyssinia (*ʿarḍ al-Ḥabasha*) and Syria (*al-Shām*). One among them is specifically named by Muqātil as 'the monk Baḥīrā'.[76] According to the *Tafsīr*, these select few true believers are precisely those *ruhbān* referred to within verse 82 of *Sūrat al-māʾidah*.[77] All of these figures are Christian monks, yet at the same time being sincere followers of both Jesus and Muḥammad. In a certain sense then it appears that monks could have been recognised as the 'true Christians',[78] those faithfully adhering to the original message of Christ and therefore being open to the prophethood of Muḥammad.[79] In terms then of the most essential Muslim exegetical understanding of the *dīn ʿIsā*, those types of monks and ascetics, remaining faithful to their fundamental principles, would have indeed been a close analog to the righteous of their own community.

The narrative of the encounter with Baḥīrā also reinforces the notion that such a holy man could be a purveyor of esoteric knowledge. This is an ancient Mediterranean and Near Eastern motif[80] that pre-dates both Christianity and Islam but seems to have been later absorbed into those traditions in the figure of the monk and ascetic. As illustrated in the account, Baḥīrā has acquired his knowledge of the sacred through a book in his possession (*ilayhi yaṣīr ʿilmahum ʿan kitāb fīhā*). The claim that he is able to effectively foresee future events and recognise the prophetic career of the young Muḥammad likewise emphasises his intimate connection to the supernatural. In the context of late antique understanding, a bond like this was accessible only to an elect few. Fellowship with the divine would have been reserved for those who displayed, in the words of Robert Kirschner, 'a personal holiness that was demonstrable and visible'.[81] Through this exclusive relationship to the supernatural, the holy man came to be viewed as 'the divine conduit, the funnel between heaven and earth'.[82]

This account was not only a feature within the Islamic tradition but was widely circulated among different confessional groups as well, in which case the basic framework of the account remains intact but the name of the monk is sometimes altered to either Nesṭūr[83] or Sergius.[84] There is frequently a sectarian agenda to the story as it appears in other traditions and is thereby employed as a polemical or apologetical device. The redaction of the story by the Byzantine historian Theophanes (d. 817), for example, takes on a decidedly polemical approach, stating that the monk had been exiled for his depraved doctrine.[85] The writings of the Melkite theologian John of Damascus (d. 749) make a similar claim that Muḥammad had been instructed in theology by an Arian monk, reinforcing the position that Islam was originally formulated as a Christian heresy.[86] In the later Muslim tradition as well the story becomes part of a discourse which reinforces the legitimacy and superiority of Islam at the expense of its rival in Christianity.[87]

It is immaterial for this research to concentrate on whether or not the account of Baḥīrā should be interpreted in historical or apocryphal terms.[88] The more important matter here is the question of what function the story serves in its early Islamic context and why monks were situated in the framework. This research takes the position that the accounts of both Baḥīrā and the unnamed monk in the *Sīra* can be seen as indicators of the continuity of the late antique pietistic veneration of monastics into an Islamic context. Though perhaps not applying to all Christians, or even all Christian monks, some of these men would have remained exemplars for a radical version of righteous behaviour. Since the development of the early *umma* would have been predicated on this tenet, yielding to the idea of a 'Believers' movement, it makes sense that these monastic figures may have held significant influence in its pietistic orientation.

Such a proposition is reinforced by other Muslim encounters with monks, particularly those Muslims interested in observing or learning the pious lifestyle. For this reason, the ancient typology of the *Apopthegmata Patrum*, or 'Sayings of the desert fathers', has frequently occurred in Islamic mystical texts and hagiographies.[89] In many cases the accounts picture a Muslim mystic seeking spiritual advice from a monk, a fellow ascetic in this context and seeker of wisdom. The same Mālik ibn Dīnār, mentioned previously in the 'wall of iron' example, is also claimed to have been enamoured with books and so visited a monastery in search of this kind of learning. He was then able to borrow a book from the monastery's collection.[90] In another passage from the *Ḥilyat al-awliyā'* a Muslim traveller, Muḥammad ibn Ya'qūb, happens upon two monks while journeying across the Syrian desert. According to the account, Muḥammad had accidently strayed from his path and was becoming afraid that he would die in the desert. As he is near exhaustion, he sees two monks from a nearby monastery and hastens over to speak with them. Their conversation is as follows:

> I said to them, 'where are you going?' 'We do not know' [they replied]. 'Do you know where you are?' And then they responded, 'Yes. We are within His dominion, His kingdom, and within His presence' (*bayna yadaihi*). I then began to chastise my own spirit (*nafsī*) as I said to myself, 'both of these monks have realized the trust in God (*tawakkul*)[91] but have you not?' So, I then asked them, 'could I ask for your companionship?' They responded, 'As you like.' So, I went with them. When night approached, they readied themselves for prayer, and I also prepared to pray.[92]

Although the passages from the collections cited above are more concerned with the clarification of ascetic practices within Islam, these types of traditions provide considerable insight into the early Muslim perception of Christian monasticism. In general, the Christian monastic figures appear to be extraordinarily pious and knowledgeable in matters of religion. When taken in conjunction with certain Qur'ānic verses and their exegesis, as well as evidence from the *Ḥadīth* corpus, it would appear that the view of monasticism in the early Islamic period was rather accommodating. A magnanimous attitude toward such figures would have necessarily been applied to their places of prayer and work also.

As has been shown, in al-Zamakshari's use of the term *mu'minūn* for example, the connection between groups of 'Believers', Muslims and Christian ascetiscs may have indeed transcended confessional boundaries in the formative stages of Islam. The monks that the exegete references in his commentary of *Sūrat al-ḥadīd* are marked by their devotion and 'true belief' with precisely the same term often utilised in the Qur'ān to depict the fledgling Muslim *umma*. This bond amongst such communities would have been forged from their most general, and mutual, understanding of the importance for rigorous devotion in worship and way of life. As has been discussed, such a sentiment would not necessarily have applied to all Christian ascetics, but rather specifically to that select body of righteous holy men that continued to embrace the most intense penitential practices.

These types of figures, it can be argued, are represented in the Qur'ān as paragons of righteousness, regardless of confessional distinction. As put by the ninth-century Muslim author al-Jāḥiẓ, when *Sūrat al-mā'ida* speaks of monks in laudable terms, it is referring to precisely those types of men 'like Baḥīrā and the likes of those monks whom Salmān had served'.[93] It would therefore appear that these kinds of pious monks were capable of traversing confessional barriers and were perhaps still interpreted as idealised beacons of righteousness into the early Islamic period. These figures, according to the commentary of al-Jāḥiẓ, are distinct from the reprehensible Christians that have taken a distinctly confessional stance. In this sense, the Christians of Salmān defy categorisation along confessional lines, even within the confines of Christian sectarianism itself. It would therefore be reasonable to suppose that these kinds of pious monks were also capable of traversing larger confessional barriers; those of a more interreligious nature. If we take Donner's suggestion that

> the community of Believers was originally conceptualized independent of confessional identities . . . Believers could be members of any one of several religious confessions – Christians or Jews, for example – if the doctrines of their religious confession were consonant with strict monotheism and not too inimical to the Believers' other basic ideas,[94]

the monks of Salmān would surely figure into such a movement and perhaps provide an additional lens into the appreciation of monasticism by early Muslims.

Their uncompromising manner of asceticism, austerity, wisdom and piety seem to parallel the concerns of an early 'believers' movement, unhindered by confessional allegiances. Bearing this contextual framework in mind, it should have been quite sound – from the standpoint of an early Muslim audience – to accept that Christian monks, long seen as individual archetypes of spiritual virtue, would ultimately reveal the path to Islam. This cycles back to the model suggested by Richard Miles in the first chapter. Here, we can see that sectarian identities in this period were not necessarily fastened to a static reality – they were often dynamic, and moreover, contradictory at times. As Jack Tannous, Christian Sahner and Fred Donner have all recently shown, religious networks in the Near East in the early centuries of Islam were exceptionally porous in nature. A firm command of specific doctrine, law and ritual would not have generally been within the dominion of the common people. In the absence of finite principles of faith, determined by higher authorities, their religion was one of a *lived praxis*, the core tenets of which would have been shared across diverse communities. In the words of Sahner, 'Levels of lay catechesis were probably very low, and in the cities and villages of Egypt, Syria, and Palestine where Muslims and Christians first rubbed shoulders, it was not always clear where the practice of one faith ended and the other began.'[95]

At the centre of this rather obscure and fluid milieu stands the figure of the Christian holy man. Rites of vistitation to their monasteries, reverence for their virtuous behaviour, and the seeking of their esoteric council continued to resist rigidly defined confessional boundaries well into the Islamic period. Such traditions were still widespread in the late ninth century and were of markedly crucial import to piety-minded Muslim ascetics, as evidenced by the formulation of the *Kitāb al-ruhbān*. This is precisely the 'residual, ecumenical īmān' that superseded doctrinal formulas or unyielding constructs of creed. Just as Tor Andrae insisted that interactions between these like-minded groups 'bear witness to the fact that Islam, during the first centuries, dared to learn, and in fact did learn, from Christian ascetic piety', we must accept that, within the narrative of Salmān's conversion and as part of the greater Muslim perception of monasticism, these men served as paradigms for an intermediary phase between the twilight of authentic Christianity and emerging Islam – the confessional barriers between which were virtually inconsequential across the early centuries of Islam.

For a devout practitioner of asceticism, like Ibn Abī al-Dunyā, there was much wisdom to be gained through dialogue with Christian ascetics. These communities had 'crucified' themselves to the world, as stated in the aforementioned Canons of Jōḥannan Bar Qūrsos, obviously a powerful symbol for demarcating a life of purity against an existence in the physical realm. One could perhaps make the case that Ibn Abī al-Dunyā was attempting to proselytise a comparable sentiment within his own religious community via the *Kitāb al-ruhbān*. These monks, along with their kernels of wisdom that might be passed along to others, have little to do with any particular sectarian group or confessional affiliation. It is simply with their unconditional conviction for a pious lifestyle that mystical devotees of Islam, the *zuhhād*, could most empathise. On this vehemence concerning the distorted condition of mankind, its institutions and its avaricious trappings, one might be further invited to see an analogous understanding within the *Kitāb dhamm al-dunyā* (*Condemnation of the World*), another work from Ibn Abī al-Dunyā. Here the author expresses contempt for the material world with direct reference to the Prophet Muḥammad himself, who is said to have professed, 'the world is a prison for the believer, a paradise for the unbeliever' (*al-dunyā sijn al-mu'min wa-janna al-kāfir*).[96]

Notes

1. A. Mingana (ed.), Book XV of the *Rīsh Mellē*, in *Sources Syriaques* (Leipzig: Otto Harrassowitz, 1908), 141.
2. Al-Balādhurī, *Futūḥ al-buldān* (Beirut: Dar al-Kutub al-'Ilmiyya, 1983), 76.
3. *Histoire nestorienne/Chronique de Se'ert*, ed. Addai Scher, *Patrologia Orientalis*, tome 13, fasc. 4, no. 65 (Paris, 1918), 602.
4. Sidney Griffith, 'Disputes with Muslims in Syriac Christian Texts: from Patriarch John (d. 648) to Bar Hebraeus (d. 1286)', *ARAM* 3 (1991), 259–60. This is listed as 'The Monk of Bet Ḥale and an Arab Notable' by Griffith, who was able to access a copy of this text from the Diyarbekir Syriac MS 95. I have not been able to see this for myself and can therefore only rely on his synopsis.
5. See footnote 40 in Griffith, 'Disputes with Muslims'. Griffith also importantly states that, as far as he has found, this tradition does not exist in any Islamic text. Furthermore, it seems reasonable that this reference to 'mountain dwellers' actually alludes more generally to solitary Christian ascetics, preferring to isolate themselves in remote areas. The research presented by Irfan Shahîd, relying on the *Ahsan al-Taqāsīm* of al-Muqaddasī, associates the Golan with 'holy mountains' as an interface between Islamic *zuhd* and Christian asceticism. See Shahîd, *Byzantium and the Arabs in the Sixth Century*, vol. 2 (Washington, DC: Dumbarton Oaks, 2002), 91.

6. Though not only applying to monasteries, this was assuredly an impetus for the falsification of documents guaranteeing the rights to ecclesiastical property. The foremost example of this type of forged agreement in circulation during this period, according to Tritton, is the so-called Covenant of ʿUmar. See A. J. Tritton, *The Caliphs and Their Non-Muslim Subjects: A Critical Study of the Covenant of ʿUmar* (London: Frank Cass & Co., 1970), chapter I.
7. Primarily concerning the monastic tenet of celibacy, as previously mentioned.
8. Ofer Livne-Kafri, 'Early Muslim Ascetics and the World of Christian Monasticism', *Jerusalem Studies in Arabic and Islam* 20 (1996), 107.
9. Al-Ṭabarī, *Jāmiʿ al-bayān ʿan taʾwīl āy al-Qurʾān*, vol. 10 (Egypt: Dār al-Maʿārif), 505.
10. Ibid. 505–6.
11. Edmund Beck, 'Das christliche Mönchtum im Koran', *Studia Orientalia* 13:3 (Helsinki, 1946), 6.
12. Brouria Bitton-Ashkelony, 'Demons and Prayers: Spiritual Exercises in the Monastic Community of Gaza in the Fifth and Sixth Centuries', *Vigiliae Christianae* 57:2 (2003), 201.
13. So important was this theme of humility in the practice of asceticism in Late Antiquity that it became a sort of game between competing hagiographers as to which of their subjects displayed the highest degree of spiritual perfection. See John Wortley, 'The Spirit of Rivalry in Early Christian Monasticism', *Greek, Roman and Byzantine Studies* 33 (1992), 385–404.
14. Talal Asad, 'On Discipline and Humility in Medieval Christian Monasticism', in *Genealogies of Religion: Discipline and Reasons of Power in Christianity and Islam* (Baltimore, MD: Johns Hopkins University Press, 1993), 125.
15. Khalid Dinno, 'Jacob of Serugh: The Man Behind the Mimre', in *Jacob of Serugh and His Times: Studies in Sixth-Century Syriac Christianity*, ed. George Anton Kiraz (Piscataway, NJ: Gorgias Press, 2010), 53.
16. See Hymn 3:107 in Dinno, 'Jacob of Serugh', 55.
17. Ibid. Hymn 3:110, 57.
18. Ibid. Hymn 192:202.
19. Ibid. Hymn 192:203.
20. Ibid. Hymn 35:9, 56.
21. See *Lisān al-ʿArab* of Ibn Manẓūr (Beirut: Dār Iḥyāʾ al-Turāth al-ʿArabī, 1418/1997), entry for the root *rahiba* (volume 5), in which the words *khawf* (fear) and *fajʿa* (fright) are provided as related meanings.
22. See Claire Fauchon, 'Les forms de vie ascétique et monastique en milieu

syriaque, Ve–VIIe siècles', *Le Monachisme Syriaque*, Études Syriaques 7, ed. F. Jullien (Paris, 2010), 37–9. The Syriac term also carries the sense of celibacy, as the *iḥidayē* is isolated from both worldly affairs and from the bonds of married life. A virtually analogous term for these consecrated celibates is *qaddīshē*, or 'saints/holy ones'. See Sidney Griffith, 'Asceticism in the Church of Syria: The Hermeneutics of Early Syrian Monasticism', in *Asceticism*, ed. V. L. Wimbush (Oxford: Oxford University Press, 1998), 223.

23. Ibid. 233.
24. Ibid. 39.
25. See Ibn Manẓūr, *Lisān al-ʿArab* entry for the root w-q-a, volume 15.
26. Al-Ḥakīm Tirmidhī, *Kitāb ithbāt al-ʿilal* (Rabat, 1998), 114.
27. Al-Ghazālī, *Iḥyāʾ ʿulūm al-dīn*, ed. ʿAydarūs (Dār al-Salām: Cairo, 2003), vol. II, 1496–528.
28. Ibid. 1496–7. Qurʾān 35:27 is invoked in this statement.
29. Ibid. 1497.
30. *Admonitions of Mār Ephrēm*, in *Syriac and Arabic Documents Regarding Legislation Relative to Syrian Asceticism*, ed. Arthur Vööbus, 20, no. 9.
31. *Rules of Jōḥannan bar Qūrsos*, in *Syriac and Arabic Documents* . . . ed. Vööbus, 59, rule 11.
32. *Canons of Tīmāteʿos II*, in ibid. 208, no. 1.
33. Al-Ṭabarī, *Jāmiʿ al-bayān*, 505–6.
34. Muqātil ibn Suleimān, *Tafsīr Muqātil ibn Sulīmān*, vol. 1, ed. Shiḥātah (Egypt, 1979), 497.
35. Ibid. 497.
36. Sebastian Brock, 'Early Syrian Asceticism', *Numen* 20:1 (April 1973), 2.
37. Ibid. 2.
38. Tor Andre, *In the Garden of Myrtles: Studies in Early Islamic Mysticism*, trans. Brigitta Sharpe (Albany, NY: State University of New York Press, 1987), 9.
39. Ibn Saʿd, *Ṭabaqāt al-kabīr* (11 vols) (Cairo: Maktabat al-Khanjī, 2001), vol. 5, 153.
40. A. J. Wensinck, *Muḥammad and the Jews of Medina*, trans. and ed. W. H. Behn (Berlin, 1982) [original title, *Moḥammed en de Joden te Medina* (Leiden, 1908)], 75–6. See also Eugen Mittwoch, *Zur Entstehungsgeschichte des islamichen Gebets und Kultus* (Berlin, 1913), 17, in which the *sujūd* is also paralleled within Judaic prayer rites. For a further exploration of the origins of the Muslim prostration, see Robert Totolli, 'Muslim Attitudes toward Prostration, sujūd: Arabs and

Prostration at the Beginning of Islam and in the Qur'ān', *Studia Islamica* 88 (1998), 5–34.

41. While it is difficult to establish the precise mechanisms of prayer in the early period based solely on Qur'ānic evidence, it certainly involved standing, bowing, prostration, sitting, and the reciting of God's name. See Fred Donner, *Muhammad and the Believers: At the Origins of Islam* (Cambridge, MA: Belknap Press of Harvard University Press, 2010), 61.
42. Annemarie Schimmel, *Mystical Dimensions of Islam* (Chapel Hill, NC: University of North Carolina Press, 1975), 148. Some of these mystics associated the word *ṣalāt* with the root *waṣala*, meaning 'to arrive'. In this sense prayer became the moment of arrival before God.
43. Thomas W. Allies, *The Monastic Life: From the Fathers of the Desert to Charlemagne* (London: K. Paul, Trench, Trübner, & Co., 1896), 3–10.
44. Adalbert De Vogüé, 'To Study the Early Monks', *Collectanea Cisterciensia* 37 (1975), 68.
45. John Cassian, *The Conferences*, 9:2, trans. Boniface Ramsey (New York: Paulist Press, 1997).
46. Bitton-Ashkelony, 'Demons and Prayers', 202.
47. Ibid. 205.
48. See John Chryssavgis, 'The Desert and the World: Learning from the Desert Fathers and Mothers', *Greek Orthodox Theological Review* 53:1–4 (2008), 147–8.
49. William Harmless, *Desert Christians: An Introduction to the Literature of Early Monasticism* (Oxford University Press, 2004), 61.
50. Ibid. 228. See also *Patrologia Graeca* 65:389, ed. Migne.
51. Vööbus, *History of Asceticism in the Syrian Orient*, vol. II, 288. The author here states, 'Since the night has always been regarded in the Orient as a proper period for dealing with deeper thoughts and things holy, just that much more did it mean to the monks.'
52. Mary W. Helms, 'Before the Dawn: Monks and the Night in Late Antiquity and Early Medieval Europe', *Anthropos* 99 (2004), 178.
53. Ibid. 178.
54. Ibid. 178.
55. *The Diwans of the Six Ancient Arabic Poets: Ennabiga, 'Antara, Tharafa, Zuhair, 'Alqama and Imruulqais*, ed. W. Ahlwardt (Paris, 1913), 2, lines 38–9.
56. Ibid. 152. For translation, see *The Dīwān of Imrū' al-Qays*, trans. Arthur Wormhoudt (Oskaloosa, IA: William Penn College, 1974), 5, lines 18–19.

57. Gerhard Böwering, 'The Light Verse: Qur'ānic Text and Ṣūfī Interpretation', *Oriens* 36 (2001), 117.
58. R. Bell, *A Commentary on the Qur'ān*, vol. I (Manchester: University of Manchester, 1991), 60.
59. Particularly the word used for 'niche' in this passage, *mishkāt*, Böwering claims to be of Abyssinian Christian origin. As explained, the *mishkāt* is classified as a hapax within the Qur'ān; whereas an alternative word for 'niche', *miḥrāb*, becomes the dominant term in Arabic literature. See Böwering, 'The Light Verse', 119.
60. Expressly given the similarities to the image in pre-Islamic poetry, in the use of 'light' and 'lamps' in this religious context. See Böwering, 'The Light Verse', 119.
61. Ibid. 116.
62. MS Rampur 565 *al-Muntaqā min Kitāb al-ruhbān*, fol. 191a, section 10, lines 20–2.
63. Daniel J. Sahas, 'Monastic Ethos and Spirituality and the Origins of Islam', *Acts of the XVIII International Congress of Byzantine Studies, Moscow, 1991*, issue 2 (1996), 30.
64. Fred Donner, 'From Believers to Muslims: Confessional Self-Identity in the Early Islamic Community', *al-Abhath* 50–1 (2002–3), 9–53 at 19–21.
65. Columba Stewart, 'John Cassian on Unceasing Prayer', *Monastic Studies* 15 (1984), 162.
66. Cassian, *The Conferences*, 9:3. The phrase 'unceasing prayer' is taken from I Thessalonians 5:17.
67. Al-Ṭabarī, *Jāmiʿ al-bayān*, 505–6.
68. For a comprehensive analysis of the tradition, see Barbar Roggema's *The Legend of Sergius Baḥīrā: Eastern Christian Apologetics and Apocalytpic in Response to Islam* (Leiden: Brill, 2009). In chapter 2 specifically, Roggema discusses the Muslim origins of the narrative.
69. It appears that the name Baḥīrā is indeed of Christian origin, likely coming from the Syriac monastic term *bḥirā*, meaning 'proven one' or a more general honourific title meaning 'elect'. See both F. Nau, 'L'expansion nestorienne en Asie', *Annales du Musée Guimet* (Paris, 1913), tome 40, 215, and T. Nöldeke, 'Hatte Muḥammad christliche Lehrer?', *Zeitschrift der Deutschen Morgenländischen Gesellschaft* 12:4 (1858), 704.
70. The age of Muḥammad is not provided in this account, though it seems to be generally accepted that the *Sīra* version places his age around twelve or

thirteen years. See Stephen Gero, 'The Legend of the Monk Baḥīrā, the Cult of the Cross, and Iconoclasm', in *La Syrie de Byzance à l'Islam, VIIe–VIIIe siècles* (Damascus: Institut Français de Damas, 1992), 48.

71. Though the descriptions of this characteristic vary, it seems most commonly to be associated with a mark between the shoulders. Ibid. 47.
72. Ibn Hishām, *al-Sīra*, 147–9.
73. Ibid. 152–3.
74. Muqātil ibn Sulaymān, *Tafsīr* 2, 185.
75. Ibid. 185.
76. Maqātil ibn Sulaymān, *Tafsīr* 1, 497.
77. Ibid. 497.
78. Roggema, *The Legend of Sergius/Baḥīrā* refers to Baḥīrā being recognised as one of these few remaining 'true Christians', 37–8.
79. Jane McAuliffe, *Qur'anic Christians: An Analysis of Classical and Modern Exegesis* (Cambridge: Cambridge University Press, 1991), 289.
80. Peter Brown, 'The Rise and Function of the Holy Man in Late Antiquity', in Brown, *Society and the Holy in Late Antiquity* (Berkeley, CA: University of California Press, 1982), 131. Here Brown references the θεῖοσ ἀνήρ, or 'divine man', of classical antiquity.
81. Kirschner, 'The Vocation of Holiness in Late Antiquity', 120.
82. Ibid. 120.
83. Perhaps indicating that he was a Nestorian monk. See R. Gottheil, 'A Christian Bahira Legend', *Zeitschrift für Assyriologie und verwandte Gebiete* 13 (1898), 197.
84. See Gero, 'The Legend of the Monk Baḥīrā', 48.
85. See C. De Boor (ed.), *Theophanis Chronographia* (Leipzig, 1883–85), vol. 1, 334, as well as Theophanes, *Chronographia, The Chronicle of Theophanes*, trans. C. Mango and R. S. Scott (Oxford: Clarendon Press, 1997), 464–5.
86. Daniel J. Sahas, *John of Damascus on Islam* (Leiden: E. J. Brill, 1972), 132. For a complete assessment of this tradition in Christian literature, see Sydney Griffith, 'Muḥammad and the Monk Baḥīrā: Reflections on a Syriac and Arabic Text from Early Abbasid Times', *Oriens Christianus* 79 (1995), 146–74.
87. Suleiman Mourad, 'Christian Monks in Islamic Literature: A Preliminary Report on Some Arabic Apophthegmata Pratum', *Bulletin for the Royal Institute on Inter-Faith Studies* 6 (2004), 81–98 at 84.
88. See K. Szilágyi, 'Muhammad and the Monk: The Making of the Christian Baḥīrā Legend', *Jerusalem Studies in Arabic and Islam* 34 (2008). As a note it should be mentioned that Irfan Shahîd suggests that the basic story of this

encounter 'must have an element of truth in it' and that, given the proximity of several monasteries to the major caravan routes, it would have been entirely possible that interaction could occur between the Arab merchants and the monks. See Shahîd, *Byzantium and the Arabs in the Sixth Century* 2, 215.

89. Mourad, 'Christian Monks in Islamic Literature', 85.
90. Al-Iṣfahānī, *Ḥilyat al-awliyā'* 2, 375.
91. The term for 'trust in God', *tawakkul*, is part of the technical language associated with *zuhd*, or Muslim asceticism: the concept being that the ascetic must have a profound faith in God's ability to meet their needs. In this way the presence of *tawakkul* is an essential component to the ascetic life in Islam. See Leah Kinberg, 'What is Meant by Zuhd', *Studia Islamica* 61 (1985), 33–4.
92. Al-Iṣfahānī, *Ḥilyat al-awliyā'* 10, 288. It should be noted that this passage continues for some length as the monks and the Muslim traveller pray together. In the end, the monks are so impressed with Muḥammad ibn Ya'qūb and the devotion to his faith, that they both convert to Islam. As such the story is clearly designed to be read as an apologetic narrative, demonstrating the superiority of Islam over Christianity. For the purposes here, however, the more interesting part of the narrative is the manner in which the Muslim traveller initially interprets the pious statements delivered by the monks.
93. See J. Finkel (ed.), *Three Essays of Abū 'Uthmān 'Amr ibn Baḥr al-Jāḥiẓ* (Cairo, 1926), 15.
94. Donner, 'From Believers to Muslims', 11.
95. Christian Sahner, 'Swimming against the Current: Muslim Conversion to Christianity in the Early Islamic Period', *Journal of the American Oriental Society* 136:2 (2016), 265–84 at 266.
96. Ibn Abī al-Dunyā, *Kitāb dhamm al-dunyā* (Beirut: Mu'assasat al-Kutub al-Thaqāfia, 1993), 13.

Index